Oh! Canada?

The Departure

The story of one family's move to the "big country"
from the "old country".

Divinder Purewal

Tellwell Talent
www.tellwell.ca

ISBN
978-1-77370-547-7 (Paperback)

Oh! Canada?

Dedication

"A journey of a 1,000 miles
begins with a single step."
~ Lao-Tzu ~

This book is dedicated to many people, including my kids who've heard me talk about this "bucket list project to write MY book" about 1 million times since we arrived in Canada in 2005 and have read this book over and over again as what they call "unpaid editors!"

However, the real thanks goes to my wife.Usha, aka "Anisha" in this book.

Usha, imagine Jimmy Fallon writing out his legendary "Thank You" cards with the piano music playing in the background...

Thank you...for taking many millions of steps by my side, behind me and ahead of me over the past 30 years. You have been the power behind all that I have done and continue to do.

Thank you...for being ridiculously patient and helping me become the best version of myself that I could be and seeing beyond the noise and bravado that was me aged 18 and looking like the lovechild of Borat and Groucho Marx!

Thank you...for having faith that the stories I told you, would – ultimately and literally - come to life. It took a lot to believe that I would do all the things that I told you I would when it took me four years to install a doorbell!

Thank you...for not running away, screaming, from me when aged 18 I told you, aged 17, "I'm going to marry you, we're going to have two kids and live in Canada..." see I told you!

Thank you...for allowing me to take you 5,000 miles away from 99.99% of the people you loved in the hope that our lives would get better, I hope you'll agree it worked.

Thank you....for being you, and having my back, even when I couldn't see that's what you were doing.

I love you more than I can ever say!

D xx

Special thanks to the following people:

Sheila Patel, sister-from-a-Guji-mister, unofficial and unpaid editor

Sandeep Kapur, Milan Kapur, Saaras Kapur and Ambar Kapur, her I.T support team

Sheila, my darling, I will never forget all the hours you guys spent correcting all the – deliberate - grammatical errors I made. I will send you a signed copy of the book, as promised!

Just don't sell it on eBay!

D x

Jane Halil,

Jane, love, I have known you, as one of my best friends since our kids were 5 year olds, back in East London. You have always been that wise old bird who would keep me grounded if I ever looked like I was getting too big for my boots.

When you got sick you lost a lot of your spark but retained your ability to love me and admonish me appropriately.

I don't know if you recall the exact occasion when we chatted when we came back to England, when you were first diagnosed with terminal liver cancer. I remember we were sitting in your garden and you asked me the following question: "Why haven't you finished that Oh! Canada? Book, yet?" I shrugged my shoulders and replied "Oh I will, when I get the time, the kids are still at school and still need me and work, well work's work, isn't it?!'

You took my hand, looked in my eyes and replied: "Don't make excuses! Don't wait for the perfect moment, cos it don't exist! When I was younger I would tell my husband, Bo, let's wait until next year to go on holiday, we'd have saved another few hundred pounds and can go somewhere better than we can this year. Well here's the irony, my darling I now have the money but my days are literally numbered! Don't be told you're dying before you start to live!"

Here's to living, Jane!

D x

Foreword

Context, like clean underwear, is everything!

I emigrated to Canada on July 10th 2005 when I was 36 years old, with my wife Anisha, aged 34, and my son Kamran aged 8 ½ and my daughter Sonya aged 5 ½.

Our plan was simply to start a new life, have a new adventure before we got too scared to take any more risks.

Several years on, when I meet new people, they usually ask me one of the three questions below:

1. "Why would you leave exciting London for boring, wet Vancouver?"
2. "What made you choose Canada of all the countries to live in?"
3. "I have a cousin in England, named Bob, do you know him?"

Number 1 is easy to answer, having been born and brought up in London and having spent almost 36 years there, I was tired of the rat race and hamster wheel and all the other rodent- related metaphors that come with life in London or any other large city.

To me, London had become a lot like Disney Land, it had lots of great stuff that you didn't mind seeing occasionally but you really wouldn't want to live there!

Vancouver is a fabulous place to live with ocean and mountains making for a great backdrop to a modern small city that has a really laid-back charm.

Number 2, I have a younger brother who I have always got on with really well and when he emigrated to Canada many years ago, it made my heart hurt and after visiting him for a number of years my wife and I decided that Canada would be a great place to bring up our kids.

Number 3, yes I do know your cousin Bob and he borrowed a few thousand dollars from me a few years ago and said you'd repay his debt, so please cough up!

This book, is written by me for a number of reasons.

Firstly, as I descend rapidly into middle age I have found that my memory is fading and fast. This book is an attempt to capture what happened before it leaves the archives of my brain forever.

Secondly, but just as importantly, I want my kids to appreciate the back story to the life they love in Canada.

I also want to say, that emigrating to Canada was 99% my decision and one that took many years to accomplish.

There were many obstacles along the way but I am glad to say that so far, it's been a great, but occasionally bumpy, ride that we have weathered with a lot of laughs and a smile on our faces.

"When writing the story of your own life,

don't let anyone else hold the pen..."

~ Tyra Banks ~

I can't say there was one angry-George-Costanza-moment when I said "That's it, Divinder hates his life in England! Divinder wants to move to Canada!" as I flipped over a table!

No, that process took many, many years and involved me feeling that my life's script was being written by someone else, someone who really hated me!

Let me explain.

I'm that average bloke that tries really hard, but just doesn't quite make it.

Imagine a real life version of Mr. Bean, only brown, slightly chubby and bald!

When I was at high school, in England, I sat my 'A' levels (Grade 12 exams) - for the first of three attempts - I was "so done with school" that when I finished my last exam – for the first time - and despite the advice of a lot of people, who obviously knew how stupid I was, I burned all my notes on a huge bonfire in my garden.

You see in my mind, I was living out a scene from one of those iconic 'Brat Pack' movies from the 1980's where teens didn't give a damn about society's conventions but somehow things always sort of worked out in the end.

Unfortunately for me I wasn't the hero of the movie, instead I was one of those weird looking extras, usually with buck teeth and ginger hair who stands in the back looking jealously as other people's lives because when my exam results came back, a few months later, I had failed- in a way that many people didn't think was possible – so had to beg other people for their notes.

It didn't get any better at university.

I took a degree in Political Science because I had aspirations, but not the grades or temperament, to be a lawyer.

I took my exams and on the day of the last exam missed the note, pinned to the faculty pin board, that the exam time had been switched from the afternoon to the morning so slept in until my friend practically knocked my front door off its hinges with his crazy attempt to wake me up.

Thankfully I was allowed to sit that exam and came out with a 2:2 degree, missing a 2:1 by 2 %.

So as you can see, I never really had good fortune, in fact a good friend once said "Divind, if it wasn't for bad luck, you'd have no luck at all mate!" and he was right.

I'm not saying that everything in my life was bad, that would ignore Anisha, the bubbly girl I met at school when I was 18 and she was 17 when I'd gone back to sit my 'A' levels again and married 7 years later.

It would also ignore my two wonderful kids who thankfully took after their mum in brains and looks.

I'd left university in the early 1990's at a time when just having a degree, any degree at all, was enough to get a job.

I somehow managed to fall into a career in recruitment and even more amazingly managed to survive swimming with the many sharks that made that particular "profession" their own.

As much as I loved being married and being a dad, I'd never got my career going, unlike my wife Anisha who'd started off working for a small Knightsbridge based publishing house and had worked her way up to being an HR Manager with a major London law firm and, somewhat annoyingly, loved her job.

I'd like to think that I managed to keep my jobs, and there lots of them, because I was likeable, funny, had the gift of the gab, a quick wit and was never likely to rock the boat.

My biggest flaw was, coming from a family where I'd seen many uncle die as alcoholics, I didn't drink alcohol, so really didn't enjoy all the networking bullshit that went with my job so found that my career was still on the starting block when others had forged ahead and even lapped me!

So here I was, a thirty-something recruitment consultant working in the City of London and unlike the MacDonald's advert of the time not "loving it".

I'd come to the conclusion that my life was in free fall and I suspected that I had a back pack rather than a parachute attached to me!!

It felt like a very premature mid-life crisis.

I hated my job but loved the company that I worked for but could never see my long-term career being that of a recruiter.

I had tried for many years to make the switch into Human Resources but was told time and time again that "once an agency recruiter, always an agency recruiter"

I felt trapped, completely helpless and in desperate need of a new adventure.

'Desperation is the step-mother of re-invention'

Monday June 16th 2003

That Monday had been the usual manic rush as Anisha and I tried to get ourselves, and our kids, ready for the day ahead.

My kids hated waking up as much as their mum did.

Every day was a fight to wrestle them into their school uniforms before their grandmother came over and took over their care for the day.

Kamran would be crying and pleading, "Dad, five more minutes sleep please, please, I beg you!" as Sonya who had mastered the art of letting me dress her as she was still half-asleep just lay there.

Anisha's mum, Rani, had arrived at just after 6:45am, after letting herself in she made her way upstairs and then took over trying to wake Kamran up.

We left the house and Anisha's dad, Mohan, waited patiently in his car ready to drop us off to Ilford station.

We sat in the car in silence as we tried to get ourselves ready for the day.

When we arrived at Ilford station, we said goodbye to her dad and then joined the hundreds of other commuter walking on auto-pilot like well-dressed zombies to the train platform.

The Walking Brain Dead!

We waited for the 7:16am to Liverpool Street station and I smiled as I realised that a woman stood in front me, who had just looked back and given me the dirtiest look ever, had tucked her skirt into her knickers!

The train arrived with a loud thundering sound and when the train stopped, we all attempted to get a spot in the carriage before the doors chopped us in half.

From 8am to 6:15pm I played the role of an average recruitment consultant in a busy head hunting firm in Moorgate, a role that I had mastered over the previous decade.

The day itself was pretty uneventful, except for one drama-filled hour and later that evening, I met Anisha at Liverpool Street station as we made our way home. Anisha had this annoying habit of asking me about my day, which actually meant that I would have to ask her about her day and listen as she gushed about what a great career she had.

"So Divind, tell me all about your day in the exciting world of headhunting."

I smiled because usually I would say, "Imagine yesterday, but worse" but today I had a story to tell, "OK, today was interesting because I had to fight with a client who tried to con me out of a commission!"

Anisha looked at me quizzically "Fight? What sort of fight?"

I sat upright and started telling her my story "You know that dodgy bloke Fred at that German bank? The one who always claims that he already knew the candidate that I sent him to avoid paying our fee?"

Anisha nodded but her slight hesitation suggested that she was just nodding to keep the story going.

"Well he tried to tell me that the candidate that he just offered a job to, came to him a week earlier through another agency. I started asking him a bunch of questions about how that could have been the case when he'd told me that he'd never seen that resume before."

Anisha nodded again.

"Well it turns out that he was trying to do a deal with an agency where his wife's nephew works. You see, the scam is that Fred sends resumes to this nephew bloke, who then calls the candidate and tells them that if they want the job they have to be represented by him and his agency. Fred then gets a backhander and then tells the real agency that the resume was sent earlier to one of his colleagues and the candidates are coached to say they forgot they'd had their resume sent to his bank."

Anisha was open mouthed, she looked genuinely shocked.

"And the best part is that most candidates will happily play along with the scam as it means getting a job but they got caught out as this candidate, Raj, is a colleague's cousin and he called me and told me all about the little deal."

For once, Anisha looked somewhat interested in how one of the stories ended.

"So what happened Divind?"

"I called Fred and asked him to send me a copy of the offer for Raj and he spun me the line about how he'd got the resume from another agency a few days earlier. Poor old Fred had no idea that I had Raj in the office and that he'd been on speakerphone!"

Anisha's eyes bugged out as I carried on with my story.

"Raj then said 'I have never heard of the other agency. If you're making me an offer it will be through Divinder or not at all' I placed the phone on mute as Fred started stuttering like Hugh Grant in a bad 1990's rom-com! It was brilliant!"

"So what happens now?" asked an excited Anisha, probably thinking about what she'd buy with the commission I was about to make!

I rubbed my hands together "Now old Freddy-boy has two choices: number one, pay up and I keep my mouth shut about his little scam or number two rescind the offer and risk Raj suing him and then have me spread the news that he's dodgier than a Tory MP. Trust me Ani, Fred and his nephew-in-law don't want me telling the world that they're playing with a loaded dice. It's payday either way!"

I smiled and Anisha high fived me and then interlocked her fingers in mine and held onto my hand.

I could see that she was happy that I was happy, which was rare these days.

We arrived at Ilford station at 7:16pm, a whole twelve hours after we'd left that same station.

We walked upstairs and headed to the taxi car park where Anisha's dad waited for us.

Unlike the quiet journey to work I regaled him with my "Frank story"

Later that evening the kids, Anisha and I were having dinner with the 8 o'clock news playing in the background on the TV.

I looked up and said "bloody hell, more doom and gloom" as I always did and pointed at the TV as it churned out the nightly news.

I grabbed the remote control and turned the volume up on the TV.

"And today Government statistics showed that the average speed of a vehicle travelling in the city of London is approximately 11 miles per hour. This is exactly the same speed as it was one hundred years ago in 1903. In other news the bank of England announced that interest rates would be going up by a quarter of one per cent next month in order to curb the rampant housing market. Breaking news, we are just getting reports that a child of 9, who was shot earlier today, in a drive-by incident in South London, has just been declared dead at Queen Mary's Hospital. This is the ninth shooting this week and the fifth resulting in a fatality. In sports news, West Ham today signed another player from the Beazer home leagues...

Hearing the sad and depressing news I'd put down my cutlery and shook my head "What's the world coming to eh Ani?"

Anisha looked up with an expression on her face which said "Here we go again"

"What do you mean Divind?" she said, knowing that this was the cue for me to rant and rave.

I pointed at the TV again "The bloody news! Think about it, we're not shocked by the murder of a nine year old child anymore. In fact we're more interested that another high school dropout is going to join a football club for the national debt of Ethiopia! Sometimes I think everyone's gone mad and only I can see that the Emperor is not only naked but he's doing star-jumps and cart wheels at the window!"

Seeing that I was upset, Anisha picked up the TV remote control and turned the volume down.

I took another mouthful of food and stared at her incredulously "Hey what are you doing? I was watching that!"

Anisha glared at me.

She had perfected the art of the glare.

From speaking to her dad, she had inherited this skill from her mum who been trained by her mum before her.

She pointed the remote control at me and said "God, I wish I had a mute button for you! Even after eight years of marriage, I don't understand you Divind! One minute you're moaning about the fact that all we hear about is death, destruction and more taxes and the next you want to hear more!"

Angrily, she slammed the remote control on the table with such force that the back plate flew off and the batteries fell out.

I picked the remote control up, placed the batteries back in and then turned the volume up another two or three notches.
"Listen Ani."

I said with a slight pleading tone that I hadn't planned for.

"All we ever seem to do these days, is rush home from work in a train carriage that would be deemed unfit to move live animals. Then we run over to your mum and dad's house, bring the kids back home and throw them in the bath. Once they're all clean, we quickly eat our dinner and then spend the rest of the evening watching TV. I can't tell you how fed up I am with our crappy little routine and our hum-drum lives. At least let me see what's happening in the rest of the world, who knows it might even make me feel better."

Anisha rolled her eyes.

In addition to being an Olympic glarer she was also a world-renowned eye-roller.

"Here we go again Divind, with that old "this is not what I thought my life was going to be like" speech. Divind, this is getting really, really boring. I've noticed that you do this every few months when you've had a bad day at work. Divind let's face facts, you're a 34 year old recruitment consultant, you have two young kids, a job that just about pays the mortgage and you are rapidly losing what little hair you have left on your head through worrying about how rubbish you think your life is and about how little hair you have left on your head."

I looked at her with an attempt at being hurt by her words, but the truth was, she was right, this little speech of mine had been wheeled out more often than I cared to admit over the past few years.

I knew I had to say something, if only to stop her having the last word, which all husbands know is the kiss of death!

I attempted to speak "Ani, in my defence, let me just say... but it turns out she hadn't finished yet!

"No, Mr. Interrupter, you let me finish – for once!" she said this in a voice that bordered on shouting and I was suddenly scared that I'd lit the firework!

"Why can't you just accept the fact that our lives – like most normal people's lives - are about getting up in the morning, at least three hours before we really want to, and then going to a job that you hate, to pay for a house that we can't afford?"

I looked over at my kids, Kamran aged 6 and his sister Sonya aged 3 who were watching our verbal tennis match with their heads bobbing back and forth as Anisha and I spoke.

I loosened my tie "Well, thanks for that pep talk Anthony Robbins!! Remind me never to ask you to talk me off the ledge!!"

Anisha folded her arms across her chest as I carried on "Don't you think I realise that my life has become this horrible parody of "Ground Hog Day" where every day is exactly the same as the one before and we all count down the days to the next weekend as soon as Monday rolls around. However that's no reason to accept this is the way the story has to end."

Anisha got up, picked up her dinner plate and walked towards the kitchen.

As she entered the kitchen she looked back and threw one more volley at me "Really? Why's that then Einstein?"

I stood up and walked over to Anisha and taking her hand in mine, partly to show affection but partly so she couldn't slap me, and looked her in the eyes.

"Ani have you forgotten all those days we spent at university talking about how we would never let the system break us? Don't you remember how we used to laugh when we saw all the sad, broken people as they trudged off to work every morning to go to jobs that they hated? Whatever happened to all our dreams eh Ani? I remember you wanted to start a catering company and I dreamed of writing that great novel. What happened to those two people eh?"

Anisha moved in closer and stroked the bald patch at the back of my head, something she knew I loved or hated depending on the situation.

She softened her voice, something she always did before she delivered her killer shot.

I tensed up in readiness for the coming verbal onslaught "Divinder, darling, those dreams went away faster than your hair down the plug hole after a power-shower! You need to understand that all those dreams are just that now, they're things to fantasize about. Reality has a habit of biting you in the bum when you least expect it. No matter what we do, we have to remember that we are now two, well one and a half, responsible adults with two kids and a huge mortgage. This is why we need to get on that hamster wheel five days a week so that we can spend two days at the weekend socialising like it's going out of fashion. Now finish your roast chicken before it gets any drier than it already is."

I gave her a sad look and walked back to the table adjusting the hair that she had ruffled and pushing my plate away in a dramatic fashion sulked and said "Funnily enough I'm not hungry anymore."

Anisha left her plate in the sink and came back to the table to carefully cut the food up for three year old Sonya who was struggling with her knife and fork. Meanwhile, Kamran, was wolfing his dinner down like he was trying to stop someone invisible from stealing food off his plate!

I looked over and smiled at him and ruffled his mop of hair "So Kamran, what did you learn at school today son?"

Kamran looked up at me like he might have an answer but instead shrugged his shoulders and stuffed a large roast potato into his tiny mouth and started to chew furiously.

Seeing her brother's attempt at dislocating his jaw, Sonya gave Kamran a disgusted look and responded to me instead. "Daddy shall I tell you what I did at school today?"

I smiled my sweetest smile at Sonya and nodded.

My kids were little versions of my wife and I, Kamran was an easily distracted little man who always looked for the funny aspect of any situation and didn't take himself or life too seriously.

He made friends easily and was the type of kid that never bothered anyone in a negative way.

Whereas Sonya, well she was a mini-me of Anisha, studious, serious, hard-working and always pushing herself to do better in whatever she did. She was very discerning about her circle of friends and as such was happy in her own company.

Sonya walked over and sat on my lap "Well Daddy, in the morning I played teachers with my old best friend, Priya, but she was being really bossy so I told her that I hated her!"

I stifled a laugh as Anisha furrowed her brow in dismay.

Sonya continued her character assassination of her one time best friend.

"She's such a baby that she started crying when I told her I hated her and then she told Miss Carter that I was being mean. After that Miss Carter said that if "I couldn't say anything nice then I shouldn't say anything at all." So I didn't speak again for the rest of the day!"

Sonya definitely had the stubborn Purewal genes!!

Anisha crouched down to Sonya's height "Sonya what did Priya do that made her act so mean?"

Sonya jumped off my lap like she'd been pinched and said, "SHE decided that SHE was the teacher and SHE said that I had to put my hand up whenever I wanted to say something. I had my hand up for about two hours and SHE never let me say nothing!! And then, SHE said that I had to clean all the board rubbers. I am not inviting her to my birthday party!"

Now it was Anisha's turn to stifle a laugh, "Sonya, darling, you'll be friends again, just you see."

Sonya shook her head, folded her arms across her chest and shouted "Nah-ah! Never ever, even in a million years!!" and with that stormed off upstairs to her room looking like a toddler version of George Costanza's dad!!

After dinner I took up my regular position by the kitchen sink as the Chief Bottle Washer.

I rinsed the plates as Anisha stacked them in the dishwasher.

Sonya had calmed down enough to join us back in the living room.

As we put away the dishes the kids were watching a programme on the TV and were fighting over who got to hold the "sacred" remote control.

Anisha was being very quiet and there was a tension in the air. I tried to break the atmosphere "You know what Ani? We need a plan B"

Anisha looked a little puzzled "Why's that then Sherlock?" she asked with a slight mocking tone.

I ignored the fact that I had been demoted from Einstein to Sherlock and carried on "I'll tell you why, because plan A has failed miserably and to tell you the truth it was a pretty poor plan to begin with."

I gave Anisha the last plate and she placed it at the back of the dishwasher, closed the dishwasher door and then hopped up onto the counter opposite me.

In the other room, we could hear the sound of a small tussle.

I looked at Anisha, as she was the strict parent whilst I was the fun parent, and she hopped off the counter and walked over to the kitchen door "If I have to come in there then you'll both be going to bed. Now stop whatever stupidity you're up to and behave!"

The commotion stopped instantly.

Anisha came over and stood in front me. "OK Sherlock what's Plan B?"

I smiled and said "Wait here, I'll be back in one minute." and with that, I jumped off the counter, banged my knee on the opposite cabinet and then hobbled past her excitedly and headed upstairs to our bedroom.

I came back a minute later with a bulky brown envelope in my hands.

I carefully handed it over to Anisha who opened it up slowly.

She took out the first sheet of paper and read the title out loud. "Canadian: immigration information." "What's this then?" she said in a sarcastic tone.

I tried to be equally sarcastic and replied "Funnily enough SHERLOCK, it's all about emigrating to Canada!"

Anisha slapped me gently cross the arm with the bulky envelope and said "I know that, I mean when did you get this and don't you think WE should have talked about it first?"

I looked at her with puppy-dog eyes "Ani, it's just an information pack. It only arrived yesterday and I haven't even had a proper look at it yet. I thought we would look through it together."
Anisha handed me the envelope back.

I looked at the envelope and then looked at Anisha.

I genuinely wanted to stand right in her personal space and scream **"DO YOU KNOW HOW MUCH I HATE MY LIFE RIGHT NOW??? I NEED AN ESCAPE PLAN AND SOON!"** but I kept my cool because history had taught me that shouting equaled sleeping on the sofa "So that's it then Ani? You get to say no and that's it?"

Anisha looked hurt that I was laying this at her feet "Ani, you're always telling me that you hate your life as much as I do but you don't want to escape?"

Anisha took my hand but I pulled back angrily.

She lowered her voice, half to soothe me and half to keep the kids from hearing our fight.

"That's just it Divind, I think we'd be escaping one routine for another. Do you honestly think for even one minute that our life in Canada would be like that advert you see on TV? Do you think I haven't noticed that stupid grin on your face every time that advert comes on?"

I looked at her with a perplexed expression "What advert?" she laughed and said "That bloody Canadian tourism advert! I see you sitting there hypnotized as they show shots of gorgeous, fit- bodied women in red Baywatch swimsuits jumping into crystal-clear lakes as Canada geese fly overhead in slow motion. Not forgetting the group of saluting George

Clooney look-a-like Mounties as they ride by on horseback. Is that what you think life in Canada would be like?"

I didn't want to end the evening with a fight so just shook my head and took the envelope and headed upstairs again.

After a few minutes I was followed by Anisha and the kids.

I had already changed into my pyjamas and was standing in front of the bathroom mirror brushing my teeth.

I looked at the brown envelope on the window-sill in front of me and sighed.

Sleeping with the light on!

I was sitting in my bed when I heard Kamran call me with his nightly request "Daddy can you tuck me in and, you know, close my wardrobe door please."

Kamran was convinced, maybe because I may have told him so, that the ghost of the wrestler Andre the giant or "A the G" as Kamran called him, lived in his wardrobe, so I had to make a huge performance of checking the cupboard to make sure the ghost of the 7 foot something wrestler wasn't hiding in some corner of his 6 foot wardrobe.

This was a routine that I did every night before Kamran would fall asleep.

I walked into Kamran's room and opened his wardrobe carefully and theatrically looked in every corner, between the hangers and on the shelf all the while saying "Andre, are you in here?"

"OK darling, no sign of A the G in the wardrobe. Now good night, love you lots, have sweet dreams and see you in the morning."

Kamran smiled, reassured that he wasn't meeting the ghost of a wrestling legend that night and said "Daddy can I ask you a question?"

I smiled back and replied, "That depends. If this is another one of those can I have a Play Station 2 questions then no. If it's something else then of course you can."

He looked a little happy that I'd mentioned the PS2, "It's not about the PS2 but now you mentioned it can I get a Play Station 2?" I put on a fake angry voice and said "No you can't, now good night darling."

He was in a curious mood so continued "Daddy I do have another question, is your hair going into your head?"

I looked at him because this had been the silliest thing I'd ever heard him ask me in a long time.

"Eh? What do you mean son?" I asked, sort of dreading his reply.

He tilted his head a little and said "It's just that I asked Mum why you went upstairs all angry and she said you had another one of your hair brained ideas!"

Now, I have to explain something, I am the middle child of five boys and as such always felt that I never had my own identity so was always a people pleaser.

You see I was a slave to my two older brothers who would say, "We'll take you the park or the shops if you get my shoes" and they never followed through with their promises and I was a surrogate parent to the two younger brothers who I had to look after from a far too young age.

As such, I always tried to please others and I hated being picked on and felt that Anisha had just done that by making my idea look stupid in front of the kids.

I quickly tucked Kamran in and then left his room to kiss an already sleeping Sonya on the forehead before heading back to my bedroom.

Anisha was sitting in bed watching the medical drama "ER" on the TV.

I walked in and closed the door behind me and then locked it for good measure.

I stood in front of the TV, something that I was careful to do rarely as Ani had a crazy crush on most of the male leads in "ER" especially George Clooney.

I pointed a boney finger at her and in my best attempt at an angry voice said "What's the big idea telling Kamran that I'm stupid?!"

Anisha tried to carry on watching her show around me but I just started dancing around and after a few seconds she then turned the TV down and replied "Oh I'm sorry, was that meant to be a secret!?"

I crossed my arms and said, "Do you see me laughing?"

Anisha saw that I was annoyed, so turned off her precious TV show.

"OK," she said with a soft voice "what part of handing me an immigration pack did you think I would be happy about? 'Oh my God Divind, this is the answer to all our problems! We'll just quit our jobs, sell our house, kiss good bye to all our friends and family in London and start all over again FIVE THOUSAND MILES AWAY in a place that we know nothing about.' Get real Divind!"

There was something in her rational and practical tone that I didn't care for so I did what any angry and illogical man would do and grabbed the duvet and pulled it off of her!

As I walked away I looked back "I'm serious! All we do is complain about our lack of a real life and I'm just trying to do something positive. I don't see you doing anything other than watching TV all night!! By the way did you just fart in the bed?! This duvet stinks!"

Anisha blushed as I took the duvet with me and headed downstairs to the sofa in the living room.

Sofa, so good!

I lay on the sofa in ten different positions, trying desperately to get comfortable but couldn't quite manage it as the sofa was just a little too short for me to lay on properly.

After a few minutes Anisha headed downstairs and sat down on the sofa, she managed to sit on my feet.

"Oi! Get off my feet! Why did you think I came downstairs? I don't want to see you right now, you are crushing my feet like you crush my dreams, like you always do! That should be your name Anisha the Dream Crusher!"

Anisha rolled her eyes and started her inquisition "Are you still upset because I didn't let you buy that ride-on lawn mower last summer?"

I shook my head unconvincingly.

"Divind we have about 20 feet of lawn and we really could do without spending money - that we don't have - on stuff that we don't really need. This is just like that time when you bought that bread maker, "Ani wouldn't it be great if we had fresh bread every morning?" We spent a hundred pounds on a huge oven, which was so much hassle that we used it three times Divind, THREE TIMES! Those loaves were the most expensive ever baked! It's now a dust collector sat on our already crowded kitchen counter."

I sat up on the sofa as my back started to spasm but made it look like I was listening to Anisha "Why do you always treat me like I'm your oldest child? I admit that I can be a little impulsive sometimes but you never let things go."

She looked at me like I had just thrown her dirty laundry out on the street!

"Impulsive? Divind the last time you went to IKEA to buy a sieve you spent three hundred pounds on a futon!! Then there was the time when you bought that DVD box set of the Godfather."

I needed to defend myself so said "Excuse me lady, you know that I watch that DVD all the time!"

Anisha shook her head "You might watch it NOW Divind, but you bought that set FIVE YEARS BEFORE we even had a DVD player!"

She moved closer to me and in a hushed voice said, "I'm not saying that you're a little kid but you have to admit there are times when you run with ideas even when you know that they're not great ideas."

She ran her fingers across my head, where once there was hair.

I looked at her "Ani, I have had to face people saying no to me my whole life. First, my Mum and Dad said that I would never get a decent education. I proved them all wrong, I got my degree despite them."

Anisha nodded in all the right places as my rant continued.

"Then I was told by all my friends that I wouldn't have a chance of dating someone as good as you because I was so dark and had acne. Well they were wrong again. Even when we started looking at this house we had everyone saying that we couldn't afford it, but look, we've been here for eight years now and we proved everyone wrong. I just have this really strong feeling that Canada is the next big thing that people are going to pooh-pooh but I think it's right."

I think my speech worked because Anisha kissed me on the forehead and leaned in close "Divind, I do love you, I don't always know why, but I do and I want you and I to succeed as a couple and a family. But I really don't see that moving 5,000 miles away from all our friends and family is going to solve anything."

I had her on the ropes!!

"But that's where you're wrong Ani! Going to Canada would give us a chance to start all over again. The exchange rate is almost $3 Canadian dollars to the pound and houses are half the price they are here. We'd be so much better off. Think about it, I could even finish off that book that I've been writing forever. I tell you Ani if I had six months to finish it off

I reckon I could be a full time writer. Just imagine that eh? Me, earning a living for writing about my life. That would be wicked."

I could feel Anisha softening her attitude "OK JK Rowling let's talk about this when we're less tired. Now come back to bed." I grabbed the duvet as Anisha lead the way upstairs. As we got to the top of the stairs I slapped her bum and walked past her and said, "Couldn't sleep without me eh?"

She smiled and replied "You know it!" and then in a loud whisper said "yeah it's nothing to do with the fact we only have one decent duvet means I would probably freeze to death!" and then slapped my bum.

De Ja Pooh!

Monday December 1st 2003

The clock radio came alive playing the Sonny & Cher classic "I got you babe."

The irony and aptness of this fact struck me immediately and made me smile as that's the song that Bill Murray's character heard each day in the movie "Ground Hog Day".

I hit the snooze button and snuggled closer to Anisha.

The clock radio came on again ten minutes later and this time with some loud DJ talking with far too much energy for that time of the day.

I got up and scratched my head.

I looked at my thinning hair in the mirror and pushed my hair forward to see if it would disguise my receding hairline. I looked over at a still sleeping Anisha and smiled to myself.

I hadn't done too badly:

Marrying my high school sweetheart.

Having two great kids.

A comfortable home.

Suffering no real health issue.

Some money in the bank.

In fact, you could have said that I had a life that was pretty stress-free if you excluded the fact that I hated the twelve hours between 7:30 am and 7:30pm every week day!

It was now 6:30am. I knocked on the kid's bedroom doors "Everybody wake up! It's nearly 7am and we need to be out of here in less than 40 minutes. Last one down has to wash all the dishes tonight!"

I heard the kids groan at my daily dad joke and that was my cue to grab a shower.

By 6:45am I'd finished my shower and was dressed and back in my bedroom.

Anisha was busy braiding a still sleepy Sonya's hair and Kamran had shuffled into our bedroom and had flopped down on our bed.

After a few seconds he rolled over onto his belly.

He stared at me with droopy eyes "Dad, do I have to go to school today?"

I looked him over, he didn't look sick "What's wrong darling? Are you ill?"

I asked with genuine concern and moved closer to him. He suddenly opened his eyes and replied, "Nah, I'm not sick but I think I've learned all that school can teach me."

I laughed, thinking he was joking and then turned my laugh into a cough when I realised that he was serious.

I composed myself and said, "You still have a few things you have to understand, so run along and get ready, there's a good boy"

He didn't move, instead he sat upright on the edge of the bed, "But Dad, why do I have to go to school?"

I gazed at my first born and thought "I'm going to have a Kodak moment!!"

I'm going to have a bloody Kodak moment!

What's that I hear you ask?!

A Kodak moment is one of those memorable experience's, that you wish you had a photo of, where my son and I would look back at in years to come and say "that was a great bonding moment and we took our relationship to another height!"

So I did that thing that Anisha said I should do, and crouched down to Kamran's height, I lowered my voice and spoke very carefully.

This was important as he'd remember these words for many years to come.

"Well darling, you go to school so that you can get clever." he nodded, so far so good.

He raised his arm. "Yes darling?" I said in my best caring dad voice "But Dad, I'm already clever, you always tell everyone that I am a clever kid."

Now it was my turn to nod, "It's true you are clever, but you go to school so that you can get even cleverer – I think that's a real word - than you already are and then you go to university. Then once you finish university you can get a good job that pays a huge salary and then me and your mum can both retire and get fat!"

Kamran stood up, patted me on the shoulder in a reassuring way and said "But Dad, I don't want to be clever."

I stood up too and asked "Oh yeah, and why's that then?" that's when he dropped the boom "Because Dad, I want to be just like you!"

Kamran winked at me and shuffled off leaving me laughing.

All aboard!

At 7:00am, like every other weekday, Anisha and I left the house.

We no longer had my mother-in-law get the kids ready at our house and instead dropped the kids off with them to have their breakfast at their house.

We walked the 100 yards to Anisha's parent's house. Anisha's dad, Mohan answered the door as his wife, Rani, made the kids their breakfast.

Mohan opened the door and greeted his only grandchildren "Good morning my darling Kamran and sweet Sonya. How are you both?" he leaned in close for a kiss but the brats smiled for a second, gave him a quick kiss and then pushed past him to see their beloved "Nani" as they called their maternal grandmother.

Mohan was a 65 year old retired civil servant who moved to England from his native Tanzania in the early 1970's.

Mohan had a very generous nature and always saw the best in everyone he met.

He was also extremely positive in his outlook on life and his glass was always half full.

Before he retired he had a 25 year career with the civil service both in Africa and England and loved his job.

He retired in his late 40's when a car accident damaged an already weak spine rendered him medically disabled.

As I waved at the kids he stepped out into the street, "So Divinder, are you looking forward to what this glorious day has in store for you?"

I looked at him and appreciated that he saw each day as a do-over so was asking out of genuine interest

I shrugged my shoulders like a schoolboy being asked why I'd taken the wings off a butterfly.

Before I had a chance to respond Anisha did it for me, "Ignore him Dad, he's having one of his "life is so crap" days."

Mohan looked at me with a disappointed expression on his face, I recognized this look as I'd seen it first when Anisha had told him that she wanted to marry me!

"Divinder, why would you say that your life is the "C" word?"

In addition to being a very nice guy Mohan was also deeply religious and considered the word crap to be a swear word. I was grateful he didn't hear the other "unholy" words we used at home!!

Just as I tried to open my mouth, Anisha, who seemed to have assumed the position of my lawyer, replied for me "Don't worry Dad, he'll get over himself, he always does. Kamran, Sonya love you both, be good for Nana and Nani and study hard, especially you Kamran Singh PUREWAL!"

We walked to the bus stop at the top of the road in silence.

As we approached the crowd of passengers waiting for the bus I broke my self-imposed vow of silence. "Seeing as my life is so "the C word" what excitement do you have to look forward to today in your great life as a HR professional?"

Anisha faked a big yawn. "First thing this morning I have a meeting with an employee who has a body odor problem. The manager doesn't feel that she is capable of telling him that he smells even though he can empty a moving elevator just by getting in!"

I laughed out louder than I wanted, causing the rest of the bus stop passengers to give me a dirty look.

You see, I laugh like a braying donkey on helium and it's pretty annoying!

Anisha carried on with her description as I tried hard not to snort-laugh "I have to think up a diplomatic way of telling him that he needs to address this little issue. What would you do, and don't say send him a can of deodorant!"

I made out like I was about to say something else but then thought better of it.

Four packed buses drove past and when the fifth bus arrived all the passengers jammed themselves on with all the other people heading for the bright lights of the city of London.

I looked at my watch, it was 7:28am.

My work day was 40 minutes away from starting and I felt my stomach knot up.

At 7:35 the bus arrived at Ilford train station and emptied except for a few old people who seemed to ride the bus all day just because they could with their free bus passes.

We got off and joined the throng of people headed for the stairs down to the train. The herd of people was so large that it felt like a conveyor belt and heaven forbid anyone if they were to fall down!!

At 7:39 we heard the crackly public address system and a nasally voice screeched "The 7:40 train from Shenfield will not be stopping at Ilford, repeat the next train coming through the station will not be stopping. We apologize for any inconvenience and thank you for using our service."

The station was suddenly a sea of swear words and I was even more tense than before.

Anisha took out her book and I took this as a cue that she didn't want to talk anymore about Mr. B.O.

Ten minutes passed and when the next train arrived it was so busy that people fell out when the automatic doors opened. Being London, passengers on the platform stepped over and on the backs of the people who had fallen and took their place on the train.

At 8:10am Anisha and I finally got on the fifth train and even managed to get two seats, together.

I settled into my seat and wallowed in the fact that in 10 years of travelling to the City I had only ever had a seat three times.

I was over-happy and said "What are the chances of getting two seats together eh Ani?"

Anisha wore a massive fake smile "Yippee Divind! I feel truly blessed! Now do me a favor, sit both of your arse cheeks on your side of the seat. I don't know why men have to sit down like they're riding a small, invisible pony!"

I shuffled over a few inches to my left and then I dug Anisha's ribs accidentally-on-purpose with my elbow.

Anisha carried on reading her book as I started to read the headlines on the Daily Mail.

After a few minutes the train stopped at Stratford station and the carriage quickly filled up.

I looked up and noticed a large woman standing in the aisle a few feet away from him. She was wearing a flowing yellow dress and a large red coat that didn't quite button up.

I nudged Anisha and whispered "Psst! Ani, see that woman over there, the one in the yellow dress and red coat, is she pregnant?"

I swear, Anisha looked up for a millisecond and then shook her head casually.

I felt that Anisha couldn't have made a proper body mass index assessment in that millisecond so kept my eye on the 'women in red'.

A few stations came and went and I looked over again and was convinced that she was pregnant.

I nudged Anisha again "Psst! Ani, are you definite she isn't pregnant? She sure looks pregnant to me!"

Anisha looked at me angrily and through gritted teeth whispered "She's just fat. Believe me I've been pregnant twice so I know the difference between pregnant and fat. Now shut up and let me read this book. You're like a bloody annoying mosquito under a duvet!!"

It was bothering me that she might be pregnant and I had a seat so once more I nervously nudged Anisha who nudged me back - hard "Psst! Ani, what if she's fat AND pregnant, have you thought about that?! Have you? Hey, have you??"

Anisha gave me a really dirty look that made a few male commuters opposite wince in sympathy.

I picked up my paper again but couldn't concentrate so I looked at the woman, caught her attention and mouthed "Do you need a seat?"

The big woman smiled back and replied somewhat loudly: "Thanks love, but I'm just fat!"

I smiled awkwardly and started to look at the sports pages as Ani nudged me really hard in the ribs for being an idiot.

At 8:22am the train arrived at Liverpool Street Station and the stream of commuters from the train were joined by those on the "The Tube". Liverpool Street Station resembled a cattle market at the best of times but during rush hour 6:30am to 9:00am and then again from 4:00pm to 7:00pm it was crazy- busy.

I kissed Anisha on her forehead as she continued her journey.

I stepped out of the station, plugged in my Sony Walkman and walked the eight minutes to my office.

As I walked along I saw the same people that I saw every day and, like every day for the past 4 years, my smile at them was greeted with a frown.

Ever since 9/11 there had been a real shift in some people's reactions to people with brown skin.

Some people can't seem to tell the difference between an Indian and a terrorist. It's easy to work out, Indians own the businesses that the terrorists want to blow up!!

And so it begins, again!

I reached my building and said hello to a few people waiting for the old elevator in the reception area.

Two young white girls giggled a "hi" back at me and the tall older white man glared at me like I was wearing a tee-shirt with the words "I ♥ Osama" written across the middle in 3 inch letters!

The elevator arrived after a few minutes and I held the door open for everyone to get in.

The girls laughed and said thanks as they got in and the old man carried on glaring at me.

He was staring at me so intently that I was sure I had snot hanging from my nostril so discreetly touched my moustache to check.

The journey from the ground floor to the main floor, all of 30 feet, should have been no more than five seconds but it took about a twenty seconds in this old building.

The rumor was that the elevator was run by an old man turning a rusty hand crank.

I spent the whole time looking at the floor numbers as if they could possibly jump from 1 to 5 and then back to 2 again.

Finally the doors opened up and I got off one floor early.

The idea of staying in the elevator with 'old glaring guy' was too much.

I walked into the office to greet "my people"!

"Good morning fans, Divinder is in the house!"

The large room had ten desks placed side by side and occupied an area of roughly 40 feet long by 30 feet wide.

I worked on the Hedge Fund team, which was made up of me and my two colleagues Terrence and Arnold.

Terrence was 40 years old and had been with the company for seventeen years.

He was the team leader and had the same dry sense of humor as me.

Arnold was the new guy having joined the team 3 months ago having previously been a bookmaker for five years.

He was very full of himself and liked to brag about all the celebrities that he was apparently friends with.

I shrugged at Terrence by way of an apology and he looked at his watch "So glad you could make it in Divind. Are you working part time hours now or what?"

I laughed "Terrence mate, if I told you that I had to wait for four packed trains to go past before I got on, would you believe me?"

Terrence shook his head in a theatrical way "No I wouldn't. What really happened?"

I sat down at my desk and powered up my desktop "I'll tell you what really happened Terrence, I was kidnapped by a gang of sex-crazed women who wanted to ravish me for my body."

Just as I started my story my manager Marion walked in.

Marion was a five foot nothing dynamo who spent 10 years as an equities trader before becoming a head hunter. She tolerated me as I did just enough to keep my head above water.

She looked at the clock on the wall "Well Divinder they would have to be crazy if they wanted to ravish you! Now that you have finally decided to turn up I have a treat for you, you have just been chosen to interview a walk-in!"

Everyone in the team, except me, cheered.

A "walk-in" was code for someone who has just turned up without an appointment.

Seeing a walk-in was normally reserved for new team members as most walk-ins were either kids just out of college or people who have been laid off after 30 years as an accounts clerk. Either way most "walk-ins" didn't have resumes so it was going to be a very long and painful experience.

The rule in the team was that whoever came in the office last got the first "walk-in."

Arnold decided to join in the banter "Good one Marion!! I'll tell you someone else who's always late, my mate George Michael! I met him last night with Andrew Ridgeley at China White..."

Terrence gave Arnold a dirty look "Arnold why do you always have to name-drop every opportunity you get? I was just saying to Sean Connery the other day "that Arnold, he's always name dropping!" and you know what? Roger Moore agreed!"

Everyone groaned as Marion handed me a scrap of paper with the name "Frankie" on it. "Hurry up now Divinder, don't keep old Frankie waiting!"

I reluctantly took the interview pack and a clipboard and headed downstairs to the first floor reception.

As I walked down the stairs I met my colleague Maurice.

Maurice was a 42 year old recruiter who looked like a younger version of Benny Hill.

He gave the impression that he was a lady's man, but in reality he was happily married with two kids.

Maurice and I had a running gag where Maurice called me Abdul and I called him Hymie because of his Jewish background.

"Alright Abdul?"

I smiled and waved the interview pack at him. "I'm cool Hymie, how's it hanging?"

Maurice clutched himself "To the left. I just heard you got a "walk-in" Abdul. What time did you get in?"

I winced "No joke Hymie, but I've already done a day's work just getting here this morning and now a "walk-in" Just shoot me now!"

Maurice patted me on the back and we made small talk as we headed for the reception. I walked in first. I said a cheerful hello to Pat the receptionist and then called out for Frankie.

One of the young girls from the elevator stood up as the old man adjusted his hearing aid and gave me a dirty look. The young girl said, "I'm Frankie. Frankie Morris."

I smiled and took a step forward.

Just then Maurice walked over and guided her towards an interview room.

As he walked past me he showed me the resume with the name Frankie Morris written across the top.

The old man stood up and walked over to the receptionist, Pat, and asked her a question.

Pat pointed at me and the old guy looked like he just won the lottery but lost the ticket!

Pat tried to introduce us "Divinder this gentleman, Frankie Manson, is here to see you. Frankie please follow Divinder."

The old man reluctantly followed me and it was hard to tell who was more upset!

I lead him into one of our new glass-walled interview rooms that were located in the reception and asked him to take a seat.

Frankie took a seat in the oversized chair and unbuttoned his blazer jacket.

I realised I hadn't introduced myself so extended my right hand, "Hi Frankie, my name's Divinder."

Frankie looked at me like I'd just completed a rectal exam, without gloves and hadn't washed my hands!

After having my hand extended for ten-awkward-seconds without him taking it, I pulled my hand back.

"Okay, how can I help you Frankie?"

Frankie avoided making eye contact with me and sat upright in his seat and in a deep Cockney accent he asked "No offence mate, but isn't there anybody...er...English available to interview me?"

I stared at him, a little shocked with just how "Frank" old Frankie was being, but hoped it wasn't showing.

I decided to be equally Frank.

"If by 'English' you actually mean someone born in England, then that would still be me, but I'm guessing what you actually mean is someone white-English, then I'm afraid not. You see we usually ask candidates to make an appointment rather than just walking in off the street. If you do want to make an appointment I would suggest you avoid seeing the following people"

I started writing names on a piece of paper.

"Eva Joseph, she's Jewish as is Paul Wise, Phil Marks, Andrew Adams, Daniel Cohen and Maurice Simons. I would also add Terrence Robinson and Arnold Cooke to your no touch list as both of those men have a touch of the old tar brush being Anglo-Indians. Then there's Veronica White who somewhat ironically is actually black. Oh and Phil Lee, well he's a chink so you might want to avoid him too. Other than that, we have a fair blend of Micks, Jocks, WOPS and WASPS for you to choose. Have a nice day."

I handed the "hit list" to him and left Frankie in the interview room and rather than head back to my desk I left the clip board and interview pack with a surprised open-mouthed Pat at the reception desk and walked down the stairs and across the street to well-known American coffee shop with a mermaid logo.

You for coffee?

I ordered a tall skinny latte and just as I passed over my hard-earned five pound note I heard a familiar voice from my past, Pat Horgan.

Pat was a tiny Irish man who was my manager when we both worked for a teaching agency. I'd left a few years ago and hadn't seen Pat since.

Pat was one of those naturally very outgoing people and he would introduce himself by saying "My name's Pat Horgan, small H, large Organ!"

"Hey Divinder! Long time, no see, man!

I turned around as Pat approached me with a huge smile on his face.

We shook hands and then did that man-half-hug where we bumped chests.

"Hi Pat, how did you know it was me just from the back of my head?"

Pat tapped the middle of my bald patch. "I'd know that bald patch anywhere! Can you pick up satellite TV on that thing?!"

I stroked my bald path and laughed awkwardly.

"So Mr. Horgan, small H, large organ!! What have you been up to since I last saw you?"

Pat smiled and his whole face lit up. "Well, first I got married almost two years ago. My Maureen finally made an honest man of me. Second I became a dad six months ago and third we are emigrating to Australia in six months!!"

I shook his hand again "Bloody hell Pat, you don't mess around!! Well in that case let me get that coffee for you."

"Thanks mate, that's very kind of you!" he said it like I'd just given him one of my kidneys!

We sat at a table and caught up for the next fifteen minutes. "One question, why Australia?"

Pat took a quick sip of his coffee and smiled again "You know what Divind, I just think that London is done."

I nodded, as he carried on.

"It was great when it was just me and Maureen but now that we have little Naomi I see the city in a different, scary light. Maureen has a brother in Melbourne and he's always saying what a great life we could have down under. So we looked into it and it turns out there's a huge need for short Irish teachers!! Seriously it works out great because Maureen is a qualified nurse and we have been sponsored by a teaching hospital and that's why our paper work went through so quickly. It gets even better when you consider that because of the exchange rate we could probably buy a house - outright. No more poky little flat in Clapham!"

It was my turn to smile now and I was genuinely happy for Pat. "That really is great news mate. Aren't you even a little bit scared that life in Oz won't be any better than what you have here? It's funny but I've recently been looking at emigrating to Canada but Ani keeps telling me all we're doing is swapping one hamster wheel for another."

Pat was just about to answer when his cell phone buzzed.

He looked at the text and pulled a face.

"That was my boss letting me know that I'm needed at a meeting now. You know what Divind, we could go out there and have the greatest life ever or we could fall flat on our faces but you know what? You'll never know if you don't try. Here take my business card and call me if you need a chat. Great to see you again, give my regards to Anisha and the kids."

Pat left and jumped into a black cab as I blew on my still hot coffee and took a long walk back.

Into the lion's den

An hour later, having trudged around a few high end shops where a month's salary wouldn't even buy a pair of socks or a single cuff link, I reluctantly walked back to my desk with my half- finished now cold coffee in hand.

Terrence looked up as I walked in and could tell that I was upset. "That must have been a great candidate you've been at it for ages."

Arnold saw Terrence's line as a chance to have a laugh at me "You've been at it for ages! I bet Divinder's wife says that a lot!"

Arnold started laughing loudly and I turned and gave him a withering look and mouthed "Bell end" which made him shut up immediately.

"What happened Divind?" asked a concerned Terrence "I've never seen you looking so annoyed."

I tried to brush it off "Let's just say that if Hitler has a nephew called Frankie I just met him and he won't be on my Christmas card list anytime soon."

"Sorry mate." said Terrence with a half-smile.

"Don't worry about it" I replied but my face was angry and I could feel the room closing in on me.

I took a seat at my desk and busied myself with listening to answer phone messages and checking emails.

Maurice came in a few minutes later with a huge smile on his face.

He walked over to my desk and tapped me on the shoulder. "Bad luck Abdul. You guys should have seen the gorgeous bird that I just interviewed. Bloody hell, she could have been a part time model! Meanwhile old Abdul got lumbered with the poster boy for the Ku Klux Klan!! I saw you leave after about a minute, what did he do? Put a pillow case over his head or what?!"

I pushed my glasses back to the bridge of my nose - with my middle finger - as Maurice walked off laughing.

Terrence saw that I was distracted so emailed me:

From: Terrence.Robinson@JonathanHawk.co.uk
Sent: December 1st, 2003 10:15 AM
To: Divinder Purewal Divinder.Purewal@JonathanHawk.co.uk
Subject: Lunch?

Hey Divind, let's grab a **really, really** early lunch

TR
Terrence Robinson/ Manager, Investment Management and Hedge Funds/ Jonathan Hawk/ Moorgate, London

---

I looked at his email and realized that I needed to vent and Terrence was as good a sounding board as anyone. I replied

From: Divinder.Purewal@JonathanHawk.co.uk
Sent: December 1st, 2003 10:16 AM
To: Terrence Robinson Terrence.Robinson@JWren.co.uk
Subject: Lunch?

Great.
Thanks.
Divinder Purewal/ Senior Consultant, Investment Management
and Hedge Funds/ Jonathan Hawk/ Moorgate, London

From: Terrence.Robinson@ JonathanHawk.co.uk
Sent: December 1st, 2003 10:15 AM
To: Divinder Purewal Divinder.Purewal@ JonathanHawk.co.uk
Subject: Lunch?

Hey Divind, let's grab a **really, really** early lunch

TR
Terrence Robinson/ Manager, Investment Management and Hedge
Funds/ Jonathan Hawk/ Moorgate, London

Cheeky brunch for two

We were sitting at our table in one of those anonymous looking pubs that have popped up all over England with dusty, fake cob-web covered farming implements hanging from the ceiling and photos of C-list celebrities who'd once had a drink there posted on the bar wall.

I looked over at Terrence as he read the menu. "Terrence why are you reading the menu mate? We both know that you're going to order the fish and chips like you always do!"

Terrence smiled. "Am I that predictable?"

I nodded "Yes, very."

Terrence put his menu down "What's wrong Divind?"

I shook my head.

"You just don't seem to be your usual happy self lately? Is Marion giving you a hard time again? She can be a complete cow but that's why they pay her the big dollars."

I shook my head again "No it's not Marion - for once. I feel just like I did a few months ago. Do you remember when I said I felt as if my life was just drifting along without any real purpose and that unless I got out of London I was going to go mad?"

Terrence nodded "Yeah I do Divind. I feel the same way mate, I'm still hoping that Phil will give me the green light to transfer to the Sydney office."

I sipped my drink "No news on that one yet, Terrence?"

He shook his head "Nothing at all. Phil did say he'd put it to the board soon. Where do you want to go?"

I shrugged my shoulders "That's just it Terrence, I want to emigrate to Canada and Ani wants to stay put in the hope that I either just accept my lot in life or win the lottery. I really wish I didn't feel so out of whack."

Terrence nodded again.

Just then, the server came over and asked us if we were ready to order. Terrence ordered fish and chips and I chose calamari and yam fries.

As we waited for our food I told Terrence all about the fight I'd had with Anisha the previous night.

"That's tough Divind, you wanting to start all over again in Canada and Ani wanting to stay here seems like a rock and a hard place. What's the big appeal about Canada anyway? I know you keep going on about how well your brother's doing out there but that's no guarantee that it would be right for you. No offence Divind but your skill lies in having a laugh for eight hours while pretending to work!! I can't imagine there's much demand for that in Canada!"

I looked around my table and saw a stale pea so threw it at Terrence.

"Seriously Terrence I feel like I am drifting along on a sea of nothingness. If I don't get some inspiration soon I am going to go nuts!"

Thankfully Terrence decided against making the obvious joke.

He could see that I was looking for someone to just listen to my ranting.

After we finished lunch we walked back to the office and I headed for the washroom.

Meanwhile in an office across London...

Anisha was sitting at her desk when an email came in from her manager asking her to attend an emergency meeting taking place later that afternoon.

From: Chris.Gold@FeavinCrookes.co.uk
Sent: December 1st, 2003 11:24 AM
To: Anisha Purewal Anisha.Purewal@FeavinCrookes.co.uk; DL London HR
Subject: Emergency meeting, 2pm

Hi guys
I hope you're all well.

In light of last quarter's revenue numbers I need to share some news from the partners.

No need to panic…well not yet anyway!

Cheers,
CG
Christopher Gold,
Senior Vice President,
Human Resources,
Feavin Crookes Limited

Anisha walked over to her friend Kaye's desk and sat down on a nearby chair. "Hey Kaye, any idea what the emergency meeting's all about?"

Kaye looked over her glasses and chewed her pencil "I have a pretty good idea and if it turns out to be true, then I'm outta here!"

Anisha laughed "Eh? Where did that come from? I thought you loved your job Kaye?"

Kaye scrunched her face a little "I usually do but I just heard from Julie, in corporate finance, that the company didn't make the huge profit it had hoped it would so it's looking to make some "headcount changes" she made air quotes "also known as redundancies. The crappy part is that they're going to ask everyone to take on more responsibilities for no more pay. I guess that's what your meeting's going to be about."

Anisha tried to reassure Kaye while trying hard to hide her own fears "I thought we were doing alright. If we're laying people off then why did we just take on those four temps to help with the new payroll project?"

Kaye pulled up an email from their colleague Julie and showed Anisha. "Julie reckons they've done that so that they'll be ready for the extra work that'll happen when they make the cuts and by taking on temps they can avoid paying any benefits and holiday pay."

Anisha stared across the office towards Julie's desk and made her own air quotes "Does Julie understand what the word "confidential" actually means? Do me a favor Kaye, keep this under your hat for now. Let me find out what's happening and I'll fill you in later. Do you fancy some lunch?"

Anisha and Kaye headed off to the company restaurant and grabbed their trays, plates and cutlery. They shuffled along and after looking at all the greasy food on offer each grabbed a sandwich and a packet of crisps.

As they sit having lunch Anisha looked off in the distance. "What's the matter Ani? You seem miles away."

Anisha snapped out of her day dream "Kaye can I ask you a question that needs a really honest answer?"

Kaye smiled "Is this one of those "would you kiss a tramp for a million pounds" questions? Because you know I would do it even for a thousand quid!"

Anisha laughed

"No it's not that but it's good to know that you're that cheap! Divinder and I were having a chat last night and he said something that seems to have stuck in my head. Am I one of those "my way or the highway" people?"

Kaye popped a grape in her mouth as she thought about the question.

After a few seconds Anisha poked Kaye's hand her with her plastic fork. "Oi! What's taking you so long to say no?! Am I really that bad?"

Kaye laughed as she rubbed her hand "I'm only joking! Before I answer that sort of question I need all the facts. What happened and does it involve a bread oven or a sit-on lawn mower?"

Anisha moved in close to have a quiet chat "Divinder sent off for the Canadian Immigration application pack. We had a big fight, he slept on the couch – well for all of five minutes - but we're cool again."

Kaye stared at Anisha's face for a moment "Why now?"

Anisha lowered her voice "He's having another bad streak at work so wants to uproot us all and pitch up 5,000 miles away in Canada all "re-invented" as he calls it."

Kaye popped another grape in her mouth "What's so bad about wanting to re-invent yourself? Seems to me that all Divinder wants to do is start all over again. If I remember you're the one who always says you wished that life was more interesting."

Anisha looked wistful "Yeah I know I complain, but who doesn't?"

Kaye smiled a huge smile "I don't! Apart from the fact that I might lose my job I am pretty happy with my life thank you very much! I realised years ago that life is never going to be a Hugh Grant film where some gorgeous bloke with brilliant hair and teeth like one of the Bee Gees, sweeps me off my feet and all I do is eat chocolates all day. My dad's fighting throat cancer - again - and my mum is getting the early signs of Parkinson's disease. I don't worry about the small stuff anymore because I realise that every day that I wake up happy and healthy is a bonus."

Anisha nodded "Is this the part where we pull out lighters and candles and sing Kumbiyah?!"

Kaye laughed "Don't laugh Ani!! Work is my sanctuary, it's where I come to get away from what's happening at home. If Divinder wants to swap one routine for another then I would go for it. What's the worst thing that could happen? You go there and hate life in Canada and then you come back home again."

Anisha nodded again.

"But that's the problem Kaye, we couldn't come back. There would be so many people just waiting for us to fall flat on our butts and that sort of pressure makes you just accept whatever comes your way. Besides which, what would I do with my mum and dad? It's the curse of the only child."

Kaye slapped the table "Take your parents with you!"

Anisha looked incredulous "What? You must be joking! I love my mum and mad but that's because they live in their own house and have their own life. It would also mean that Divinder would divorce me!"

"But I thought Divinder got on with your folks."

Anisha took a sip of her orange juice "He does but for the reasons I gave earlier. If we lived together we would never speak to one another again. No, I think it's best if we just accept our lot in life and just get on with it."

They finished off their lunch chatting about their upcoming meeting.

For whom the bell tolls!!

Later that afternoon Anisha was sat in a board room waiting for the arrival of her manager Karen and the VP of HR Chris.

Anisha started to day dream again and absent mindedly started doodling on a piece of note paper.

When she looked down she gasped, when she saw that she had written the word "Canada" over and over again.

After a few minutes Karen and Chris arrived.

Karen approached Anisha "Hey Ani, I hope you haven't been waiting long, Chris and I had to tie up a few loose ends."

Anisha smiled "It's all good, I was just catching up on some emails."

Chris nodded. "So Anisha, I'm sure you've heard the gossip that we're making 'headcount changes', I just want to tell you that the partners have been disappointed with the first quarter's profits. In fact they have asked me to work out a number of cost cutting options and as you're a senior member of the team we'd like to hear your views before we proceed. We want to reduce headcount by two people."

Chris handed Anisha a list and the very first name was Kaye's.

Anisha looked at the list "Can I get a bit of background here and ask why we're looking at making cuts? It seems to me that we've had one bad quarter and suddenly we're looking at making permanent cuts."

Chris looked surprised at Anisha's frank approach "To be honest Anisha, the cuts have been in the pipeline for months, this bad quarter has just given the partner's a good reason to pull the trigger. I don't like this any more than you, but the bottom line is I need to have an approved list of leavers by the end of the week or the partners are going to make their own cuts, and we don't want that."

Anisha kept seeing Kaye's name getting bigger on the page. "What criteria are we using to make these cuts? I see you've got Kaye's name at the top of the list. Kaye's a top performer and always gets a really high appraisal rating. What sort of message are we sending if we let her go?"

Karen stepped in before Chris had a chance to answer "Ani, I know it's hard to look at that list, especially as Kaye is a good friend of yours, but as Chris said, we need to control these cuts or we'll find ourselves being told who's out of the door and that's no good."

Anisha bit her lip, something she did when she was nervous as Chris looked at his watch and excused himself. "Karen, Ani, I'll leave this in your capable hands."

Chris left the room and Anisha tapped her pencil on her laptop "Karen, what about that idea that I spoke to you about a few weeks ago when we had requests from ten people to work four days a week."

Karen looked surprised "What about it?"

Anisha pulled up a spreadsheet on her laptop "Well if we approved all those people to work condensed work hours, we would save enough money from their salaries to cover one and half people. If we then add in the fact that "Part time Pauline" has just been waiting to leave after 30 years we would kill two birds with one stone."

Karen sighed "It's not that simple Ani, if we approve the shorter work requests we still have to pay them their benefits."

Anisha became animated and shook her head "You would, but only at 80%. You see, by working one less day their benefits get pro-rated and we effectively save 20%. This would be a good win-win solution. Can we at least think about it?"

Karen looked at the spreadsheet on the screen "OK Ani but that needs to be our plan B, let's discuss plan A. Please send me that spreadsheet when you get a moment and don't share this with anyone, OK?"

Going Underground

That evening I met Anisha at Liverpool Street Station, like every other evening.

I kissed her on the cheek, like I did every evening, but that evening she seemed a little distracted.

"What's with the long face Ani? You look, like how I feel."

Anisha half-smiled and put her head on my shoulder "I've just had one of those crappy days that you seem to have monopolised."

I wanted to make some smart arse comment but the look on her face said, "do that and you die mister!" so instead I chose Oprah mode, took her hand in mine and said "Do you want to talk about it?"

Anisha shook her head "Not really."

I decided it was now OK to make a smart arse comment "Good! What's for dinner tonight?"

Ani bit her lip, I knew this meant she was nervous "Oh I forget to tell you we're having dinner with mum and dad."

Now Anisha's mum is a superb cook and I love her parents more than I loved my own parents, so I knew there was something else making Anisha nervous.

"That's cool, what's she making?"

Ani dropped eye contact with me and said "Indian food." and then whispered "and Uncle Gulshan is coming over too"

I stared straight ahead, something that Anisha said I did when I got annoyed, and replied "In that case, bring me back a doggy bag."

Anisha took my hand and with a pleading voice said "Oh come on Divind. How long are you going to bear a grudge?

I pulled my hand out of her hand, much to the amusement of two Japanese tourists who started giggling. "A grudge? Let me remind you that this is the idiot who asked your Dad why we were handing out sweets when OUR daughter Sonya was born. Please forgive me if I never get over myself."

Anisha tried to calm me down but the fuse had been lit "This so-called idiot is also my dad's older brother. Divind you need to let things go. He's an old man and you have to remember that he's seeing things through his own experiences. People of his generation never celebrated the birth of a daughter. Please come over, for me."

I was annoyed that Anisha couldn't see why I was annoyed.

Several years earlier, when our daughter Sonya had been born we were so happy that our little family was complete and that she was healthy, and more importantly didn't have my huge nose, that we gave out sweets to all our friends and relatives.

Everyone accepted them graciously except Gulshan uncle who handed the sweets back and said "better luck next time with having a baby boy."

"Please don't use that "for me" card Anisha. You go and have dinner with your family and I'll get a KFC bucket for me and the kids."

Anisha made her version of puppy dog eyes and pouted a little "Is that the last word?"

I held my ground, all the time thinking "I hope the couch has somehow magically got longer and more comfortable since the last time I tried to sleep on it."

"Yup I'm serious. After the sort of day I've had I wouldn't be the best of company either so if I heard him brag about his precious Sunitta-this or his Sunitta-that I would probably strangle him and that would look bad."

Anisha dropped her pout "OK, fine, I'll remember this next time we have one of those boring Purewal gatherings. Just you see."

Ding-Ding! Round One!

We travelled the rest of the way home in silence which is really hard for me to do because I swear I'm the inspiration for Shrek's donkey!

Both of us were annoyed that the other couldn't see that they were wrong.

When we finally arrived at her parent's house Anisha went in ahead of me.

She saw her mum in the kitchen so loudly announced "Divinder is being an idiot and taking the kids for KFC."

Just then Anisha's dad walked out of the living room, newspaper under his arm. "Divinder, are you still angry about what he said about Sonya?"

I nodded "Yes Dad, come on kids we're going to KFC."

Sonya and Kamran cheered and ran towards me, like I was a conquering hero.

I walked down the street with a kid on each hand. Kamran was so excited at the prospect of KFC, on a school night, that he did the signature MC Hammer dance as he sang "KFC time!" to the tune of "Hammer time"

Kamran stopped singing and dancing long enough to ask me a question "Daddy, I thought we were having Indian food with Nana and Nani. They said that Gulshan granddad is coming for dinner."

I stopped walking and crouched down to his height "Listen darling please don't call him Gulshan granddad. You have two granddads and he isn't one of them."

Sonya, trainee lawyer, came to her brother's defence "But Daddy, Mummy said that because he's old and Nana's big brother that we had to call Gulshan granddad."

I scratched my head "OK, here's the deal, you can call him Gulshan granddad but just not in front of me. OK?"

The kids both nodded their heads without really understanding why.

I got through the front door and turned off the alarm.

The kids rushed in and threw their school bags on the stairs and I grabbed the car keys. "Go upstairs and get changed out of your school uniform."

I said that just to get two minutes breathing time.

When they came down a few minutes later I ushered the kids out "Right guys let's jump in the car. I don't know about you guys, but I'm starving!"

The kids ran to the car and jumped in, they put on their seatbelts and waited for me to lock up. Kamran leaned over and tooted the horn impatiently and shouted "Hurry up old man! There's a drumstick with my name on it!"

Ding-Ding! Round Two!

Thirty minutes later and the kids and I were sat around the dining table with a plate of chicken bones in front of us and bulging belly's.

Sonya looked very uncomfortable "Daddy I think I ate too much." and with that, a little burp escaped her mouth. "My tummy hurts."

Not to be outdone Kamran stood up opened his mouth and burped like a fog horn. "That's better!"

Sonya and I both gave Kamran a dirty look and then I burped too and we all laughed!!

Meanwhile at the in-laws house Gulshan was boring everyone with the fact that his precious daughter Sunitta, or Sunny as he called her, a Cambridge educated lawyer was on the fast track to being a partner at a big London law firm.

"Did I tell you that Sunny has been approached to head a new government initiative to recruit more Asian females into the legal world? We are so proud of her. Anisha you should have heard about that, after all you're still a secretary at that law firm aren't you?"

This was what Gulshan did best, he'd throw out passive aggressive comments and then dared people to be offended, all the time hiding behind the fact that he was the families elder statesman and therefore somehow not to be questioned.

Anisha's mum, Rani, jumped in. "Actually Anisha is a Senior HR Manager with one of the top five law firms in London. Anisha could have been a lawyer if she wanted to. She chose a husband and kids over a career. Isn't that right Anisha?"

Anisha smiled at her mum and obnoxious uncle.

She suddenly wished that she had joined Divinder and the kids with their KFC.

Gulshan had only just started "So Anisha, beti, what's new with that husband of yours and the kids? I see he's still boycotting me. Is he still upset that I didn't break-dance when you had a daughter? He needs to realise that there are certain traditions that need to be upheld. Isn't that right Mohan?"

Anisha glared at her dad who avoided her anger by staring at his food.

Just as her mum was about to speak for her again, Anisha spoke.

"Divinder's good and the kids wanted KFC so he decided to take them. I'll be honest with you Gulshan Uncle, Divinder is still upset about you rejecting the sweets we sent. To be really honest I'm not your biggest fan either."

Gulshan spat out the rice in his mouth all over his plate, amazed that someone had talked back to him.

"REALLY?" he said in an over the top tone.

"Is this how your ONLY daughter shows respect Mohan, Rani? Unlike me, with my four kids, you only had one child and you were unable to bring her up properly! Listen here, I am older than you so you HAVE to respect me! Do you understand?"

But Anisha wasn't in the understanding mood! "I tell you what I understand, you have bullied everyone in the family just because you happened to be born first. Nobody likes you, they're just scared of you. Divinder's right, you're just an old bully stuck in the past. I'm going home, I've suddenly lost my appetite!"

With that she grabbed her coat and bag, walked angrily through the kitchen and slammed every door she encountered.

Ding-Ding! Round Three!

Anisha entered the house and slammed the front door for effect.

I looked at my watch and then at her, but before I even had a chance to utter a single word she pointed an accusing finger at me. "Don't even think about saying "I told me so" or God help me I will make you wear that KFC Bargain Bucket on your head and don't ask where I'd stick that drumstick that's in your hand! Now pass me that chicken and share the French Fries, fatso!"

I handed her the bucket of chicken that she snatched from my hand!

The end is nigh! Well sort of, for some people anyway...

Monday December 8th 2003

Just a week after the emergency meeting with Karen and Chris, Anisha was summoned to a staff meeting in the company board room. The whole team was in attendance. Anisha grabbed a seat by Kaye.

"Good morning Anisha darling." said an upbeat Kaye.

Anisha smiled "Hello madam, I guess D-day has arrived!"

They both laughed, nervously.

"Any idea what's going to be said today Ani? I know you said all would be revealed but I feel like one of those sad Hollywood nominees on Oscar night with their face on a massive TV screen hoping that I don't say the f-word when they pick someone else for the award!!"

Anisha smiled and looked anxiously at the door, just as Karen and Chris came into the room.

Chris had a large brown envelope under his right arm.

As Karen and Chris took their chairs the room became silent except for the scraping of seats on the wooden floor.

Karen stood up and walked to the head of the room

"Good morning guys, thanks for coming together at such short notice. As you're all aware this last week has been a tougher one than usual. There have been numerous hushed meetings and I just wanted to say that we appreciate your patience. Before I start, I just want to say that I have heard the rumors that we were going to make redundancies today."

She stared directly at a red-faced Julie, who squirmed in her seat.

"I am happy to say that the management team have come up with a plan that allows everyone to breathe easy again and should allow us all to get back to work without that fear. Well, for this week anyway!"

Her joke created a ripple of mild laughter around the room as well as a few groans.

Karen handed over to Chris who took her place at the head of the room.

Ani smiled at Karen who walked past her but Karen again avoided-making eye contact.

"Thanks Karen. I am pleased to announce that after a lot of thought and after crunching a lot of numbers Karen and I have decided to adopt an approach that will allow us to both offer more flexible working hours and save on the bottom line."

Kaye leaned in close to Anisha and whispered "Ani, fame at last! They're going to go with your idea!! Do me a favour, don't forget to mention the little people when you do your speech eh!"

Chris was just finishing off his speech "Of course none of this could have been possible without the sterling work of one of our unsung heroes, to whom I would like to present this spa voucher for £250."

Chris paused for dramatic effect as Anisha felt her face redden with embarrassment.

Anisha discretely adjusted her skirt as she got ready to stand up and accept her voucher.

Then Chris seemed to speak in slow motion "Could I ask Karen to come back here please?"

Anisha looked across at Karen who deliberately avoided her gaze a third time.

Karen walked the ten feet to where Chris was standing and took a place beside him as someone took a photo for the company's monthly magazine.

Chris extended his right hand as he handed Karen the envelope with his left hand

"Karen please accept this voucher as a small token of our esteem. You really have shown true spirited team work with this win-win solution that you suggested. Guys, Karen has crafted a comprehensive plan where Pauline can leave after all her great service and all the people who requested condensed work weeks will be approved. Let's give a big hand for Karen."

Anisha reluctantly clapped with the rest of the team as Kaye whispered in her ear "Let's grab a coffee eh?"

Anisha nodded and followed Kaye as they made their way through the crowd.

As they are about to leave the room they were stopped by the office creep, Annette, "Hey ladies I've heard that champagne is on the way to toast Karen's creative brilliance."

Anisha bristled and dismissed Annette "I would love to stay Annette but I have to rearrange my knickers drawer. Feel free to have my share of the bubbly."

Tea for two

Anisha and Kaye were sat at the counter at a local café.

Kaye broke the silence "At least it was a nice speech eh?!"

Anisha gave her a "look" that was usually reserved for Divinder, the kids or occasionally her parents.

"Yup, speech of the year!! This is so bloody typical of what happens to me here at Feavin Crookes. I have given Karen so many great ideas that she then rehashes as her own inventions. It really ticks me off because I should be doing what she does and earning the salary she gets."

Kaye placed a hand on Anisha's shoulder "If it's any consolation Ani, I told everyone that you came up with that idea on Tuesday. They all know that you're the brains in the operation."

Anisha forced a smile "Thanks for trying to cheer me up Kaye but the truth is that everyone knowing that this was my plan doesn't pay the mortgage and I could really do with a spa day, god knows I need that right now more than ever!"

Anisha told Kaye all about her argument with Gulshan uncle the night before and about the fact that she feels as trapped in her life as Divinder does but is worried that he'll use that fact to rush them into emigrating to Canada.

Kaye drained the last few drops of coffee from her cup "I tell you what Ani, it sure stinks being you!! Let's go shopping down the West End! No-one's going to miss us, especially if the bubbly's going to flow!! Come on let's go, right now!"

Anisha chugged down her coffee and they left arm in arm.

"You're right, let's do it!!"

Is it home time yet?

I sat at my desk staring at my pc screen, pretending to read a resume.

Suddenly my phone rang, making me jump a little.

I picked up my headset and answered the call. "Good Morning Jonathan Hawk, Divinder speaking. How may I help you?"

The caller introduced himself as Jean-Christophe Papin. "Hi good morning my name is Jean- Christophe Papin. I work as an Investment Manager at Parachute Investments in Knightsbridge. I've been given your details by Morris Micklewhite at Caine & Company."

I sat up in my seat, Morris was something of a legend in the city and if he gave out a referral it was money in the bank.

"Hi Jean-Christophe. How is Morris?" the other voice had an upper class French accent that screamed old money. "He's still the reprobate that we all know and love! By the way please call me JC, only my mother calls me Jean-Christophe and only then when she's very angry with me!"

I laughed and put on my best Hugh Grant telephone voice "OK JC, my name is Divinder and I am the senior consultant in our hedge fund and investment management team. How can I help you?"

JC coughed into the phone, the harshness of the sound making me wince a little "Sorry about that, I'm fighting some allergy. Well, as you probably know, we have just signed a partnership deal with a major Japanese bank."

I didn't know about anything as numbers always scared me but said "Yup, it's all over the wire" and then I cringed and felt like a right muppet for uttering that stupid phrase as I didn't even know what "the wire" meant.

Maurice heard me and mouthed "The wire? You knob head!" and it almost put me off my stride.

"Anyway, we need to recruit seven analysts, preferably with a background in the Far Eastern market and solid OTC experience. We even know some of the guys we want to headhunt."

I did a fist pump like Tom Cruise on Oprah's couch!!

"That's fantastic. Now it would really help me if we could have a face to face meeting. Where are you guys based?

JC started giving me his address "We're based at 16 Beauchamp Place, just around the corner from Harrods. Could I be cheeky and ask you to come over this afternoon? It's just that we need the get the ball rolling ASAP."

I nodded and then realised that he couldn't see me. "That's no problem at all JC. Would 3pm work for you?"

I could hear the sound of a keyboard being tapped "Let me check the online calendar."

After a few seconds JC replied "That would be superb. I won't be here but please ask for Tristan St-John-Smyth, he's our CEO and likes to be involved in all recruitment issues. Thanks Divinder."

I placed the phone down slowly and threw my hands in the air.

I looked over at Maurice and Terrence "Can you guys hear the sound of the cash register guys? Ker-ching!!"

Maurice cupped his ear "No Abdul! All I hear is you squawking about the wire!"

I laughed at Maurice's lame attempt at a joke "Maurice ask me why?"

Maurice shook his head so I threw a soft rugby ball at his head, it caught him over his right eye. "OK stop with the onslaught Abdul!! Why?"

I walked over to his desk "Because I just picked up seven, yes Maurice ONE, TWO, THREE, FOUR, FIVE SIX, SEVEN, investment analyst roles at Parachute Investments from a referral from none other than old Morris Micklewhite. Even better the guy I just spoke with said that they know a lot of the people they already want. So up yours Maurice Simons, UP YOURS!"

Maurice looked sick and gave me the middle finger as I laughed and walked triumphantly back to my desk.

Just then Marion called out my name "Well done Divinder. Would you mind taking Arnold with you?"

My reaction was obvious "If I say no will you let me go by myself?"

Marion smiled.

"Of course not but if you'd said "no problem" it would have made you look like you had some say in the matter!"

Arnold smiled a creepy grin at me that made me want to punch him in the back of the head.

Mind the gap!

Arnold and I sat opposite one another in the carriage.

I was reading a copy of the London Evening Standard that I'd found behind my seat.

Arnold waited for the train to stop and when the passenger next to me left, he took the seat beside me.

To tell you the truth, Arnold wasn't a bad bloke, he was just a little smug and lived in a fantasy world and was fluent in bull shit.

He tried engaging me in the dreaded small talk that I hated.

"So Div, you don't mind if I call you Div do you Div?"

I talked over the paper, avoiding what I imagined would be his smug gaze. "My name's Divinder, so I really would prefer it if you'd call me Divinder."

Arnold sounded genuinely hurt when he replied "But I've heard Terrence call you Div, you never correct him."

I put my paper down "Arnold, I have worked with Terrence for four years and actually like him. He's a personal friend, we even meet up outside of work and the occasional weekend."

Arnold looked like I'd just told him his dog had died! "Why don't you guys like me?"

I have to admit I was somewhat surprised by the honest question so it took me a second before I answered. "What makes you think we don't like you Arnold?"

Arnold looked like I had just walked right into his trap!

He raised his chubby right hand up and started to count off five pieces of "evidence".

"Number 1, I know you guys go out every Friday for a pub lunch and you always book me into interviews from 12 to 2pm so I can't come with you. B, you and Terrence pick up all the best clients and I am left picking up the crumbs that no one wants."

I tried to interrupt him. "About the pub lunch...."

Arnold shushed me and raised his forefinger on his left hand. "Div..... inder, please let me finish."

I nodded and raised both my hands in mock surrender.

"Now where was I? Oh yeah number 3" he pointed his middle finger at me "I know that you all have a nickname for me, 'double A', "Annoying Arnold". D, you all draw straws when it comes to who's taking me out on interviews and number 5, the worst one, you all think that I lie about who I know! I do go to the same clubs as George Michael and Andrew Ridgley. You know how hard it is to work when you know everyone around you hates you? Do you?"

I waited until he stopped talking "Can I speak now?"

I asked and he nodded "Yes, actually I do know how hard it is to work when you know everyone around you hates you, because that's exactly how it was for me at Jonathan Hawk when I first arrived. Do you mind if I address your questions now, point by point?"

Arnold said "Go for it"

"Number 1, the pub lunch. Yes it happens every Friday and it's the most boring gathering you could ever attend. The place is full of big mouthed city types bragging about how much they made that week and then not seeing the irony in asking everyone else to buy them a drink as they are a 'little short on cash flow'."

Arnold frowned a little, scrunched his face and adjusted his glasses as I carried on.

"Number 2, when I started at Jonathan Hawk, I was given a phone book and told to start at A and go through to Z. I banged my head against a brick wall for months before I got my first placement. At least when you got here, Terrence and I each gave you five warm clients to start you off."

Arnold tried to interrupt me and it now it was my turn to put up my forefinger in the same way that Arnold had done to me a few minutes earlier.

"Let me finish Arnold. Number 3: 'Double A', it's true we do call you Annoying Arnold because you don't stop talking! It's like you have verbal diarrhea! Earlier today when Terrence saw that I was pissed off because of some racist idiot you felt you could butt in. Number 4, taking you out on interviews isn't our favorite thing to do with you and that's because you take over and say dumb stuff."

Arnold looked perplexed "Dumb stuff? Give me an example!"

I placed the newspaper on the seat next to me "OK do you remember last month when you went to see that German client with Peter?"

"Yeah what about it?"

"Well when the client told you that the Head of Operations had died suddenly earlier that week you told her you had the perfect candidate and could get the resume over "dead quick""

Arnold looked slightly sheepish "OK it was a bad choice of words. Is that all you have?"

I shook my head and continued with what was fast turning into a character assassination.

"Then there was last week when you told Brian Curry at the Indian Bank of Trade and Credit that he had 'the perfect surname for an Indian bank!' You can't say stuff like that without it backfiring on you. Number 5, you can't keep on making up stuff about celebrities being your friends. This bragging doesn't impress us at all!"

Arnold looked really upset.

I hadn't planned on kicking him when he was down, but he was just getting to me.

After a few seconds of silence he spoke "What would you suggest I do?"

I looked at him with a "watcha talkin' bout Willis?" look on my face.

Was he really asking my advice on how to be less annoying?

Me, as someone who my wife often described as the living body of an annoyance!?

"My advice is this, number one - listen more than you talk. My wife always tells me that I have one mouth and two ears for a reason and that I should listen twice as much as I speak."

Arnold nodded like he was being told something life changing.

"Number two, stop making up bull shit stories about famous people and pretending you know them and just think about what you're saying. I'm sure you're a nice bloke but you put up too much of a front. We're here now. Do me a favour, let me lead the meeting and if I look at you and raise both eyebrows feel free to jump in."

He nodded and looked like a deflated balloon.

Nothing like the smell of old money in the afternoon!

We entered the lobby of a very grand looking building in Knightsbridge and I pressed the buzzer for Parachute Investments and shouted into the microphone that we were there to see Tristan St- John-Smyth.

After a few seconds a loud static buzz rang in my ear and the door opened.

We both walked along the wooden clad corridor to a reception desk manned by a huge white security guard wearing a black uniform and a peaked cap.

He stood up when he saw us and I swear he was about 7 feet tall and about 4 feet wide!

"Good afternoon gentlemen. Could I ask that you kindly sign the visitor's book and empty your pockets into the grey tray on the desk please?"

We did as instructed and then signed our names.

The security guard looked at the sticks of gum, wallets and pens in the tray and then told us we could have the contents back and asked us to follow him to the elevator.

I whispered to Arnold "It's like bloody Fort Knox!"

Arnold laughed and loudly said "Luckily I disguised the gun in my pen!"

The security guard looked back at Arnold and glared at him for a second as we waited for the elevator to arrive.

I mouthed "stupid stuff" and Arnold nodded and put his head down.

All three of us entered the tiny elevator and the guard pressed the button for the 8th floor.

Arnold hated silence so tried to make small talk with the guard "What's the weather like up there mate?"

I put my leather briefcase in front of my face in embarrassment.

The security guard tried to give Arnold an out "Sorry sir?"

Arnold didn't take the hint.

"Well you're tall so I thought I'd find out what the weather was like up there. It's a joke." the security guard laughed sarcastically "Oh I see. Ha-ha, that's the first time I've ever heard that comment. This is your floor. I'll see you both when you finish." he made it sound like a threat!

We squeezed past the guard and walked to yet another reception desk.

We both approached the young woman at the desk and smiled at her. She smiled back. "Hello, are you here to see Tristan?"

I smiled again "Yes we are. I'm Divinder and this is my colleague Arnold" I handed her both our business cards "We're from Jonathan Hawk."

The Receptionist took both cards and then picked up her phone and pressed the button for an internal line.

"Hi Marjorie, please let Mr. St-John-Smyth know that there are two gentlemen here to see him from Jonathan Hawk. OK I'll ask them to take a seat. Thank you."

She stood up and asked us to take a seat on a nearby leather couch.

"Mr. St-John-Smyth will be a few minutes late so can I get you a cup of tea, a coffee or some water?"

I shook my head. I was already nervous and a bladder full of freezing cold water wouldn't be a good thing.

"No I'm fine thanks. Arnold?"

Arnold shook his head in reply.

We both took a seat and I picked up a copy of their company report from the coffee table and pretended that I knew what all the graphs meant as Arnold started to fiddle with his cuff links. "Are you nervous Arnold?"

He shrugged "No, not really. I just rub my cuff links for good luck."

I looked at his cuff links and they looked pretty impressive. "They're pretty flash cuff links, Arnold, are they from Next?"

Arnold laughed dismissively "NEXT?? Mate, they're from my old school."
I felt a little stupid "I'm guessing that you mean private school?"

He nodded

"Which one did you go to?" he touched the face of his cuff link "It's
a small one in Bristol called The Masonic School."

I wanted to make out that I'd heard of that school but it was obvious
I didn't have clue. "Masonic, eh? Do you have to expose your left nipple
and pull up your right trouser leg when you meet a fellow school mate?!"

Arnold started to laugh out loud, somewhat louder then he'd expected.

"No mate, but we do have a secret handshake! I'd show you but I'd
have to kill you afterwards!"

Just as I was about to ask another question a short jockey-like man
approached us. I extended my hand but he shook Arnold's hand.

"Hi I'm Tristan." he said in a voice that was straight out of
Downton Abbey.

Arnold had the decency to introduce me "Hi I'm Arnold and this is my
senior colleague Divinder."

Tristan looked at me for a second and waved at me and said "Hey."

Tristan started walking "Please follow me, I don't have a great deal of
time before Mr. Yakamota arrives"

We followed him into a large board room with oak panels and portraits
of scary looking old white guys with handle bar moustaches.

I realised that I needed to take control of the meeting as Tristan
assumed that I was Arnold's flunky.

"Tristan, thanks for seeing us at such short notice, we really appreciate it."

Tristan gave me another quick look and then became mesmerized
by Arnold's cufflinks.

He tapped Arnold's sleeve with his pen "Masonic?"

Arnold smiled "Sorry? Did you say moronic?"

Tristan laughed and looked at Arnold's cufflinks "Are you a Mason Old
Boy? Did you attend Masonic?"

Arnold laughed awkwardly "Yes, yes I did. Sorry I honestly thought
you said moronic!"

Suddenly I was a by-stander at an impromptu school reunion!!

Tristan seemed hell bent on seeing if Arnold was for real.

"What year did you finish?" Arnold puffed out his chest like a sad peacock "I finished in '96."

Tristan nodded and asked us to take a seat.

I was just about to ask him a question when he said "Did you know spunker Forbes?"

Arnold smiled again, like they were sharing a private joke while I just thought "why would anyone call themselves or let other people call them spunker?"

"Spunker junior or Spunker senior?"

Tristan slammed the table, I thought we were being kicked out and then he said "Hurrah! Good man! Only a true Mason Old Boy would know there were two spunkers. I was there up until '90. The best years of my life!"

Arnold agreed "Indeed, the happiest of days."

I forced a laugh "OK, now that the school reunion is done can we move onto the candidate overview?"

Tristan gave me a dirty look.

I have always found dirty looks from public school boys to be the dirtiest as you never know what they're judging you on!

As much as I tried to manage the conversation Tristan was only interested in speaking to Arnold "So Arnold, how did you get into the murky world of financial recruitment?"

Arnold shuffled in his seat "I spent a few years in the back office at Barclays Global and then when 9/11 happened I decided to get out and have a go at recruitment. It's been really good so far. So Tristan, what are you guys looking for?"

Tristan took out a job description and handed it to Arnold.

Arnold passed it onto me and I quickly read through it as they carried on their trip along memory lane.

"This looks pretty straightforward" I said as if I understood what they were looking for but knowing that I would show Terrence the details later and he'd explain what they actually needed "I have a couple of resumes with me and was hoping you could have a quick look at them."

I reached into my briefcase and placed three resumes on the table in front of Tristan.

"I'll leave these with you to have a look at them. When I spoke to JC earlier he mentioned that you have a couple of people that you'd like headhunted. Do you know anything about that?

Tristan looked at his expensive watch "I do. Do you have business cards? I need to prepare for my next meeting now."

Arnold handed him his card, which he placed in his pocket, as I placed my card on top of the resumes with a paperclip.

Tristan walked us to the door that he then opened. "I'll have to kick you guys out now as the Asian invasion" he made 'Chinese' eyes' is about to start" as he spoke he looked over at me "No offence"

I shrugged "None taken. Before we go could I get your business card please Tristan?"

Tristan reached into his shirt pocket and gave his card to Arnold who placed it into his presentation folder.

As we walked out with Tristan, towards the reception desk, he placed his hand on Arnold's shoulder "Arnold I'll get JC to email you the names of the guys at Goldman's later today. It'll be like shooting fish in a barrel! Oh, and by the way, I'm arranging a stag party for spunker senior this Saturday. I'll call your cell, now that I have your number. Ciao!"

With that he shook Arnold's hand and walked away through another door as I stood with my arm outstretched.

We took this as our cue to leave.

A few minutes later and we were sat on a tube train again, heading back to the office. I was unusually quiet whereas Arnold was eager to debrief. "That went well didn't it Div....inder?"

I pulled a face.

"If you say so Arnold" he looked puzzled "Mate, Tristan just handed us seven vacancies and is even going to give ME the names of five people that he'd like me to headhunt. That sounds like a pretty sweet gig for US."

I pulled another "watcha 'talkin 'bout Willis" face "Us? This is my deal, I got the referral from Morris"

Arnold shook his head like a chimp "No way! Are you for real?! He didn't even want to acknowledge that you were there! I'm talking to Marion about getting half the commission!

I lost it, right there and then at Holborn station on the Central Line!

I grabbed Arnold by the lapels on his jacket and pushed him against the carriage doors.

I was suddenly aware that I was causing a scene, so let him go.

Arnold adjusted his tie and tried to compose himself again.

"Arnold that isn't going to happen. This is why people dislike you, you can't try to pull that sort of crap and expect them to give you the thumbs up. And the fact that he ignored me really ticked me off! What makes you public school boys think you're better than the rest of us plebs?"

That's when Arnold unwittingly pressed all my buttons at once "Do you want a burger with the chip on your shoulder?"

I got right in his personal space again "Listen double A, you have no idea what I have had to do to get to where I am today. I went to one of the worst schools in East London, suffered racism like you could never imagine. So don't you ever suggest that I have a "chip on my shoulder" I'm going to sit over there before I do or say something that I might regret later."

I moved across the carriage and took a seat and tried to calm down, but failed.

After a few minutes the train arrived at Moorgate Station and Arnold had the sense to walk a few steps ahead of me.

As we arrived at the office the elevator door opened and out stepped Marion.

She smiled, her shark-like-smile "Ah, just the man I wanted to see. Divinder can I see you for a minute?"

I sighed dramatically "Sure. Am I in trouble, again?"

Marion laughed as Arnold skulked off into the elevator.

Marion opened the door to a nearby boardroom "No, not this time Divinder."

I took a seat opposite Marion as she took her laptop out. "So Divind, what's wrong?" I gave her a surprised look "Terrence had a word with me earlier, he's worried that you're getting depressed again."

I relaxed a little.

Marion had a reputation for being a ball buster and the boardroom was where she always delivered her knock-out punch.

"It's nothing really. I've just had a really crappy day. First thing this morning I met Hitler's nephew and now I just came back from a client meeting, that I set up, and I was treated like Arnold's servant. By the way that idiot is going to try to get half my commission just for going to the same school as the idiot client we just met with."

Marion giggled, something she only ever did when she was nervous.

I always said bad news comes in threes and this looked like the last bit of news "Sounds like a great start to the week! Anyway I wanted to see you about that recent pay rise request you made."

I tried to make light of the situation, but my gut told me that I was not about to hear some great news "Finally, some good news!" she screwed her face up "Actually it's not what you want to hear."

I straightened up in my chair "Listen, Marion you told me last year that if I hit my target you would look at increasing my salary"

Marion bristled, no one ever told her to listen "I'm not denying that, but you didn't technically hit your target did you?"

She pulled a spreadsheet up on her screen and asked me to look at it with her so I moved around to her side of the desk. I found my name and pointed at the screen "Look I only missed my target by 200 pounds! If I give you the money can we say that I did hit my target?"

Marion giggled again

"You know that's not how it works. I did speak to Phil and he said that he's happy to look at the situation again this time next year. It's not all bad news though, because we are prepared to make you a Team Leader in recognition for all the work you do with Arnold."

I didn't even pretend to understand and went straight into sulk mode.

"So, let me get this straight, I'm getting a paper promotion but no pay rise?"

Marion closed her laptop and stood up "Listen Divind, you know as well as I do that business is slow and Phil and the board are even looking at laying people off so this is the best I could do." she walked over to the door and opened it, which meant that she was done and I could leave.

"Think about it and let me know later today if I can make the announcement at the quarterly meeting tonight."

Purewal P.I!

Back at my desk I tapped on my keyboard and found the revenue forecasts for the team.

Employee: Title:	2003-2004 revenue target	2003-2004 revenue actuals
Divinder Purewal Senior Consultant {Investment Mgt}	£160,000 GBP	£ 159,800 GBP
Employee: Title:	2003-2004 revenue target	2003-2004 revenue actuals
Maurice Simons. Senior Consultant {Private Banking}	£160,000 GBP	£ 145,000 GBP
Employee: Title:	2003-2004 revenue target	2003-2004 revenue actuals
Peter Purcell Senior Consultant {Private Banking}	£160,000 GBP	£ 165,000 GBP

I hit the print button and headed for the printer to retrieve my "evidence" which I then folded and quickly placed into my inside jacket pocket.

There may be trouble ahead....

Later that evening I sat with Terrence at Jonathan Hawk's quarterly meeting and drinks.

This was just an excuse to get drunk on the company's money every three months.

Terrence commiserated with my day from recruitment hell "Sorry mate that sounds like a pretty crappy day. At least you can toast your sorrows with a few free drinks eh?"

We raised our glassed, his was beer and mine was Sprite and we toasted quietly.

"To not working here!" and we laughed!

The meeting began with Marion standing at the front. "Hi guys, really great results for this last quarter of 2003. The board have asked me to let you all know that they're very happy with how you guys have done in such a quiet market."

Marion applauded and the rest of the team joined in.

"Now just before you all get too drunk, at our expense, I thought I would take this opportunity to tell you all about some upcoming promotions for January 2004. If I could get the following consultants to come up to the front: Peter Purcell, Maurice Simons and Divinder Purewal."

Peter, Maurice and I walked to the front of the room to golf claps and a few sarcastic wolf whistles.

Marion handed each of us a small white envelope.

"I am very proud to promote three members of my team from Senior Consultant positions to Team Leader roles. Please give it up for Peter, Maurice and Divinder."

The rest of the team started to whoop comically as Peter and Maurice took theatrical bows. Meanwhile I opened my envelope and saw a spa voucher for £200. I turned to Marion and showed her my prize.

She shrugged her shoulders and gave me a sheepish grin.

"The bar's open so please enjoy the evening and remember this venue is like Las Vegas: what happens here stays here!"

I approached Marion "We need to chat"

Marion looked like she was expecting my reaction and simply said "OK, follow me."

We headed out of the main room and into a smaller room with a table.

Marion took the lead "Let me apologize for not waiting for your reply but I guessed that you were highly unlikely to decline a promotion so made an executive decision."

I took the folded A4 sheet out of my jacket pocket and handed it to Marion.

Marion read the details quickly and dropped the paper on the table.

"Why are you showing me this?" she asked with a real accusatory tone.

I was in no mood to play nice so, picking up the paper, I went for it "I need you to tell me how Maurice gets promoted when he's £15,000 under his revenue target and I don't?"

A black look came over Marion's face and she spat her words out "I don't need to explain myself to you, I'm your manager, not the other way round!"

Usually I would be the compliant little Indian boy but I honestly felt an injustice and was ready to walk away from the company. "No, Marion, you owe me an explanation because right now this looks like favoritism and that isn't right."

Marion had somehow managed to calm down almost immediately and in a very calm and measured voice replied, "If you must know, I promoted Maurice because he started on the same day as Peter and it would have looked bad if we promoted one and not the other."

That's when I lost it for the third time that day, if you include walking out on "Frank" Frank and the earlier bust up with Arnold.

"Come on Marion, that's a pretty lame excuse. What about the fact that he's £15,000 under target? Are you, Phil and the board just going to ignore that little fact?"

'Calm Marion' suddenly made way for 'Crazy pointy-fingers Marion' and I didn't like her at all!

"Now you listen to me Divinder, you know that Maurice lost a £17,000 fee earlier this week and if that had come in he would have been £2,000 over his target"

I stupidly hit the self-destruct button "That's like saying that if my uncle had tits he'd be my aunt!"

Marion wasn't used to people answering back "Excuse me? You are skating on very thin ice, mister!! I know you've had a bad day but you're very close to getting a warning from me right now, for insubordination. Just back off OK?"

I looked at her and she was physically shaking with anger.

I knew that I had to back off but the stubborn idiot in me needed to have one last word "I will back off, but one final question: whose idea was it to give me £200?"

Marion seemed surprised by my question "Mine, why?"

I spoke very slowly and deliberately, letting my words hit their mark "Think about it Marion, £200 is the exact amount I missed my target by. Feels like insult to injury."

With that, I walked out of the room, grabbed my coat and headed to the train station to meet Anisha from work.

We have lift off!

I reached the bench, besides the ticket barrier, just seconds before Anisha did.

I gave her a kiss on the cheek and we started to walk, hand in hand, towards the 7:35pm train to Shenfield.

Anisha was as quiet as I was.

This was never good.

I started to think about what I'd done that day, sure in the knowledge that I'd annoyed her at some point and was waiting for the dam to break.

A few more seconds passed in silence and I was conscious of the fact that we hadn't exchanged more than two words.

I was just about to say something when she broke the silence "Divind, I've been thinking about Canada...

I looked at Anisha with the most intense stare I could manage.

"Ani after the sort of day I've had I think I need to warn you that I am just looking for a fight so please don't pick that scab again."

Anisha sighed

"No Divind I was going to say let's look into it!"

I smiled the biggest smile I could without looking like the Joker from Batman!

"Don't mess with me Ani. I have had the day from hell and if you are winding me up God help you!! First I get Alf Garnet, then a pompous public school knob-head treated me like a servant and then I get told that I will be getting promoted but without any pay rise."

Anisha smiled back and patted my shoulder "Let's just say we've had equally crappy days today" then without really engaging my brain I said "Good! I mean, that's terrible!! I mean, please tell me all about your day, in full, on the train."

Thankfully Anisha laughed as we took a seat on the train going home.

Over the next five minutes Ani told me what had happened at work.

Ani was close to tears so I kept my smart arse remarks to myself.

I shook my head "I can't believe that Karen did that AGAIN!!! Do you want me to send the boys over to give her the once over? Just say the word."

I punched my left palm with my right fist and scrunched my face for effect.

Anisha laughed.

"Divind, firstly the only boys you know are your brothers and your dad and collectively you guys couldn't fight your way out of a wet paper bag! Secondly Kaye made me realise that there's a whole life out there, in Canada, that we could be missing out on."

I was a little taken back by what Anisha was saying "She's a wise old bird that Kaye."

Anisha giggled.

"Really? You've always said – and I quote 'Kaye's the closest thing to a living Muppet!'"

I blushed but my dark face hid the redness

"Yes..... I did say that.... but what I meant by that was....that..... Kaye's like a very clever, living Muppet! Like Beaker the scientist!"

Anisha laughed again and threw her head back, hitting the seat with a thump.

She carried on laughing as she rubbed her head gently and then wiped a tear away.

I hadn't heard Anisha laugh so much in a long time so just smiled back at her.

She regained her composure again "OK Divind, so what exactly do we need to do to emigrate to Canada? That huge pack of forms looked pretty scary."

I sat up in my seat and was suddenly excited in a way that I hadn't been since I discovered free soft drink refills at Costco!

"It's not that bad Ani. There are about 40 forms that we need to fill in and from what I can gather getting into Canada is a little like a board game."

Ani looked confused "You what? A board game?"

I took out a piece of paper and a pen from my jacket and started making a quick sketch.

"Basically the Canadian government wants to attract as many educated and skilled people as it can. It realizes that if you earn more, you pay more in taxes."

Ani nodded as she rubbed the back of her head.

I carried on with my description "We just need to get over 65 points to get reviewed for immigration purposes. So they give you points for certain skills. For instance speaking English as a mother tongue gives you 10 points, writing English fluently also gives 10 points."

Anisha looked at my rough drawing "So would they make an exception for you?"

I didn't follow what she meant so said "What do you mean, exception?" she laughed and said "Well you said Canada wants as many educated and skilled people as it can get, you're neither educated nor skilled!!"

I slapped her forehead and it made her bang her head on the exact same spot on the seat!

Thankfully she laughed through her tears and said "Have you worked out how many points we get?"

I added a few columns to my sketch "I've worked out that we get about 70 points. That includes our academics, work experience, English skills as well as other stuff like how much money we'll bring with us."

Anisha suddenly looked all serious again "Divind, do you think we're going to Canada for the correct reasons?"

I deliberately avoided her gaze "What does 'correct reasons' mean Ani?"

Ani saw that I was avoiding her gaze. "Divind, look up."

I looked up, with slightly scared eyes. "We've had a few bad days and all of a sudden we're looking at leaving. Are we being cowards?"

I locked my gaze and gave an impassioned speech "Ani I can't tell you how frustrated I am with my life right now and I really don't see it changing any time soon. I don't want to dread going to work every day for the rest of my life. We've also outgrown the house and there's no way I'm paying an extra £100,000 for an extra bedroom and another bathroom for a house in Woodford." she nodded "But what if we get there and hate it? Can we come back?"

I laughed out loud making an Indian teenage girl give me a really dirty look that made me laugh even louder! "Ani we haven't even filled in the papers yet, let's not start looking at how we get back just yet eh!"

The point of no return!

That night we put the kids to bed as usual and then we went downstairs to read the immigration forms.

I emptied the whole pack onto the table.

Anisha picked up the first form:

APPLICATION FOR PERMANENT RESIDENCE IN CANADA.

She started to read the questions and with a pencil ticked off the boxes that applied to us.

I couldn't help smiling.

Another dream was finally becoming reality.

Anisha started ticking boxes like she was being paid to do it and when she hit page 7 she stopped and placed her pencil in her mouth "This seems pretty straight forward. When do we get to the tough part?"

I smirked.

"Hey whoa there Nelly! This is part one of a four part process. First we submit our application. Then they review our application and according to these notes that can take between 15 and 20 months."

Anisha opened her mouth in shock and the pencil landed on the table. "20 months?! What if we change our minds in that time?"

I made sure I had eye contact and spoke very carefully "We can't change our minds once we submit our paperwork. They won't care because the cheque would have cleared by then."

Anisha raised her right eyebrow "What cheque?"

I shook my head.

"Did you think it was free to emigrate? We have to pay $1400 as a family just to get our application into the process. Those lumberjack shirts aren't cheap you know!! Do you still want to go ahead?"

Anisha nodded "You better fill this form out today because if I have a good day tomorrow I might change my mind!"

I laughed – nervously. "I still have to tell you about the rest of the process. Assuming we get through the initial application process we then have to have a medical to see what sort of shape we're in. Canada has enough home-grown people on welfare so doesn't want anymore. Then if we get through that we might have to go through an interview at the High Commission and then after that we just have to sell the house, quit our jobs, take the kids out of school, pack all our belongings into a container and then we are Canada bound!!"

Anisha took a deep breath. "OK, let's do it!"

We ploughed through the paperwork and after four hours the forms were completed.

Anisha placed all the forms into a huge brown envelope "So Divind we just need to get photocopies of all 4 passports, our birth certificates and marriage certificate as well as bank statements yeah?"

I just nodded "That's it, then we wait."

Just as Anisha was about to put the envelope in her work bag she looked at the first form again "Divind it says here on this fee payment page that children under the age of 7 are considered infants but we need to think about how old Kamran will be when the process gets completed. He's only a few weeks away from turning 8."

I tutted, something that Anisha hated me doing.

"You worry too much Ani. I reckon that we could get all the papers back by the middle of January. Why pay an extra £60 if we don't need to Ani? Think about it Ani? That's almost $150"

Anisha shrugged her shoulders and went off to bed as I tidied up in the kitchen.

Work: a true 'four letter word'!

Wednesday February 25th 2004

Anisha and I had just picked up Kamran and Sonya and were walking the short distance back to our house.

Kamran was holding my hand as Anisha walked with Sonya.

Kamran looked up at me "How was work Dad?"

I hesitated before I replied "It was as good as it usually is son."

Kamran smiled impishly "So it was another crap day then?" unfortunately for Kamran, and I, his mum heard him!

"Where did you learn the word crap?" she asked, rhetorically whilst looking directly at me.

Kamran pointed at me and gave me the sort of look he gave before he threw me under the bus "From Daddy. He says it all the time when you tell him to stop playing PlayStation with me and help you instead."

Anisha sneered at me so I pretended to discipline Kamran "That's a very bad word Kamran, just don't say that anymore OK?"

Kamran nodded but I felt it was just for his mum to see.

I unlocked the front door and walked into the porch.

I looked to the left hand side of the porch where the mail slot was located.

There on the floor was a large padded brown envelope with the Canadian flag in the top right hand corner.

I picked it up excitedly and ran back out to Anisha!

"Ani it's arrived!! It's arrived!!"

I was conscious of the fact that our neighbours were looking out of their windows as I screamed at the top of my voice but didn't care as I ran back into the house!

Anisha walked over to me "What's arrived?"

I think I shouted "A LETTER FROM THE CANADIAN EMBASSY!! I THINK WE'RE ALREADY IN!!"

Anisha ran over to me as I threw my briefcase on the table and started to rip up the envelope.

I quickly emptied all the contents onto the table.

The envelope contained the whole pack that we'd sent 6 weeks earlier had been returned in full.

Anisha looked at the pack and then at me again "Divind why have they sent all our forms back?"

I started to speed-read the short letter that came with the application pack.

Dear Sir/ Madam,
Wednesday 19th February 2004
Reference: Can.Imm/12986708-05

Thank you for your recent application for immigration to Canada.

Unfortunately, your form was completed incorrectly. Please see the bold item on the list below, then amend and return the updated application pack * as soon as possible:

• Insufficient application fee payment
• Application form(s) not completed fully
• Unclear resume and or references

Kindest regards,
Canadian High Commission, Grosvenor House, London.
* Due to the fact that the application wasn't completed as required by Canadian law your application will be sent to the back of the queue

---

My eyes bugged out because I knew I'd messed up "CRAP!!"

Kamran told me off "DADDY! That's a bad word!"

Anisha picked up the pack and looked for the application fee form. She found it at the very back of the pile.

"No Kam, this time crap is exactly the right word!"

When she next spoke she did so with a bad imitation of my voice "Why pay an extra £60 if we don't need to eh Ani? Think about it?" Why did I listen to you?! You are such an idiot! For the sake of £60 we are now 6 weeks further back in the application process! I'm tempted to say forget it!! I'm going to my mum's house to calm down. I suggest you start dinner while I'm gone! Come on Sonya let's go see Nani."

Anisha stormed off back to her parent's house with Sonya in hot pursuit.

I took her advice and decided to start dinner to calm her down.

Kamran switched the TV on as I started dinner "Dad, why is mum so angry?"

I shrugged "I messed up" he made a sad face "You mean, you messed up again?"

I nodded "Yes, I messed up, again, again."

Kamran walked over and put his arms around my legs "Don't worry Daddy, Mum will calm down, eventually. Can I ask you a question?"

I crouched down to his height "Of course you can darling"

Kamran nuzzled in close like a little puppy looking for a cuddle.

"Daddy can I get a PS2 for Christmas?"

I stood up, realizing that he was working me over with his Mum out of sight. "Oh, that again? Listen Kamran we are going to Canada soon and the PS2 from here won't work in Canada."

"Why's that Dad?"

I sighed, having told him the same thing about a dozen times before "We have different electricity from them."

Kamran looked like I was lying "Eh Dad? Different electricity? What does that even mean?"

He was scanning my face as kids do with their parents when they don't understand what they've been told, but I have nothing "Honestly Kamran, I don't know how to explain it but we can't take one from here to there OK?"

He raised an eyebrow as a yes.

A few seconds later he spoke again "Dad, was there a PS2 when you were a kid?"

I stopped peeling the potatoes "No there wasn't. Besides which we were pretty poor so we couldn't have afforded one."

Kamran smiled like a therapist taking notes with their patient. "Oh, I see. Was there anything like a PS2 when you were small?"

I made a face and replied "I guess the Atari was similar. My god if you saw the games back then you'd laugh at what we thought was entertainment. Pong!! Space Invaders! Pac-Man!"

Kamran laughed along with me without really knowing why he was laughing "Did you ever get to play with that Antari?"

I corrected him "The At-ar-ee. We had a cousin, Peter who had one but he would only let us watch him play it."

Hearing this, made Kamran a little sad "Did you feel sad when that happened?"

I put down the potato peeler "Of course I did! I'm ashamed to admit that I hated Peter for making me feel that I had a cra...rubbish life. Now where's this line of questioning going?"

He turned away for a second, just for dramatic effect "Nowhere Dad. It just seems to me that you want me to have the same rubbish childhood that you had!"

And with that he walked off upstairs to his bedroom, leaving me laughing.

An hour later, I'd made dinner and Anisha returned with Sonya, seemingly a little calmer then when she'd left.

I plated up dinner and placed it on the table.

You could almost hear the sounds of the egg shells under my feet.

I handed Anisha a pathetically wilted dandelion from the garden and said "I've written a new cheque and I'll repost the application pack tomorrow. I'm really sorry."

Anisha didn't acknowledge me, or the pathetically wilted dandelion, and instead spoke to Kamran

"Kamran go get the calendar off the fridge."

Kamran looked a little surprised "Why Mum?"

Anisha didn't let down her angry mask "It's not every day that your Dad admits he's wrong!"

We all laughed as Sonya looked at us in dismay.

"What's so funny? It's not fair! No one ever tells me why something's funny!"

Absent friends

Thursday July 8th 2004

We were shopping in a local supermarket when we bumped into a couple of friends Naya and Kamaljeet. They had two young kids, Anish and Rashni aged a few months apart from Kamran and Sonya.

Naya was a very successful financial planner and Kamaljeet a Vet so they were real movers and shakers in the local community.

Naya came rushing over "Hi Anisha, long time no see!" she stepped forward and gave Anisha two air kisses as I shook Kamaljeet's hand.

Anisha was a little taken back and was someone you never, ever air kissed!

"Long time indeed! How have you guys been?"

Naya was one of those over-enthusiastic people who spoke as much with her hands as her voice and you stood a few feet away for fear of being hit by one of her well-manicured fingers.

"Great! We're having a birthday party for Anish next Saturday and you really should come. It'll give you a chance to see our new five bedroom house."

Anisha stepped back just as Naya's arm swung through "The 16th? Isn't Anish's birthday in December?"

Naya laughed and then turned it into a snort "Well remembered!! It is, so we always have a half year birthday party for him so that he can enjoy the good weather. We've invited all his friends from his new fee paying school."

Anisha forced a smile on her face.

She found people that spoke about money, very tacky "Divind are we busy this weekend?"

I had managed to say a quick hello and was making faces and shaking my head out of the sight lines of both Naya and Kamaljeet.

"You know Ani, I can't remember. Can we call you guys later today and let you know?"

Kamaljeet piped up "Sure, you should try to come along though, you'll have fun. All my cricket buddies will be there. See you both later!"

And with that Naya and Kamaljeet headed towards the checkouts as I pushed my shopping trolley towards the deli counter.

Anisha playfully grabbed my ear "What's with the face back there?"

I winced in real pain "I just don't like them!"

I'd fallen right into Anisha's trap!

She'd always said I had an irrational hatred of rich people. "Why, because he's an influential Vet and she's a successful business woman?"

I responded "No" without making eye contact. "Could it be that you're jealous of the fact that they're rich and drive his and hers BMWs?"

Again I responded with a resounding but weak "No."

Anisha kept pushing "So what is it then?"

I cracked under her interrogation "OK, you want to know what it is? They are just so full of themselves! Why did Naya have to mention that their son is at a fee paying school? I don't care! And anyway if they wanted us to come they would have called us. They're only inviting us because we bumped into them. You know what that was?"

Anisha humoured me "No, I don't. Please educate me, oh wise man!"

I didn't take her bait "That there, was nothing more than an unvite!"

I knew I was in trouble when Anisha folded her arms across her chest

She pointed at me "An unvite?! I don't even know what that is! Sounds like you just made it up! I still think you're jealous!"

I shook my head vigourously as I tried to define a word I had just invented!

"An unvite is.....when someone feels guilted into asking you along usually as afterthought and everyone, apart from you it appears, knows that you should never accept an unvite. And what's to be jealous of? His ill-fitting wig or jealous of her trying to social climb? I just don't mix with them and their friends. You watch, if we go we'll stand out like sore thumbs. All their mates will be discussing this property deal and that property deal while I'll be sitting in the corner grinning like an idiot as we struggle to save some money for the kid's university fund."

Anisha just shook her head "You have to give me two reasons why we shouldn't go in the next minute or we're going!"

I started stuttering, something I only seemed to do around my mum and Anisha.

I held up the forefinger on my right hand "Oh...OK, reason one, I d-don't want to go!"

She laughed like before, only louder "Not good enough. Try again. You have 55 seconds left!"

I knew I had a weak argument and that Anisha wanted to do something other than stay at home over the weekend "Why isn't that a good enough reason?"

Anisha took a step forward, right in my personal space, something she knew I despised "Because we'll just sit at home on Saturday night watching TV so this looks like a pretty good alternative."

I looked at my watch "Hey, I still have 50 seconds to give you two reasons!"

She walked off as I shouted out behind her, "Their kids are like little robots!"

Anisha made the "L" loser symbol on her forehead "If that's the best you have that's really pathetic!"

I wasn't giving up without a damn good fight! "I hate the way he asks me a question and then ignores my answer or just changes the subject."

Anisha dismissed me "Try again! You have about forty seconds left!"

I raised my arms in surrender "OK, I'll go but I'll tell you now that I won't have fun!"

I could not have known how true that prophecy was to be until that day.

"Just give it up Divinder because we are going. And you wonder why I tell people that I have three kids!"

Location, Location, Location...

Saturday July 17th 2004

We pulled up outside a large house a few miles from our house, in our 9 year old Ford Escort.

The street was packed with high end cars and I felt way out of my depth.

Anisha was right, I had a problem with rich people, I didn't like the idea that money bought access to opportunities that poorer people, like me, didn't see.

I turned to Anisha, in the passenger seat "Jeez! Look at the size of their house! You could get our place on their driveway!'

Anisha clicked her tongue, winked at me and said "It's just a house Divind. It's like I always tell you, it's not the size, but what you do with it!"

I laughed and then stopped as Kieran seemed to get the joke.

We all stepped out of the car and the kids ran ahead excitedly.

I walked up to the gate and felt like The Freshie Prince of Ilford!!

Kamran reached up and rang the doorbell.

The door was answered a few seconds later by an older Indian man who smiled at us.

The kids squeezed past him as he called back to Naya.

The old man turned around "Naya beti, there are some more guests for Anish's party"

I smiled at him and was grateful when Naya suddenly appeared from the kitchen and waved us in.

Anisha lead the way into a grand entrance hall with antique black and white tiles on the floor and an upright piano in the right hand corner.

I looked around and saw that a few of the guests were hanging around the kitchen with drinks in hand.

Naya beckoned Anisha over and started talking food "Anisha I am so glad you're here I have a new chutney recipe that is to die for. Please send the kids to the field on the back of the garden, they're all playing a big game of cricket out there."

Kamaljeet came out of a room to the left and guided me into the reception room where all the men were sitting.

He introduced me in a loud voice over the sound of the CD playing classical Indian music "Everybody, this is Divinder, Divinder this is everybody!" and with that I joined the throng of people chatting about money, property, politics but mostly bollocks.

A few of the men raised their glasses as hellos whilst others looked me up and down and seeing that I was wearing "supermarket clothes", quickly decided they wouldn't benefit from saying anything to the new guest.

Kamaljeet approached me with his globe shaped drinks trolley "So what's your poison Divind?" I looked at all the various bottles of booze and just pointed at the large bottle of coke "I'll just have a coke please Kamaljeet."

As I asked for my drink a fat Indian guy wearing about a gallon of after shave spoke "OK you can have a coke but you have to put something alcoholic into the coke. Isn't that right Kam? Coke's expensive!"

Kamaljeet laughed and placed his arm around my shoulder "Divinder is one of those rare Punjabis who doesn't drink. His wife says it because he acts like he's drunk most of the time! Apparently he's a very cheap date!" the room erupted in laughter and I wished he hadn't said that.

I really wanted to bite my tongue but didn't like the way the conversation was going "Nah, it's alright Kamaljeet, a coke would be perfect. Besides which, unlike some people, my personality isn't found at the bottom of a glass of alcohol."

I smiled at fat-after-shave man who just ignored me and started chatting with someone else.

I took my drink and sat beside Kamaljeet who whispered a joke with a nearby guest who looked at me and then spat out his drink.

Kamaljeet turned to me "Divinder you've joined us at an interesting point. Vikram here was just telling us about this great company called Encon that he thinks is going to be huge."

Vikram was the fat-after-shave man "Yeah, one of my buddies, stateside, has a friend on Wall Street" he then tapped the side of his nose for effect "ask no questions, tell no lies! Basically this trader guy reckons there's a fortune to be made with the Energy trading business. Apparently it's the new Y2K. He was telling me that for a small investment of a hundred grand you can turn that into a cool half a mill in a few months. I'm looking to start a consortium and make hay while the sun shines. Anyone interested?"

I sipped my coke as the conversation became one full of pseudo finance-speak.

Kamaljeet saw me stifling my yawns and looking at my watch.

He could sense that I was way of my depth.

"I met your father-in-law, er Mohan uncle, at the post office the other day. He told me you guys might be emigrating, is that true?"

I nodded "It's true. We've put our paperwork in for Canada."

Kamaljeet took a large swig of his scotch "Why would you want to leave England mate? This is the best place in the world!"

I shook my head "I need to reinvent myself. I don't really love my life that much at the moment and we are fast out growing out house. We looked at another house, in Woodford, and the extra bathroom and bedroom would cost us another £100,000. I would rather take my chances in Canada."

Kamaljeet took another swig of drink "Naya and I actually thought about moving to Canada once. Just after we finished Uni Naya and I travelled the world for a year to see where we'd want to live. I have a cousin in Vancouver and she put us up for a few weeks. The lifestyle looked good but once I saw beyond the big houses and flash cars I realized that I would be 5,000 miles away from everyone I know and love."

I started to tell him that I understood "That's a good point and I have thought about it and.... As I was opening up to Kamaljeet he suddenly stood up, looked at his watch, and clapped his hands "OK chaps let's watch the boys' cricket game!"

That's just not cricket!

We all followed Kamaljeet through the kitchen into their garden.

The back of the garden opened up onto a large soccer and cricket field.

"Wow!" I said loudly "That's some cricket pitch!"

Kamaljeet looked smug "It's a big reason we bought the house. You see, the local church owns the land and for a small donation all the home owners, who back onto the land, get private access to the field whenever the church team doesn't need it. There's Kamran and Anish, looks like they're going to have a big target to reach."

I looked up at the scoreboard, which was located at the opposite end of the pitch, and saw that the batting team has scored a huge 145 runs for 9 players.

As we watched the game, the bowler caught the ball and ended the batting team's innings.

Kamran and Anish ran to the wicket and patted the bowler on the back.

One by one the parents left the house and took up a position on one of the many fold-up seats around the cricket pitch.

Anisha and Sonya walked over to me, behind the wicket.

Anisha asked "Is Kamran's team batting now?" and I pointed at the scoreboard "Yeah, his team just got the last player out and I think we're here for a few more hours."

Anisha handed me a plate "I know, that's why I bought you some food" I happily took the plate from her "Fantastic! I am starving! My stomach thought my throat had been cut!"

As we spoke, Kamran approached us "Here comes Kamran, I swear he can smell food like a shark smells blood!"

Kamran ran over excitedly and grabbed a handful of food off my plate.

I tried to stop him from stealing all my food, leaving me hungry, but wanted to sound like a good parent "Slow down son! You're going to be running around in a minute, you don't want to be sick when you play, do you?"

Kamran jammed a sausage roll in his mouth "It's OK Dad, I'm the ninth batsman. I'm batting when that fat kid gets out" and with that took the last of my food and ran off to join his team

....**several hours later**....

We'd been at their house for five hours and I was actually enjoying seeing my kids having fun with the other kids and I even thought that I had been wrong to judge Naya and Kamaljeet so harshly.

We watched the scoreboard as the batting team got closer and closer to the first team's total.

Finally the "fat kid", as Kamran called him, got in to bat with the score at 143 runs with 8 balls left to bowl.

The bowler, a skinny kid, whipped the ball in fast and the fat kid closed his eyes, moved out of the way, whimpered loudly and hit his own wicket with his bat and got himself "out" in the process.

Kamran turned away from his team mates and did a fist pump as he was batting next.

As he headed towards the wicket he was met by Anish and another boy.

I couldn't make out what was being said but I did see Kamran gesticulating with his hands and seeming to plead his case but eventually he walked back towards us with tears welling in his eyes.

Anisha met him halfway "What happened darling? Why aren't you batting?"

Kamran sniffled, looked at the ground and shrugged his shoulders.

"Can we just go Dad?"

I joined Ani, by Kamran, he was shaking with emotion.

Crouching down I placed my hands gently on his shoulders and whispered "Kamran darling what did Anish say to you?"

I could tell that Kamran was just about to break down and cry but somehow he managed to remain composed.

He spoke very carefully, as if he was trying to remember everything that was said to him "Anish and his friends said that I couldn't play because I don't go to a private school! They said that people at ordinary schools are poor!"

I couldn't help myself "What a complete bastard!"

Anisha was shocked with my outburst "Language Divind! Just calm down, Anish is just a kid."

I corrected her mistake "I wasn't talking about Anish, that idiot's just a parrot for his dad. I'm going to have a word with Kamaljeet."

Anisha stepped in front of me, blocking my path "What's the point Divind? You'll only end up looking stupid."

I didn't mean to, but I lost it with Anisha "So you think it's OK for an eight year old snot to discriminate against our kid because we don't have the money to send him to a private school? No, he needs to know what his kid said."

I stepped past Anisha and walked over to Kamaljeet who was deep in conversation with Vikram.

I stood next to Kamaljeet and tapped him on the shoulder "Can I have a quick word?" Kamaljeet looked at me and then the cricket match "Can it wait? We only need two more runs to win the game."

I shook my head "No, actually it can't wait" Kamaljeet stared at me "This better be bloody good."

I did my best to remain calm and took a cue from Kamran and spoke slowly, making sure that I breathed. "Anish just told Kamran that he couldn't bat for his team because he doesn't go to the same school. Apparently only poor kids go to state schools. Kamran's very upset."

I could see from the expression on Kamaljeet's face that he wasn't seeing any issue "I'm sure that Anish didn't say that. And even if he did, boys will be boys."

Kamaljeet looked at the batsman, over my shoulder "What a brilliant shot! Well done Rikesh! Are you and I done?"

I was ready to punch Kamaljeet in the face and possibly dislodge his bad toupee. "No we're not done! Are you going to get Anish to apologize?"

Kamaljeet laughed "What for? I told you boys will be boys."

He walked off as the batsman scored a 4 and won the game.

Anisha brought the kids over and nudged me out of the garden "Divind, let's just go before you start a fight"

I agreed "I'm out of here."

All I want for Christmas is January!!

Saturday December 25th 2004

Our families were due to arrive in a few hours for the annual carnage that we lovingly called 'Christmas dinner'!!

I seemed to have spent the whole day in the garden cleaning the plastic chairs and table for that night's dinner.

Anisha popped her head out of the kitchen door "Divind why do we have to have everyone here, every year? 24 people, sweaty, Indian people at that, in a room this small ought to be illegal!"

I laughed as I shivered in the cold "Ani, just think, this could be our last Christmas dinner in this house. We could be in Canada this time next year"

Anisha wasn't having it "That's beside the point. We have been in this house for nine years and every year we have had to host the Annual Christmas day dinner. Why couldn't someone else host it this one time?"

I walked back into the kitchen, partly to get warm and partly to chat in private. "We are the best people to host it Ani. No-one else could do what you do so well. I'll tell you what, if we are still here by next December, then I'll insist that someone else host the dinner. Is that a deal?"

Anisha dismissed me with a wave of her hand "I want that deal in writing.....in your blood!"

I laughed but the look on her face suggested that she was semi-serious!

Just as I was about to get back to the cleaning, the phone rang, Anisha picked it up, it was my oldest sister in law Ranjvir.

Ranjvir was a woman of a few words and most of them were insults!

"Hi. Merry Christmas and all that innit! What time is your dinner tonight?"

Anisha screwed her face up "Merry Christmas and all that to you too! Yup, dinner will be at 6pm like it is every year. What time can we expect you to arrive this year?"

Ranjvir ignored Anisha's jibe "I'm in the West End at the moment, doing some last minute shopping innit so I should be there on time. Do you want me to bring anything?"

Anisha hit the mute button "I swear she winds me up on purpose!"

Once she was composed again she unmuted and said "A bottle of wine would be great. I'll see you later....much later"

Just as Anisha was about to put the 'phone Ranjvir had the last word "Oh by the way just in case I'm slightly late could you be a darling and make me a plate of food? If you could please don't put any breast meat on that plate you always make it so dry. Bye."

She hung up and Anisha stomped her foot and came into the garden. "Oooh! She drives me mental!"

I stopped my cleaning "Who drives you mental?"

Anisha waved at me "Who do you think?"

I was at a loss as everyone I knew, seemed to annoy Anisha "My mum?"

Anisha shook her head "For once, no"

I tried again "Your mum?"

She glared at me "NO! Think, who REALLY aggravates me?"

I racked my brain "Final answer, your auntie Bunty?"

Anisha screamed "NO!" as I raised my arms again in mock surrender "Your bloody sister-in-law Ranjvir. She's driving me crazy like she does every year!

I stupidly carried on the chat when I should have continued cleaning the garden furniture "What's she done now?"

"The same thing she does every year, she taunts me by asking me what time dinner is and then turns up two hours late on purpose. Then she has the audacity to complain that the food is cold or dry or both!!

I swear if she tries to pull that on me this year you'd better make sure there are no knives within arm's reach!!"

I took a deep breath "OK, I suggest you take one of the large blue pills and then swig straight from the whiskey bottle!!"

Anisha slapped me on the arm "I'm not joking. I slave all day to make sure that the dinner is hot on the table at 6pm and she always messes the day up by turning up late. Then there's the fact that she always brings a nasty £2 bottle of wine that isn't worth wasting a hangover on!!"

"Just find a happy place" I said "and stay there!! She isn't going to change. It's only for a few hours and only once a year, thank god!!"

Anisha started to sharpen the carving knife with an evil glint in her eye and I left before she used me for target practice!

Later that evening, after the guests had all finished their meal.

Anisha's uncle Ramesh was standing by the front door, ready to leave "Thank you very much Anisha, Divinder, as usual that was a great meal. But we have to go now as your auntie needs her medication before she goes to bed."

Anisha walked over and gave him a hug "No problem Uncle Ramesh, please give Sandiya Auntie a big kiss from me."

Just as Ramesh opened the door to leave Ranjvir walked in.

She didn't care for the niceties of society like being on time and just breezed in "Hello everybody, Merry Christmas innit!!"

I glanced over at Anisha who gave Ranjvir the dirtiest of dirty looks as she looked at the clock on the wall, it was 8pm. I could almost hear the music from a Spaghetti Western when the two gun fighters have a stand-off before they shoot each other!!

Anisha spoke first, through gritted teeth "Thanks for joining us, your majesty!"

Ranjvir didn't flinch.

She had thicker skin than a rhino. "Oh Anisha, the traffic was murder! Here's a bottle of wine."

She handed Anisha a bottle of wine that was covered in a thick layer of dust. It was that old that I swear she'd stolen it off the table from the Last Supper!

Anisha was on a roll "Won't Judas miss his bottle?!"

Everyone laughed except Ranjvir. Anisha and I went into the kitchen where Anisha took Ranjvir's plate out of the oven.

The food was stuck to the plate in a sea of congealed gravy.

It looked a lot like a piece of art!!

Anisha tapped the food with a fork and it made a "thud" sound that seemed to make her happy.

"I think this is dry enough!"

I winced as she took the plate out and placed it onto a mat in front of Ranjvir who had taken her seat at the table by herself.

Anisha smiled and said "Merry Christmas! Bon Appetite! By the way the plate is very hot, it's been in the oven since 6pm, that's when everybody else managed to get here!"

Ranjvir looked at the plate and pulled a face and started to eat the food with Anisha staring at her.

Anisha went back into the kitchen and started to wash the dishes nosily.

I followed her and closed the door and then pulled Anisha away from the sink.

I didn't make any attempt to be subtle "Let me do the dishes Anisha, we can't afford to buy any new ones!"

Anisha walked away from the sink, she hated washing up and told everyone she met that she despised the "waste of time that cleaning truly is" she took her seat on the counter top and sipped deeply from her glass of white wine "I wish I could just wave a magic wand and choose new relatives!"

I laughed, as much because she had calmed down than how funny she was being "If you do master that trick could you possibly make Angelina Jolie one of your cousins?!"

Anisha laughed back and struck my butt with a nearby tea towel "Get back to work servant! You missed a spot!"

Later that evening, all the guests had left except for Anisha's cousin Anjna.

She stood at the door saying her goodbyes.

She hugged Anisha and then me.

As she stood there her eyes started welling up "That was another great dinner party guys. You're both so good at getting everyone together."

Anisha, who by now had polished off three glasses of wine, slurred "Ain't that the truth sister!"

Anisha hadn't tuned into the fact that Anjna was trying to be serious "It's a little bit sad really Ani, because your dad was saying that this might be your last Christmas in this house. Have you guys heard anything back from the Canadian High Commission yet?"

Anisha suddenly sobered up "Nothing yet if you ignore the fact that package was sent back after 6 weeks when someone" she pointed at yours truly "forgot to pay the correct fee payment and that put us back a whole six weeks."

Anjna nodded sympathetically "That's a shame although I was sort of hoping that you guys would change your minds."

I must have had a surprised look on my face when I said "Why would we do that?" because Anjna looked at Anisha and then at me and continued "Because we'll miss you all when you go to Canada with Uncle and Auntie too."

I must have been on auto pilot because I then repeated what I'd just said "Why would we do that?" again Anjna looked at Anisha who had completely sobered up and was shaking her head furiously as Anjna spoke. "Well Anisha's dad said that they would go to Canada with you!"

I looked over at Anisha just as she ran into the kitchen and pulled the door behind her and as Anjna slammed the front door!

There may be more trouble ahead!

Several hours later, after we'd cleaned the house, we were both sitting in bed.

We hadn't spoken after Anjna had dropped her bombshell.

I was pretending to read a book as Anisha watched Jamie Oliver on TV.

Anisha had taken a temporary vow of silence and every question I'd asked her about what Anjna had been met with a dumb smile.

Anisha was a huge fan of Jamie Oliver and made no secret of the fact that she thought he was a culinary Mother Theresa.

"That Jamie Oliver should be made into a saint! Saint Jamie of Oliver!"

I ignored her, the way she'd been ignoring me and smiled at her and carried on pretending to read.

Anisha turned off the TV and pulled my book down.

This was serious, she never turned Jamie Oliver off!

"Are you going to sulk all night or are you going to have an adult chat about what Anjna said?"

I knew I had a rare moment of having the moral high ground so tried to milk it "I'd like to carry on sulking a little while longer if you don't mind?"

Anisha wasn't about to let me have the high ground "Let me rephrase that, tell me what's on your mind fat boy."

I folded my arms across my chest, something that she always did when she was about to launch into her attack "Our whole plan was to escape from everyone, including your parents, by moving to Canada."

I thought I had her on the ropes "Divind I'm an only child, it's natural that they would want to come with us. After all, the only grandchildren they are ever going to have are ours."

I didn't want to come off as being inconsiderate so softened my tone and unfolded my arms, which were hurting from how hard I had them folded "I get that Ani, despite what you might think I realise that you guys are close. The problem I have is that we have never really been proper parents to Kamran and Sonya."

Anisha seemed to assume that my unfolding my arms gave her the green light to fold hers!

"Excuse me mister, but I remember every second of both labours and deliveries and even have the stretch marks to prove that I am a parent!!"

I realised that what I meant and what she'd heard were worlds apart!

"Ani you gave birth but ever since then we have become weekend parents."

Anisha shook her head like one of those trained chimps in the zoo "You are nuts! How can you say that we are weekend parents? Whatever that means!"

I sat upright on my side of the bed "OK you tell me what happens from the moment we wake up to the moment we go to bed ignoring the work part" before she could respond I carried on.

"I'll tell you. We get up at 6:30am. 20 minutes later we wake the kids up, 20 minutes after that we drag their half-asleep bodies to your parent's house and then we head off to the train station. Meanwhile your mum and dad, feed the kids their breakfast and then they both walk the kids to school. When school is over they are picked up by your parents and brought back to their house for a snack. At 7pm your dad is waiting for us at Ilford train station. On the rare occasion that we go out we call your parents to feed the kids and even give them a bath. At what point do we become parents? On Saturday and Sunday when your parents get a break and get a chance to clean their house that our kids messed and go shopping in preparation for the next week when the kids attack them like biblical locusts!"

Anisha looked furious and I was worried that I had pressed all the wrong buttons!! "That's not true! My parents love looking after the kids. What else would they do?"

I grabbed my chance to tell her all the things her parents had told me that had wanted to do in their golden years "How about just relaxing? Maybe enjoying their retirement? Socializing? Travelling? The list is endless my darling."

Anisha stared deep in my eyes and pulled the trigger "Listen Divind, if my parents don't emigrate then I'm not going either!"

The best laid plans

Tuesday January 4th 2005

We were all enjoying dinner at Anisha's parents' house.

I decided to take the bull by the horns, or the Moose by the antlers so to speak.

"So Mum, Anisha was telling me that you are looking at moving to Canada with us."

Rani beamed "Of course we are! How could I leave my little Kamran and Sonya?" she made a playful grab for Kamran who scampered off to the lounge where he disturbed Sonya who was coloring in.

I chewed a mouthful of chicken curry "That's really great. I think you'll both love the rain forest in Vancouver."

Her dad looked up "What rain forest?"

I'd caught his attention.

"Oh yeah, didn't you know? Vancouver gets even more rain than London."

I saw Anisha make a face as she tried to kick me under the table but I pulled my legs back just in time and she struck her dad's leg instead.

"Ouch! Who's kicking me?"

Anisha apologized and glared at me as I took a triumphant swig of water.

Mohan spoke again as he rubbed his leg "When we went to Vancouver for your brother Amarjit's wedding, in June 2000, it was like a heat wave! More rain than London? How?"

I nodded, in a knowing way, and avoided Anisha's Medusa-like gaze

"When I went to visit Amarjit in December 1994, I was there for three weeks and it rained for almost my whole time there, sometimes 24 hours a day! I thought I would see Noah's Ark come past his house at one stage!! Amarjit was saying that it can rain continuously from late November through to March."

Rani just smiled some more "The rain doesn't bother me, I will just spend more time with my grandchildren inside the house."

Anisha was no longer kicking her dad, now she was my translator "Mum, what I think that Divinder is trying to say – badly – is, that Canada isn't the same as England."

Mohan rejoined the conversation "What do people do when it rains that much?"

I looked over at Anisha, pushed my seat back ever so slightly and answered his question 'The truth is Dad, most people in Vancouver aren't stressed by the rain. It's the snow that comes in January that messes people up!"

I felt the breeze of Ani's attempted kick and I smiled and raised my glass to her again.

Mohan bugged out "Snow? I didn't know it snowed in Vancouver."

I went in for the sucker punch "Oh yeah, it snows! In fact, last year Amarjit was saying that they had a few feet of snow in January that brought the whole city to a standstill! Don't forget Dad you'd need to take your driving test again, they drive on the other side of the car and on the wrong side of the road."

Anisha adjusted her seat and managed to kick my right shin. My eyes bugged out and I screamed - in my head!!

"Well in that case Rani and I will just have to visit Vancouver a few times before we put in our paperwork."

With my leg slowly swelling up I carried on with my scare tactic "That's a great idea. I think you should come over for a few months at a time so that you can see how it feels to leave your friends and family behind. It is 5,000 miles away."

Rani touched my arm reassuringly "Divinder my dear, you forget that we moved from Tanzania to England so making new friends in Canada should be no problem."

I nodded and touched her arm "That's true Mum, but that was more than 30 years ago."

Anisha's dad looked sad and when he spoke again I felt bad that I been so direct "Divinder, if I didn't know better, I would swear that you don't want us to come with you."

I truly felt bad but there was method to my madness "Dad, please don't get me wrong, I really want you to come with us. I just want you both to have your eyes wide open before you leave behind the great life you've spent 30 years making here in England."

Mohan smiled again "I completely understand why you're telling us. Thank you, now who wants to go out for ice cream?"

The kids came rushing in with their jackets on.

Anisha stopped me walking through the kitchen.

"Dad why don't you take the kids and Mum. We'll clear up the dishes" from the tone of Anisha's voice I suddenly wanted to be taken out for ice cream too!

Anisha's dad knew that tone too "OK, come on Rani the kids are hungry!"

I watched from the living room window as they left and then rejoined Anisha in the kitchen.

I started drying the dishes and Anisha grabbed a tea towel and helped me.

I avoided Anisha's gaze but spoke to her general space in the kitchen "I think that went better than expected. What do you think?"

From the corner of my eye I saw Anisha flick her tea towel across my butt! The pain was immediate.

"Ow! What's that for?" Anisha was glowering at me, with a fierce look on her face "Are you stupid or do you just like to fight with me or both?"

I scratched my head for effect "Is that a trick question?"

Looking at her closed off body language, apparently it wasn't a trick question.

"I can't believe that you would try to put my parents off from coming with us. I am an only child with elderly parents. They need to be looked after by me, by us!" she pointed at me with a knife in her hand which made it seem like more a threat than anything else!

I carefully took the knife out of her hand "Ani I need your parents to know exactly what they are heading into. Wouldn't you rather have your parents 5,000 miles away and happy rather than on my door step and miserable?

Anisha disagreed "No!"

I was shocked "Are you nuts Ani? Do you realize what you're saying?" she nodded her head vigourously "Divind you have four brothers. Your parents have a lot of people they can lean on if they ever need anything. I'm an only child, I am all my parents have. If they get sick and I'm 5,000 miles away what am I going to do?"

I changed my tactic, this needed some violins "Ani, I don't want to bring your parents over to a life that they might end up hating."

I held her hand "The truth is that it does rain a lot in Vancouver. Your dad would need to take his driving test again because they drive on the wrong side of the road over there! They might end up as prisoners... just as I was in full flow she started crying!

"I do want us to start all over again in Canada but without my parents it's going to be really tough. I don't want my parents to hate living in Canada but I don't want them here without me either."

With that she walked off to the lounge, took a seat on the sofa and bawled her eyes out!

I finished drying the dishes, very slowly – I'd always been great at making Anisha cry but not so great at making her stop!

I walked into the lounge and waved a white tea towel in front of me. "Hey Ani, are we still talking?" she laughed and a little snot bubble came out of her left nostril.

She wiped her nose. "Course we are silly face. Come and sit next to me"

I walked over to where she was sitting and put my arm around her as she started to cry again.

See, told you, I could make her cry easily!

She stopped crying long enough to carry on explaining why she needed her parents.

"Moving to Canada is supposed to be a real chance to start all over again and be happy. It just seems to be falling apart. I don't want to go if my parents don't have the chance to come with us. I do want them to be happy and I think that once we're gone they'll miss us so much that they'll follow us. Just you see."

I always knew she was close to her parents but this was a chance for me to see that their happiness was tied to hers, even 5,000 miles apart.

I gave her a hug and we looked out of the window together, watching people walking along our street.

The postman only knocks once!

Monday January 10th 2005

I'd been sick all the previous weekend with a serious case of "man flu" so stayed at home that Monday.

At about noon I heard the doorbell ring.

I dragged myself out of bed, pulled back the curtains and tapped on the window.

The postman stepped back from the door and waved at me with a registered letter in his hand.

I put up one finger and then ran downstairs.

I opened the front door to our postman, Pete "Morning Pete. How are you doing?"

Pete stepped back as if he could catch man-flu from my words! "Bloody hell Divind! You look like death warmed up mate! You got that man flu that's going around?"

"Yup, I've got it bad. What you got there?"

Pete was one of those naturally very funny Cockney blokes that seemed to have found jobs as bus and train drivers or postal workers.

He stared at the letter in his hand "I would say that with my 25 years' experience with the Royal Mail it would be my professional opinion that this here is a registered letter!"

I laughed as he handed me the letter. "Thank you very much. Now, be on your way. I'm sure there's a doughnut with your name on it!"

Pete saluted and walked towards our neighbour's house. "Hmm doughnut! See you later Divind, get well mate."

I stepped into the house and looked at the logo on the front of the brown envelope. "Havering Health Authority"

I put the envelope down on the TV and made myself a cup of tea.

Just as I sat down the phone rang. I looked at the caller display, it was Anisha's work number.

"Hi Ani" Anisha sounded surprised that I was up to the task of answering the 'phone "You really sound terrible!" she always made me feel bad for the very rare times that I got sick and took a day off work "I'm sick! You never believe me when I'm sick!" she tutted "So how's it going Mr. Man flu 2005?"

I glared at the 'phone "Alright I suppose. I was fast asleep when I was woken up by old Postman Pete. We have a registered letter."

Anisha sounded excited for a moment "Please tell me the Canadian stuff has come in, I really need some good news right now"

I was suddenly worried, Anisha generally loved her job but had been in a depressing funk for the past few weeks. "What happened?"

I heard her take a huge sigh "Karen just asked me if I had any ideas to improve efficiencies. That translates as "Give me another idea that I can pass off as my own and get all the credit again.""

I almost swore but controlled myself because I was scared that my negativity would rub off on her "I hope you told her to take a long walk off a short pier! Cheeky cow!"

Ani ignored me.

"Go and open up the letter it might be from the embassy" it was my turn to sigh now "No it won't be, it says "Havering Health Authority." on the front.

Ani tutted "It's probably a date for my smear test, deep joy!"

I placed the phone on the shelf and put it on speaker mode as I opened the envelope.

I started to read the letter quickly.

It was from the Canadian Embassy!

"Oh my god Ani! It's a letter from the embassy!"

Anisha squealed with excitement! "What does it say?"

I carried on reading as fast as my eyes would let me "It says that we are approved to the next stage of the application process which is the medical! We're in Ani, we're bloody in!!"

I heard Anisha cry a little "Oh my god! Divind if you're lying I swear I will chop off parts of your body that you may still need!! What does the medical involve?"

I started reading again "We have to call the number on the letter and arrange our medicals at Hornchurch Hospital. It says here that we need to get some x-rays and then arrange a medical with one of the doctors on their approved list. Now let me hang up on you so that I can book the medicals ASAP!!"

Anisha screamed on the other side of the phone "OK bye, call me when you're done!!" before she managed to hang up she shouted "Kaye, lunch is on me love!"

I hung up and carefully tapped in the numbers on the letter for Hornchurch hospital. After a few seconds I was put through to an automated call list.

"Welcome to Hornchurch Hospital. Please listen carefully to the following selection: Dial 1 if you want to speak to a nurse practitioner. Dial 2 if you want to speak to a cardiology nurse. Dial 3 if you want to arrange an X-ray. Dial 4 if you want to arrange a medical for immigration purposes."

I hit 4.

Another list.

"For the USA press 1 For Canada press 2 for other countries press 3"

I hit 2 and waited as the phone started to ring to another extension.

Finally after a few minutes the call was answered by a woman who sounded like she needed to blow her nose.

"Dello, ibbigration abbointments, how can I help you?"

I tried really hard not to laugh or speak like she did "Hi I have just received my letter from the Canadian embassy asking me to make an appointment to have an x ray for me, my wife and our two kids. I was wondering if you have any time available, maybe even this weekend?"

She sniffed and made a slurping sound over the sound of her tapping on her keyboard. "Det me check. Blease hold."

I listened to a musak version of "Green-sleeves" hold music which made me think of the woman who answered the phone wiping her nose of her sweater.

After a few minutes she picked the phone up again and snorted, slurped and sniffed at the same time, quite a feat!

"We hab a 12 o'clock available, shall I book you in?" I didn't want to hear her snotty nose again so answered quickly "Yes please" I heard more keyboard tapping "OK please gib me your name, phone number and credit card details."

I gave her the details and hung up. I then looked through the list of approved doctors and called the one closest to the hospital.

Dr, Dr!

The receptionist at Dr. Chin's surgery was one of those super professional women with a breathy Welsh accent.

When she answered the phone she sounded like Catherine Zeta-Jones "Dr. Chin's office, how may I help you?" it took me a moment to compose myself from the effect of her voice!

I kept picturing Catherine Zeta-Jones!

I put on my best Hugh Grant voice "Hi good morning. My family and I have just been approved for Canadian Immigration and need a medical before we can proceed. Do you know if Dr. Chin has any availability this coming Saturday after, say, 1:30pm?"

I could hear the receptionist looking through a book "You're very lucky because I happen to know that Dr. Chin is available at 2pm. How many people do you need to have assessed?"

I did a fist pump. "Me, my wife and our two children."

'Catherine' spoke slowly "OK, how old are your children sir?"

I had to really concentrate on her questions as her sexy Welsh accent was driving me mental!

"My son is 8 and my daughter is 5. By the way how long does each medical take? And how much does a medical examination costs?" she asked me to hold and came back a few seconds later "Give me a second and I'll check that for you"

I heard her keyboard being tapped "each medical lasts about 15 minutes and costs £500" I thought I'd misheard her "£500? That seems a bit much for all four of us?"

"Katherine" laughed "No sir, that's £500 EACH for you and your wife and ONLY £250 each for your kids" my sticker shock was hard to hard "Bloody hell! £1500 for an hours work?! I should have studied medicine!"

Katherine was now in no-nonsense mode "Would you like me to book the appointment or not sir?"

I mumbled and then answered "£1500! Sure book us in please. My credit card number is...

Saturday January 15th 2005

After our X-rays we completed we drove the short distance from the hospital and now waited in the doctor's lounge with our sealed X-rays on our laps.

The receptionist looked more like Tom Jones than Catherine Zeta-Jones with her bad perm, bad fake tan and elasticated black trousers that were pulled up just beneath her boobs and a lacy blouse that looked like it had been a table cloth earlier that day at a cheap café!!

She wore thick glasses with lenses that were about an inch thick.

She had, what Ani said I had, a great face for the radio.

Anisha had a big smile on her face "We're nearly there Divind. What do you reckon this medical will involve?"

I smiled "I think it'll be a case of getting naked and the old rubber glove! Drop 'em and cough!"

Anisha looked anxious "Shut up, he'll just ask us a few questions and then check out weight and height won't he?"

Truth be told, I had no idea at all what the medical involved and had even tried to Google it without any success "Listen Ani I'm giving this guy £500 I want him to suffer by seeing me naked! In fact I may even bend over or do a star jump or two!"

The receptionist called my name and I walked over to her desk. "Mr. Purewal, please follow me and bring your X-ray with you" I nodded at Kamran and said "Can I bring my son with me?" she looked at his innocent face and said "Of course. I'll get Dr. Chin to see your son first."

I thanked her as she led the way to another room where a middle aged Oriental doctor was awaiting us.

Dr. Chin was about 5 foot 2 and was very wiry.

He wore his half-moon glasses on the very tip of his nose.

He spoke with very little accent and sounded like one of those evil guys from the James Bond films and I half expected him to say "I expect you to show me your moobs!" so was disappointed when he just said "Good afternoon Mr. Purewal. I guess this is Kamran?"

Kamran gave him the thumbs up "Good guess, Dr.!"

Dr. Chin smiled for a fraction of a second and then addressed Kamran directly "Kamran please lift up your shirt, I just want to check your breathing with this stethoscope."

Kamran looked at the stethoscope and said "Cool!" and then lifted his shirt as Dr. Chin warmed up the stethoscope before putting it against Kamran's chest, heart then his back.

Dr. Chin wrote a few notes on a pad and then pointed at a weighing scale in the corner of the surgery. "Now Kamran please take off your shoes and then step up on the scales, I need to see how much you weigh."

Kamran was having fun and saluted and said "OK boss"

Dr. Chin smiled properly this time and ruffled Kamran's hair.

Kamran took off his shoes and stepped onto the weighing scales.

As before, Dr. Chin took down a few measurements and then asked Kamran to stand beside a height ruler.

Once he was finished he offered Kamran a lollypop "OK Kamran you're all done. Thank you for being such a good patient. I hope you like Canada."

Dr. Chin shook Kamran's hand before Catherine walked Kamran back to Anisha.

I looked at Dr. Chin as I started to undo the buttons on my shirt "That was pretty easy. Should I lift up my shirt?"

Dr. Chin looked at me like I was nuts! "No Mr. Purewal, for you we do the full medical. Please go into that room over there and take off all your clothes and put on the green gown on the table. I would ask that you keep the gown open at the front please."

I gulped and was glad that I'd taken an extra-long shower that morning "OK"

15 minutes later I came back to the waiting room with a surprised look on my face.

Anisha's eyes bugged out seeing me walking with a wide limp "So what exactly did he do Divind?"

I repeated the rubber glove routine.

Anisha brushed me off "Shut up Divind, Kamran told me all the Dr. did was check his breathing, measure and weigh him."

I shook my head "Ani I know I've put on a few pounds over the past few years but why would weighing and measuring me take 15 minutes? I promise you that just he probed me in places that I didn't even know I had! For your sake I hope you're wearing those big granny knickers!"

Anisha laughed nervously as the receptionist called her name.

Sonya and Anisha followed the receptionist and after a few minutes Sonya returned, lollipop in hand.

I let Sonya sit on my lap "How did it go?"

Sonya winked at me "Great. The Dr. Man just measured me, weighed me and then gave me a lollipop, high fived me and said good luck in Canada."

15 minutes later Anisha came back with her eyes wide open.

She headed straight for the surgery door and the kids followed her out.

Before leaving I approached the receptionist and asked her a quick question "When will we get the results?" the receptionist smiled and replied "As long as nothing comes back negative on the X-rays and the blood samples you should get a letter from the embassy in the next 28 days. Good luck Mr. Purewal."

I gave the receptionist my best smile, one that I usually reserved for Anisha or the kids "Thanks, have a great weekend."

As I stepped out into the afternoon air I had a spring in my step that I hadn't had for many years.

I bounced over to the car where Anisha and the kids were already seated and belted in.

I was just about to open my mouth when Anisha placed her forefinger on my lips "I don't want any of your wind ups Divind, let's just go now."

I moved my head back and avoiding her gaze I took my life in my hands "So Ani how did the medical go?"

Anisha gave me a look that would have turned milk into yoghurt in about five seconds "Just drive Divind, I never want to talk about what just happened, EVER!"

As Anisha stared off out into the distance- finding her "happy place", I drove off, laughing maniacally - in my head!

Saturday January 29th 2005. Kamran's 8th birthday.

I remember that day vividly because I knew it was Kamran's last birthday in the only house he'd ever called home.

We were all sitting at the dining table eating breakfast.

Kamran was as excited as any eight year boy could be on his birthday.

We'd planned a party at school, later that day for Kamran and all his friends.

I looked at Kamran and felt a rush of love that happened a lot when it came to my kids.

It was as if, I couldn't believe that a muppet like me could have such great kids!!

He kept walking over to the presents that we'd stacked by the TV. "Dad, can I open my presents now?"

I don't know why he was asking me because we all knew that it was his mum who wielded all the power!

So pretending that I was the boss I said "No darling, I think you should wait until the party"

Kamran made puppy-dog eyes "Why Dad?"

I wanted to say "Because you'll get so excited that you'll ignore us for the rest of the day!" but instead said "It'll be nice to see you open all your presents at the same time" the puppy-dog eyes came out again. "That's not fair Dad. I bet granny let you open your presents when you were my age"

I shook my head "Actually Kamran, we never celebrated birthdays when I was your age."

Kamran had an astounded look on his face "How old are you Dad?"

I knew he knew my age but humoured him anyway. "I'm 35. Why?" he laughed "Because you make it sound like you were born in caveman times!"

It was my turn to laugh now "Listen, Donald Trump! When I was your age there wasn't a lot of money going around so we were told that only white people celebrated birthdays!... I lie. There was that one year when granny bought a cake from the supermarket and slapped a big white candle in the middle of the cake and then sang 10 verses of "Happy Bird day" at your uncle Jarnail!!"

Kamran looked disgusted "Man, you guys were so ghetto!"

I crossed my arms across my chest "Now you definitely can't open your presents!" just as Kamran was about to respond the door-bell rang and Anisha walked down the stairs.

I did that stupid thing that adults do and said "I wonder who that is?"

Anisha patted my butt "Here's an idea Divind, get up, walk over to the front door, open the door and you'll find out!"

I made out to be angry "It's because you speak to me like that and grab me the way you do, treating me as a sex object, that the kids don't respect me! You know that don't you?"

Anisha just pushed me towards the front door.

I opened the door to see Pete the postman stood in front of me with a brown envelope in his hand.

I wanted to believe that it was the Canadian paperwork but the package looked too thin. Pete handed me the envelope "Mornin' Divind. Another registered letter for you. I would love hang around but I'm dying for the toilet! Have a great day mate."

I took the envelope and thanked Pete "Thanks Pete, you too mate."

I looked at the brown envelope and turned it over in his hand. There in the top right hand corner was the postal mark of the Canadian Embassy.

I rushed in and closed the door behind me.

I half-walked half-ran to the table waving the letter over my head and grinning like I had the winning lottery ticket! "Ani, I think this is THE letter we've been waiting for"

Anisha's eyes stared at the letter in my hand "Hurry up then! Open the letter, man!"

I carefully opened the envelope, I wanted to savour every moment and started to read the letter out loud.

January 21st 2005

Dear Mr. Purewal, REF: CanImm/12986708-05

I am pleased to inform you that you, and the applicants listed below, have successfully passed the medical for emigration to Canada.

Anisha and I cheered and Kamran and Sonya not wanting to be left out joined in too.

I carried on reading out loud.

APPLICANT: Mr. Purewal, Divinder Singh
GENDER: Male
DATE OF BIRTH: 2nd May 1969
APPLICANT: Mrs. Purewal, Anisha.
GENDER: Female.
DATE OF BIRTH: 11th December 1970
APPLICANT: Master. Purewal, KAMRAN Singh.
GENDER: Male
DATE OF BIRTH: 28th January 1997
APPLICANT: Miss. Purewal, Sonya Kaur
GENDER: Female.
DATE OF BIRTH: 19th February 2000

With completion of the medical you are now cleared to apply for Permanent Residency, see page 5 of the Canadian Immigration application pack. You now have 12 months, from January 31st 2005, to have your passport validated with an official Canadian entry visa.

IMPORTANT: Failure to comply with this requirement will make your Permanent Residency null and void.

If you have any questions please contact the Canadian Embassy on 0898 677 3443 and leave a message for one of the consulate staff.

Welcome to Canada!

Anisha started to cry. "Ani, tell me you're crying tears of joy?"

Anisha just nodded as the kids hugged her leg.

I joined the family hug "I suppose we should tell our families now?"

Anisha smiled and went into 'practical Anisha' mode "Well they'll all be at the party later today so we'll tell them the good news at the same time"

Kamran tugged Anisha's shirt "Does this mean we're going to Canada, Mum?"

Anisha had this crazy-happy smile on her face and her lipstick was smeared where she'd been touching her face "Yes it does darling" then Sonya joined the questioning "When can we go?"

Anisha turned to Sonya "Not yet darling. First we have to tell our parents, sell the house, quit our jobs, buy plane tickets, not forgetting sending all our stuff in a container to Vancouver."

Kamran nodded like he understood what was ahead.

"Oh, OK. Well, just let me and Sonya know when you've done all that stuff and we'll do what we can to help."

SCHOOL GYM Saturday January 29th 2005. Kamran's 8th birthday.

Kamran was leading a game of indoor soccer with a few of his class mates.

I was in the kitchen area arranging the snacks with Anisha and Sonya.

Anisha's parents had just arrived with my parents.

My dad came into the kitchen and gave Sonya and Anisha a hug and shook my hand.

He took a handful of potato chips "Hello son, do you need any help?"

I shook my head "I think we're OK Dad. Have a seat or join in with the soccer game" my dad laughed out loud "I'm having a heart attack just watching them play!! I think I'll have a seat with your mum. Oh before I forget, Sarbjit and Ajit called to say that they wouldn't be able to make it today but they'll see you next weekend sometime."

I nodded and turned to Anisha.

I spoke quietly "Looks like we're just be telling our folks the big news today."

Anisha agreed 'That's alright, at least we'll be able to share our happy news with the oldies first."

Anisha stepped out into the hall and blew a whistle to get all the kids' attention. The kids all froze when they heard the whistle.

Anisha shouted "PIZZA TIME!! Everyone wash your hands first then grab a seat."

The kids start screaming and ran towards the washrooms.

We took this brief moment of peace and quiet to take our parents into the kitchen.

I stood in front of them "Mum, Dad, Mum, Dad please take a seat. We have some news."

My dad got over-excited "You're pregnant aren't you Anisha? I was just saying to your mum that you look like you're at least four, maybe five months pregnant!"

Anisha looked like she about to lose it and I squeezed her hand REALLY TIGHT!!

"I'm not pregnant Dad, but thanks for that!" my dad put his head down and sheepishly said "Oh sorry."

I regained the floor "As I was saying, Dad, we have some news. Our paperwork came through for Canada. We passed our medicals and we now have a year to get our Canadian visa. Isn't that great news?"

The parents all look depressed!

It was like I'd said they all had cancer and only six months to live and I should have told them six months earlier!!

Anisha tried to lighten the mood "Didn't you hear what Divinder just said? We're going to Canada!! All we have to do is sell the house now and we are off. This is the part where you should be smiling and hugging us and telling us that everything is going to be great. I don't see any smiling, I don't feel any hugging and I don't hear anybody telling us we'll be great."

Anisha's dad was the first to speak. "To tell the truth Ani I didn't think you were serious about the whole move to Canada thing."

Anisha did a double-take like that Scottish fella from the Laurel and Hardy movies!

"Dad we just spent about £3,000 on all the application fees then we had our medicals a few weeks ago. That should have been a pretty big clue that we were serious 'about the whole move to Canada thing.'" my father-in-law hadn't quite tuned into the fact that Anisha was pretty mad and continued "Are you sure you want to do this?"

Despite my hand-holding Anisha was fast approaching mad town! "You're about 12 months late with that question Dad!!"

Anisha's mum tried to calm things down "Anisha of course we are happy for you but have you really thought about what you're doing? You are taking my only grandchildren 5,000 miles away just because you don't like your job and the house feels too small."

It suddenly felt that our parents had taken a box of needles to our "happy news record" and were scratching it to pieces!!

My dad now took another swing "Divinder, Anisha, Rani and Mohan are right, this is a very big decision and you seem to have made it without asking for any adult's advice. This is like that time when you told everyone you wanted to be an architect but then gave up on that idea. What happened then eh? I even told all my friends that you were becoming an architect and then you didn't become one!"

I stared at my dad like he was nuts! "Dad this is nothing like that time! I thought I wanted to be an architect and then decided that it wasn't for me. Can we drop that topic please?" my dad wasn't in the dropping mood! "So why didn't you become an architect?"

I realised that my dad needed to have some closure "OK Dad if you must know I can't draw a straight line with a ruler and I have the mathematical ability of a frog! Happy now?!" my dad tutted as my mum was tagged into the fray "Divinder what if you go to Canada and it isn't what you think it would be? What will you do then?" the problem was we were angry because these were questions that we had avoided asking ourselves.

"Mum, in the remote chance that it happens, we'll just come back. But that's not going to happen, we are going to have a great life and it would be nice if you guys would pretend to support us in this big move."

Anisha's dad was just about to say something when Bo, one of our closest friends arrived.

Bo could feel the tension in the air "Hi Divind, hi Ani. Where shall I put Kamran's present?" I took the present and also the opportunity to go for a walk outside,

"Bo I'm sorry that you had to hear that little episode."

Bo shrugged his shoulders "What happened Divind? Has someone died?"

I laughed.

"You'd think so wouldn't you?! No, we just found out today that we've been approved to emigrate to Canada"

Bo extended his hand and then gave me a 'man hug' "That is great news!! So why are the old brown people so upset?"

Once I'd recovered from him crushing my ribs I spoke again "We just told them all at the same time and they decided to ask us, no tell us, that we were making a huge mistake. Anisha's dad asked if we were sure this is what we wanted and my dad asked me why I wasn't an architect!"

Bo gave me a sideways glance "An architect? I bet you can't even spell architect can you?!"

I punched him on the arm but bent my wrist back on his muscles "It's a long story mate. The bottom line is that they are making us doubt that is probably the biggest decision we've ever made apart from getting married and having the kids."

Bo nodded sympathetically "That's tough mate. Maybe they just need some time to let the news sink in. How long before you guys leave?"

I stared at my feet, something I did when I was nervous. "Probably summer. We need to sell the house first."

Bo seemed a little shocked. He looked me straight in the eyes "This summer?"

I returned his gaze "No Summer 2010! Of course this summer you muppet!! The Canadian embassy gives you 12 months to get your visa stamped or else your application gets scrapped and you start all again."

Having been called a muppet, Bo regained his composure "Why would you go so soon? If you have 12 months why not sell the house, move in with Anisha's folks for a while and work up until like September, October? That way you can make a bit of extra money and fly out at Christmas."

I put my arm on his shoulder in a reassuring way, both for him and me. "We did think about that but we decided that if we could get out there in July we could spend the whole of the summer holiday with the kids. They're probably going to be really homesick so if we get to go out a few times it might be easier for them. Then when school starts in September one of us could help them get settled."

Bo looked hurt "So you're really going?"

I slapped his shoulder "Don't you start!! Yup. I really think that the move is going to the best thing we could do. The kids will love the great outdoors and I can write that book that I've always wanted to."

Bo's face was all ashen and he looked close to tears "Me, Jane and Amber, we're going to miss you. You know that don't you?"

Seeing Bo's reaction made me a little close to tears myself so I did that thing that British blokes do and started talking loudly!! "I should hope so, we're really good friends to lose! Listen Bo if you get all soppy you're going to make me cry, let's talk about soccer. Now, your Newcastle, what the hell are they playing at? Cos it ain't football mate!"

Bo stood upright and puffed out his chest "Well if you're going to be like, that I'm glad you're going to Canada!"

Welcome to the muppet show!

Saturday February 5th 2005

Anisha and I pulled up outside a Realtor's office in Barkingside, Essex, just a few miles from where we lived.

Before we went in, Anisha and I formulated our "Game Plan"

This usually involved me being the good cop and Anisha being the bad cop.

This time I wanted to mix things up a little.

"OK Ani, before we go in what let's agree that we're not going to get over excited in there."

Anisha laughed involuntarily "Divind, let me remind you that you're the one that goes all giddy when we meet new people!"

I didn't find her funny. "Like when?"

Anisha turned and faced me in her seat.

This didn't look good for me!

"Like when? Like when we were looking for our first new car and that car dealer offered you free car mats if you bought the car that day, you said yes immediately."

I couldn't see where she was going so thought I had her on the ropes "What's wrong with that? They're great car mats."

"What's wrong with that " she said angrily "is the fact the car dealer waited until after you'd signed the sales contract to admit that he was prepared to offer us free insurance for a year just to sweeten the deal but you took the stupid rubber mats!"

I suddenly remembered that expensive episode. "OK I'll let you do all the talking then!"

Anisha thought she'd hurt my feelings so went into her charm offensive "Listen Divind, sulking isn't going to help us. All I'm saying is let's listen twice as much as we talk......

I knew what was coming next so stopped her mid-sentence "Ani if you say "You have 2 ears and 1 mouth" I might just punch you in the mouth!"

Ani stopped herself "You have 2, OK let's just do this thing."

I gave her the stink-eye and we walked in and were greeted by the receptionist.

She was an attractive Indian girl who Anisha would later say, "She seemed to have applied her make-up with a stick of dynamite!"

She smiled at us and had teeth like rotting grave stones!!

I hoped that my shock didn't show but guessed it did because she stopped smiling after about two milliseconds! "Good morning, how can I help you?"

Anisha spoke first "Hi, we'd like to see a Realtor, we want to sell our house."

One of the Realtors, an Indian man, aged about 30, stopped at the reception desk and smiled at us.

This bloke had that sort of weird accent that was a mix of East End meets East Punjab! "Well you've come to the right place innit! Hi I'm Dave Mistry at your service" and then he saluted "It's OK Sunitta, I'll take over from here innit."

He shook our hands with a limp wet fish of a hand-shake and then waved his hand and we reluctantly followed him.

"Please walk this way." and he started walking in a weird way that was slightly alarming and made Sunitta laugh hysterically.

When he looked back and saw that we weren't following his stupid walking style or even looking mildly impressed he started walking properly.

Anisha leaned into me and whispered. I could tell that Anisha didn't like this guy, this was confirmed when she leaned in close "This guy's like an Indian Mr. Bean! DO NOT encourage him."

I laughed at the idea that this idiot was going to sell our house for us.

I crossed my heart and whispered "I am mute!!"

Dave led us to a desk at the back of the office and offered us both a seat.

Dave then took out a pad of paper "So let's start with the formalities: what's your surname?"

Anisha spoke "Purewal. That's P U R E W A L."

Dave jotted down the details "Thanks. Now, your address and phone number please" I decided that even I couldn't mess up with that question "12 Denham Drive, Gants Hill, IG2 6QU. 0208 554 8008 at home and my cell number is 07979 344 344."

Dave nodded knowingly "Gant's Hill's eh? That's a nice area. Remind me is Denham Drive down by Eastern Avenue?"

Anisha nodded "Yes, it comes off of Eastern Avenue."

Dave placed his pen in his mouth like he was a big shot lawyer who'd just found a fatal flaw in the defence's case "Great. Now are you selling and buying?"

Anisha pulled her seat closer "No we're just selling."

Dave took the pen from his mouth and joked "Looking to become homeless eh?" he then started laughing and it sounded like a braying donkey.

Neither of us joined in.

Anisha gave him one of her legendary dirty looks "Not exactly, we're emigrating to Canada."

Dave responded with a whistle "Sweet! OK so when can I come over to see the house and take a few measurements and photos?"

I could tell even more that Anisha wasn't happy and was certain that she was about to say the "12th of never" when she actually said "We're free tomorrow afternoon if that works for you?"

Dave grabbed his desk diary "Let me just check what my day looks like tomorrow." he said and then thumbed through a diary that we could see was almost entirely empty of appointments.

He finally landed on the right date "You're in luck, I'm free at about 2pm, does that work for you?"

Anisha stood up and I copied her "That's great. We'll see you tomorrow." and with that Anisha turned and walked to the front of the office as I took a business card from Dave.

As he handed me his card I asked him a question "So Dave, what's your real name?"

Dave looked a little surprised with my question "It's really Dave."

I didn't believe him "Come on tell me the truth." he laughed "No seriously, it really is Dave. My parents have three boys, I'm the oldest then there's Jimmy and Brian."

I looked at him for any indication that he was joking but he didn't flinch "Brian?"

He nodded "Yeah, Brian" and then he opened his mouth and placed his foot in there! "I know. It's funny because all Indian people automatically assume that Dave's short for some embarrassing Indian name like Da-vinda innit!"

I immediately went red and stared at the ground then back at Dave.

I was thankful that I was dark because he probably wouldn't be able to see my embarrassment.

"You're name's Da-vinda innit?"

I nodded sheepishly

"Sorry man" he said "no offence"

I regained my composure "That's alright. We'll see you at two o'clock tomorrow."

I left the office and joined Anisha in the car.

Anisha was re-applying her lipstick when I got in the driver's seat. "I take back what I said about him" she said "I have a good feeling about him. I think he'll sell our house quickly"

I turned the key in the ignition "He's an even bigger idiot than me, and that's saying something!!"

Sunday February 6th 2005

It was 11:30am and we were all cleaning the house.

Anisha was cleaning the kitchen and I was upstairs with the kids in Kamran's bedroom.

Kamran didn't want to help as it was cutting into valuable playing time "Dad why do I have to clean my room?"

Sonya joined in "Yeah!"

I sat on Kamran's bed and asked them to take a seat too "I told you guys last night, we have someone coming over to see the house so that they can sell it. It wouldn't look nice if people saw and smelled your socks under your bed would it?"

Kamran had a cheeky look in his eye "But you and mum keep telling us that this is your house and that we only live here!"

Usually I would have laughed but Anisha was on full 'work mode' which meant that she wouldn't accept anything other than a spotless house. "Kamran I would just shut up and tidy up your little room or you might find yourself vacuuming MY whole house!"

He looked at me and realised that I wasn't kidding "Come on Sonya, us slaves better get back to work!"

Just then Anisha called me downstairs. "Divind did you put all the dirty laundry into the wash basket?"

I looked around the bedroom for any stray clothes "Yes Ani. We're pretty much all done up here do you need a hand downstairs?"

Sonya and Kamran stood in the hallway waving their hands and grimacing indicating their disgust with my offer to do more cleaning.

Anisha shouted back "Actually Divind I've done everything except vacuuming. Oh and could you get rid of the cob webs at the top of the patio curtains? I would do it but this stove seems to have chili welded onto it."

I grimaced now.

Neither of us liked cleaning the bloody stove "I'll be down in a minute Ani."

I turned back to the kids "OK you guys just need to tidy up your drawers then you can play in the loft. Please don't make a mess up there, mum would probably skin you both!"

I then sprayed some Febreeze into their bedrooms closed their bedroom doors and headed downstairs.

Anisha was scrubbing the stove top with strands of hair hanging over her face.

She blew the strands away and puffed a little when she saw me.

She looked so beautiful.

"I don't think I've ever cleaned this house as much as I have today! There's a yellow cloth on the kitchen counter by the toaster, take it and slap the cobwebs off the curtains"

I grabbed the cloth "No problem Ani. I'll vacuum afterwards."

Ani puckered up and closed her eyes in readiness for a kiss.

As I leaned for a kiss she shouted "Bugger!"

I said "Charming! I go in for a kiss and get called a bugger!" she laughed and said "Not you, for once. What are we doing for lunch?"

I shrugged "Well we can't cook in here in case we make a mess. Let's have some burgers."

Anisha pulled a face "No thanks. I don't want you coming back and messing up our freshly cleaned toilet!"

"Good point. How about Chinese? We could go to that new buffet place on Cranbrook Road" thankfully Anisha agreed "Perfect. Let's hurry up, you, go kill those cobwebs and then we can all kill some satay chicken!"

Sunday February 6th

Anisha and I were already seated and we looked over at Kamran and Sonya who are standing by the sweet and sour shrimp balls.

Anisha saw that Kamran was trying to empty the dish of all its shrimpy contents onto his plate. "Kamran! Only take as many as you can eat! He can be so embarrassing when he sees shrimp!"

Kamran froze and then stopped his shrimp rampage.

I tried to hide my own pile of shrimps that I'd hidden on my plate under some rice.

She carried on "I don't know where he gets it from!" and then looked at my own shrimp rampage and rolled her eyes.

As the kids walked back we sat them down and walked over to the buffet trays. "You've been very quiet. Is everything OK Divind?"

I smiled "I was just thinking....

Anisha interrupted me "Divind I thought we agreed that I would do all the thinking from now on!"

I laughed "Funny lady!! I was saying I was just thinking about what we're doing. I have to admit that it's happened a lot quicker than I thought it would."

Anisha agreed "You're right Divind, but I think it's better that we just get on with it rather than sit around with our lives on hold for months, even years."

I started placing some crispy duck onto my plate "I know Ani, but I'm suddenly worried that Canada is all about what I want" a weird, puzzled look suddenly sat on Anisha's face. I was scared that I'd hit a nerve. "What do you mean?"

I took a piece of sweet and sour chicken "Think about it, I'm the one who hates what I do for a living and where my life's at. I'm worried that all I've done is convince you to hate what you do too. I am really scared that you'll end up hating me for taking us 5,000 miles away from your parents, friends and everyone we know."

Anisha placed her hand on my hand to reassure me "Divind the truth is that you didn't make me hate my job. I've been drifting along quite happily with my life but you have this whole idea that you have to make your mark on the world. If you think being in Vancouver is going to make all of us happy then I'm behind you and beside you 100%. However, and you may want to write this down, if we go there and it sucks I will throw that fact in your face for the rest of your miserable life!! And trust me I will make your life really, really miserable!!"

We both laughed and Ani gave me a peck on the lips.

Kamran saw us kissing "Ugh! Go get a room!" Sonya added her two pence worth "Yeah, that's disgusting!"

The Realtor cometh!

Sunday February 6th 2005 1:58pm.

Anisha came back home having dropped the kids off to her parent's house in readiness for Dave's arrival.

At 1:59 a black BMW 4 series pulled up on our drive and Dave jumped out wearing a blue pin striped suit, white shirt with a blue collar and a bright yellow Homer Simpson tie and mirrored sunglasses.

Dave adjusted his tie and rang the doorbell.

I answered the door.

"Good afternoon Dave"

Dave took his glasses off with, what he hoped would be a slick movement that he had obviously done before but the arm of his glasses got caught in his long hair. "Aaagh my hair! Hi Da-vinda."

I invited him in.

"Do come in."

Dave walked in and removed his shoes.

He had a quick look around the room. "Nice. open-plan layout, I like it, I like it a lot!" he then took out a digital camera and started taking a few photos.

I felt a little aware that I was in his way so tried to go into the kitchen "Dave can I get you a cup of tea or a glass of coke or something?"

130

Dave shook his head "No thanks, I'll be done in a few minutes. How wide is the living room?" it was my turn to shake my head "I've no idea Dave I've never had a reason to measure it."

Dave then took a laser measuring device and started to take various readings around the room. He carefully wrote down the numbers into his note book and spoke into his Dictaphone.

After a few minutes he approached me in the kitchen "So it's just the kitchen and open-plan living room downstairs?"

I wanted to say 'No you idiot, there's another five rooms down here but they're invisible!' but thought better of it "That's it. We were thinking of adding an extension to the back of the house but with us looking to move that didn't make sense." he nodded again and looked at the stairs.

"Do you mind if I go upstairs?"

I could feel myself getting really impatient with this idiot!

He kept saying my name like it was two words, was asking me the measurements of my room and was asking generally dumb questions. "I guess seeing upstairs would help in trying to sell our house so go for it. Just a word of warning, you'll have to bend down slightly to your left at the top of the loft stairs because the staircase comes down quite sharply on the right hand side."

For the first time since I'd met him 24 hours earlier Dave seemed excited about something "You've got a loft? Sweet man, sweet!"

Dave walked up the stairs and a few seconds later Anisha and I heard a loud thud followed by muffled swearing.

I laughed into my shirt "You OK Dave?"

Dave responded angrily "Yes, I'm fine!" After a few minutes Dave came back downstairs rubbing a small purple bruise on the right side of his forehead. He sat down at the dining room table and took out his notebook and started his sales patter "Your house is in fairly good condition. I don't think you'll have a hard time selling it. It's in a nice quiet street, you're between two underground stations and you have good schools nearby."

Anisha was getting impatient too so asked him straight out "Yes we know that Dave and that's why we live here. Now the question is, how much do you think the house is worth?"

Dave was a little taken aback with how blunt Anisha was being "Ah, that's the $64,000 question. The value of the house is determined by how much someone is prepared to pay for it."

That's the moment I first lost it with Dave!! "Wow! That's brilliant!! Do they teach you that at Realtor school?!"

Dave looked like the proverbial rabbit in headlights! "What, what I mean is that your house is a typical three bedroom terrace in a suburb of Ilford."

Anisha put her hand up like she was back at school "Three bedrooms? What about the loft, doesn't that count as an extra bedroom?"

Dave looked too scared to speak! He whispered "It's only a fourth bedroom if you got planning permission for the loft. Did you get the planning permission?"

Anisha pointed at me "No, we didn't. Divinder said that we didn't bother as we didn't alter the roof line. Besides Divinder said it was a waste of £2,000"

Dave suddenly saw an opportunity to throw me under the bus and become the second stupidest Indian male in the room!

"That's such a shame." he said with a huge dose of sarcasm and irony thrown in.

"If the loft had been granted planning permission then it would have been a four bedroomed house and that would have added an extra £20,000 to £30,000 to the value of your house." Anisha gave me the dirtiest look ever!!

It was so dirty that I felt like I needed to take a shower!! "Crap! Well done again Da-Vinda!" she glared at me "OK so what are we looking at?"

Dave smiled at me and I wanted to punch his stupid face in! "I would suggest we put the house on the market with an asking price of £265,000 that way you'll probably get about £250,000"

Anisha was very unimpressed "Is that all? I keep reading about people selling for £300,000."

Dave took his second metaphoric swing at me "Those houses have the extended kitchens and the council approved loft conversions. Sorry. Also you have to appreciate that with stamp duty people are reluctant to pay a penny over the £250,000 threshold."

I didn't know what he was talking about "What's stamp duty?"

Dave started drawing on his note pad "Basically the government gets 1% revenue from all house sales up to the value of £250,000 from the person who buys the house. It's called Stamp Duty and we get taught that at Realtor school! However, as soon as you sell for a penny over the £250,000 threshold the amount payable goes to 3% on the whole amount."

I felt sick that I hadn't paid the £2,000 for planning permission "Ouch!" Anisha was back in practical mode "What are your terms?"

Dave took out a contract and started walking us through it "We have a 12 week contract and if you make us sole agent I can give you a rate of say 3.5%" we pretended to read the small print. Anisha took the contract from Dave "Dave, just give us a minute to have a quick chat. Let's go in the kitchen Divind."

We went into the kitchen and closed the door behind us "Ani, I hate the idea that we're going to pay brown Mr. Bean out there £7,000 just for sticking a For Sale sign outside our house. This house and area means that this place will sell itself."

Anisha agreed "It is what it is Divind. Let's sign the contract and get the ball rolling and Mr. Bean out of our house" we shook hands "OK let's do this."

We took our seats around the table and looked at the contract together.

Anisha read through quickly and then focused on the fee and tapped it with her pen "Make the fee 3%, Dave, and we have a deal."

Dave bit his lip for a second and started to punch random numbers into his calculator "OK. You're killing me here, but I like you guys. Well done. Mrs. Purewal, have you ever considered a career as a Realtor?"

Anisha laughed as Dave tore off a few pages of the contract and handed them to Anisha.

"Here's your copy and if you give me a few minutes I'll call the board guys to come over this afternoon. Have a good day."

With that Dave shook our hands and left the house.

We both stood at the window and watched him get into his car.

Before he drove off he put on his sun glasses, checked himself in the mirror, then started the ignition as he made a call from his cell with the sound of Shaggy's "It wasn't me!" blasting loudly from his speakers.

Anisha held my hand "There's no going back now Divind!"

I momentarily gulped for air and loosened my collar.

Later that same day Anisha and I were shopping at Sainsbury's doing the weekly shop. Anisha had left the kids with her parents.

As Anisha picked out vegetables I attempted to sneak a few chocolate bars and biscuits into the shopping trolley.

Anisha came back, lifted up the fish fingers, found my illicit goodies and put them all on the nearest shelf "You really are a pathetic human being! You know that don't you?"

I threw my hands in the air like a 5 year old kid "Why do you treat me like your oldest kid?"

Anisha raised an eyebrow "Divind, look at what you just did, I was picking out vegetables for the family to eat healthily and you saw that as an opportunity to hide sweets in the shopping trolley. Here's an idea I'll stop treating you like a kid when you stop behaving like a kid. Deal?"

I stuck my tongue out, blew a raspberry and walked off with my arms folded in a pretend sulk.

Anisha continued shopping and after a few minutes I felt my phone vibrate in my pocket. I read the message "Let's go Divind. I'm done."

I ignored the text.

A few minutes after her text, I found Anisha packing her bags.

She grabbed a receipt that was hanging from my pocket!

It was a £4 bill that I'd used to pay for some sweets with my credit card.

"You really think you're clever don't you?"

I dropped my head.

"Well let me tell you that Sonya saw you, the other day, with a bath towel around your waist and she asked me if you were pregnant! The only thing that's getting thinner about you is your hair!"

I didn't make eye contact.

As we sat in the car, in the car park, Anisha rummaged through my sweet bag and started to eat a chocolate bar.

I wasn't having that! "Oi you hypocrite!"

Anisha just carried on eating "Listen I'm trying to keep us healthy for a long life but if you want to get all fat and flabby then let's do it together!!"

I was just about to argue when my cell phone started to ring.

I looked at the phone number, it was Dave.

"Hi Dave" Dave sounded like he was calling from an echoey washroom "Hi Da-vinda, it's Dave" having not yet forgiven Dave for telling Anisha about me messing up with the planning permission I was in no mood for his stupidity so replied "Yeah I know who it is and that's why I said Hi Dave. What's up?"

Dave ignored my passive aggressiveness "I've got a runny nose and an upset stomach after a dodgy sausage but other than that I'm sweet! Listen I've got some good news"

I needed some good news so dropped my attitude "Great, what's the good news?"

I heard Dave make a slight groaning sound and then I swear I heard a muffled splashing sound!

He was calling from the toilet!!

"I've got a couple interested in viewing your house. I'm just about to show then a place in Woodford but I could be at yours in about 15 minutes. Does 5pm work for you?"

I was suddenly impressed with Dave, even though he was calling me whilst taking a dump!

Some would call it multi-tasking!

"Bloody hell Dave you only left two hours ago and there's not even a board outside the house yet?"

Dave took the compliment "It's called being proactive Da-vinda! We don't just get paid to stick a For Sale sign outside your house you know!"

I looked over at Anisha, placed my hand over the phone and said "Dave's got a first viewer, five o'clock today. Is that too soon?"

Anisha gave me the thumbs up.

I got back on the 'phone "Sure Dave, send them over. Will you be with them?"

I swear I heard Dave fart and then he coughed too late in an effort to cover the sound and replied "Unfortunately not, I have a hot date with Sunitta from the office. I think I'm on a promise!"

I stared at the phone "Dave you could have just said no" he apologized "Sorry. The couple are the Carter's. The husband is Derek and his wife's name is Carly. Give me a call when they leave. Laters!"

He hung up but not soon enough because I heard him say "Jesus, I'm making myself sick with that smell!" and then a toilet flushed!

4:55pm

We drove back and unpacked the shopping in record time.

I looked at the clock on the wall "Do you think it's worth putting on some coffee Ani? I read somewhere that the smell of coffee makes people relaxed when they view a house."

Ani looked unsure "Hey listen if you think that'll help do it. Just be quick they'll be here any minute. I'll help you" I dismissed her help "I think I can boil water and pour in over dehydrated coffee beans!"

Just as I finished making the coffee a tiny red Ford Fiesta pulled onto our drive.

I walked over to the window and watched as a white couple got out of the car which rocked as they balanced themselves.

The man, Derek, was about 6 feet 6 and built like a wrestler.

His wife Carly was just under 6 feet tall and looked to have a similar build to her husband. "Ani, look at these two! The circus must be in town!"

Anisha joined me at the window and almost jumped back when the doorbell rang. "You get the door, they scare me!" she said.

I opened the door and looked up at the giant in front of me. "Hi you must be Derek. I'm Divinder."

Derek put out a shovel-sized hand which made my hand look like a kid's hand.

I had to massage my fingers from Derek's vice-like grip. "Hello Govinder." he growled.

I didn't correct him saying my name wrong. "This is my wife Carly."

Carly waved at me with equally huge "man hands"!

I stepped into the house conscious of the fact that the three of us would not fit in our tiny porch without me being crushed to death. "Do come in, out of the rain."

The Carter's lumbered in and my nostrils started to twitch a little.

Anisha looked like a toddler against their huge frames.

Anisha also started sniffing "Hi I'm Anisha. Can I offer you guys a cup of coffee?"

Carly spoke first in a deep voice that sounded like it started in her gut! "I'm allergic to coffee: the smell of it makes me gag!"

Anisha glared at me.

What were the odds that we would get the only person allergic to coffee?

I watched helplessly as the Carter's started to wipe their feet vigorously on the cream mat sat on the porch floor rather than the doormat on the porch floor.

I noticed that Derek had something brown and smelly on the sole of his shoe and it was now all over our – once - expensive cream mat.

I tried to stop the carnage! "Derek could I ask you to take your shoes off? You seem to have brought some stuff on the bottom of your shoe."

Derek looked down at his shoes, then at the mat and went red. "Sorry about that Govendra!"

Carly tutted "That would explain the smell in the car!"

Derek looked upset "Could you smell it in the car?"

Carly nodded "Yeah I could."

Derek seemed a little surprised "Why didn't you say something?"

Carly tapped the side of her head "I just thought it was that curry from last night!"

Derek was staring at the sole of his shoe "Do you guys have anything like a cocktail stick or a skewer that I could borrow?"

We both shook our heads as Anisha was trying really hard not to puke.

I didn't want him to make any more mess "Don't worry I'll bring you some napkins and some soapy water."

Derek thanked me and then spoke to Carly "Carly love why don't you look at the house with Ursula? I'll try to get this mess off the rug."

Carly agreed and went into the kitchen with Anisha as I filled a bucket with warm water.

"As you can see the kitchen comes with a fitted dish washer and washing machine. We have a tumble dryer in the loft"

Carly seemed unimpressed "The kitchen's a bit small innit?"

Anisha tried to sell the house's benefits "Yeah it's small, but we manage to do a Christmas dinner for 25 people every year."

Carly wasn't buying "My kitchen is about 3 times the size of this. It won't do, nah it won't do."

Meanwhile I was with the man-mountain "So Surinder why are you selling your place?"

I was gagging and dry heaving in the tiny porch as the smell of the fox crap was made worse with the warm water that he was using on it. "I'm being transferred to...Edinburgh...by my company....to open a new branch."

Derek smiled "Edinburgh eh? I love Ireland! The Irish are just so friendly!"

I was very concerned that the mat was completely ruined "Yes, got to love the Irish. That stain's not coming out is it? Derek agreed and tried to make a joke of it "Nah, I think I'm making it worse. At least you've got a nice new brown rug eh?"

Derek laughed and I forced a laugh for fear that he might kill me with his bare, pooh covered hands!

I heard Anisha talking to Carly "This is the lounge that leads onto the patio."

Carly didn't seem impressed at all.

"Don't you have an extension?"

Anisha looked at her as if to say "Can you see a bloody extension you stupid, giant cow?"

Thankfully Anisha kept her cool "Not at the back of the house no, we chose to convert the loft into a play room for the kids."

Carly sniffed snootily "So where's the second bath room?" Anisha went red in the face at having to give a negative answer to every question that Carly had asked "We only have one family bathroom. I'll show you it when we go upstairs."

Carly raised her hands in surrender "I don't think I'll bother checking out the rest of the house, it seems really small and poky. Let's go Derek."

Derek nodded, placed the dirty napkin into the soapy water and handed the bowl of dirty, stinky fox-pooh water to me.

He looked slightly embarrassed as he said "As I say I'm sorry about that, mess. See ya." with that they left and squeezed themselves back into their clown car.

As the Carters' car screeched off the drive, Anisha screamed!

"Aaagh!! I can't believe that Hagrid's sister just dissed my house so bad! What gives her the right to tell me my house is small and poky after her stupid giant husband ruins that mat we got as a wedding present? I'll leave you to clean up that mess, you know what I'm like around stuff like that."

I looked at her with a "watcha talkin' 'bout Willis" expression on my face "Excuse me, why's this my job?"

Anisha just pointed at the mat "Divind you know that if I smell that I'm likely to puke!"

I shook my head "That's really convenient! I don't remember this being part of the wedding vows!!"

MACDONALD'S RESTURANT.
Saturday February 19th 2005, Sonya's 5th birthday party.

Sonya had invited her whole class and they were all in the ball pool.

We were placing the last of the presents into the boot of our car.

Anisha looked a little sad "Divind, it's just hit me that this is the last time Sonya will have a birthday in England."

I smiled "You're right Ani, but you could go nuts with the whole "this is the last time" thing" she looked at me with a weird expression "What do you mean?"

I closed the boot and leaned on the car "Well it's like your Uncle Ram who says the same crappy joke every New Year's Eve" she laughed "You mean when he says I'm not having a bath until next year and then a second after midnight says 'I haven't had a shower since last year'"

I nudged her and said "Exactly!"

We walked back towards the restaurant and Anisha grabbed my hand "Let's just enjoy the carnage and see what fate throws our way"

I looked at her and felt a crazy sensation take over "Good idea. You know I love you don't you?"

Anisha stopped in her tracks "I sort of guessed it when you married me and then it was confirmed after we had our two kids!"

I laughed "You really are a muppet! I just can't wait to start our new adventure in Canada together."

We kissed and then walked back in, hand-in-hand

I took a seat with Bo and his wife Jane as Anisha went off to buy coffee for her parents.

Bo sipped his tea and then raised an eyebrow "Hey, any more luck with the viewings after Mr. and Mrs. Skidmark?"

I laughed at the nickname rather than the memory "I'm so glad that my misfortune makes you laugh!"

Bo giggled "It's still early days mate, you see you'll be out by May."

I forced a smile on my face "I wish I had your confidence. We haven't had as many people view the house we we'd hoped for."

Bo took another sip of his tea "Well think about it, we're only in the middle of February, anyone wanting to get their kids into school will need to be moved by summer."

Bo made sense "I guess you're right mate. The frustrating part is keeping the house clean 24/7. The poor kids are even eating their cookies and chips over a bowl in case they make a mess!"

Bo laughed "Sorry mate, but that's funny!"

I agreed "I know, but the poor kids. What's really annoying is when people just don't turn up and don't even have the decency to call ahead and tell us. You feel like you've been jilted at the realty altar."

Just then Anisha joined us with hot chocolates for everyone.

She raised her eyebrow "So what have I missed boys?"

Bo responded before I could "Divinder was just complaining about having to keep the house spotless."

Anisha blew out a blast of air in exasperation "Did he tell you we've even made the kids eat their cookies over a bowl for fear of making a mess?"

Bo laughed "I thought he was joking about that!"

Anisha suddenly noticed that Jane had stayed out of the conversation and this was very unlike her. "You're a bit quiet Jane, everything alright love?"

Jane burst into tears and Bo and I started looking at our drinks as if they had the winning lottery numbers floating in them!

Between sniffling she said "I am going to miss you guys so much!" her tears started Anisha off! "Now you've got me started! Come here you silly moo!"

Bo and I looked at each other and took this as our cue to take a walk to the ball pool and check on the kids.

Bo placed his hand on my back in a big brotherly sort of way "It's a brave thing you guys are doing"

I stopped walking and faced Bo "Not really. Think about it, Anisha and I both have our degrees, after we sell the house we'll have some money in the bank, I have my brother and a lot of relatives in Vancouver and it shouldn't be that hard to get a job with our work experience."

Bo looked like he was ready for me to answer his question as I had because he came back with a quick reply "OK, I thought you'd say something like that, but what if you go there and really hate it? Would you come back?"

I thought about his question for a whole two seconds "I don't think we would Bo. If I came back I would never ever take another risk again because I would be worried that it would fail like Canada did. Nope, we just have to grab the bull by the horns and make the best of what we have."

Bo looked sad that I had dismissed the idea of coming back home.

Suddenly my shirt pocket started buzzing "Excuse me Bo, I'm either having a heart attack or my phone's vibrating!"

Bo laughed as I answered the phone "Hello Dave, Divinder speaking" it was rent-a-muppet Dave. "Hi Da-vinda, it's Dave!"

I stared at the phone and thought "I'm paying you to annoy me!!"

"Hi Dave, how are you?"

He sounded excited like he'd just found his long lost brother "I'm cool. I need you to do me a favour. Da-vinda tell me I'm the best Realtor you've ever met!"

I covered the phone and whispered to Bo "This guy is a proper bell-end!"

"OK, Dave why would I say that?"

Dave laughed "Go on Da-Vinda, please just humor me and say it."

I could hear other voices from his phone and had visions of him having me on speaker phone in his office recreating the classic "Show me the money!" scene from the movie Jerry McGuire "OK, Dave you are the one and only Realtor that I've ever met and are therefore the best one I've ever met!"

I heard the sound of muffled laughter from his line and then Dave spoke "I suppose that'll have to do. I have a cash buyer interested in seeing the house and they are first timers so there's no chain!"

I didn't want to show that I was impressed "That's great. What time do they want to view the house?"

"Well actually we're outside your house right now! Where are you?"

I looked over at Sonya who smiled and waved at me "I'm at my daughter's 5th birthday party at the McDonalds in Newbury Park. Can they come back this afternoon?"

Dave sounded desperate "Could you come back for a few minutes? I promise it'll be worth your while."

I looked at my watch "I'll call you back in two minutes I just need to make sure that Anisha is OK by herself and thirty 5 year olds"

Dave sighed "Sweet, I'll wait for your call."

I walked over to Bo "Sorry about that Bo, business calls."

We both walked over to Anisha and I told her about the potential offer and she gave me the thumbs up.

I pulled up on my drive and saw Dave leaning on his car with a middle aged Indian couple by his side.

Dave practically skipped over to my car "Thanks for seeing us at such short notice. This is Ahmed Sharif and his wife DOCTOR Fatima Sharif. Fatima has just finished her medical training at St. Barts and has found a job at King George's hospital."

I nodded at them both "Hi, please do come in." I walked ahead of them and turned off the alarm.

Dave took the Sharif's around the house as I took a seat on the couch.

Ten minutes later the Sharif's were back in the living room.

Dave approached me "Da-vinda do you mind if we take a seat around your table?"

I nodded "Sure, no problem. I'll go in the kitchen and give you some privacy. Can I make you guys some tea while I'm in there?"

Ahmed looked up, he was one of those Indian guys who had a huge head and a crazy comb-over that had to be 3 feet long! "That would be very kind Divinder. I'll have a tea with milk and two sugars please. Fatima what would you like?"

Fatima was almost round and wore a burkha that made her chubby face look like it was framed she spoke with a soft voice "Just a glass of cold water for me please."

I looked over at Dave "OK, and Dave what can I get you?" he had wild eyes and as he spoke he tapped his pen on the dining table "I'm fine, I had three Red Bulls earlier."

I went into the kitchen and closed the door.

I put the kettle on and then put my ear against the glass door to hear the conversation.

Ahmed spoke "I really like this house. I want to make an offer immediately, I don't want to miss out. Don't forget that Fatima starts her first rotation in three weeks. As long as we can agree on a reasonable price I would like to move in within 14 days. Now remind me, is the asking price £265,000?"

I started dancing around the kitchen and nearly knocked the tea pot off the counter.

Dave turned towards the noise in the kitchen. "Let me get Da-vinda."

I heard Dave get up and saw his shadow in the glass door.

"Crap!"

I quickly poured the hot water into the tea pot as Dave opened the kitchen door just as I poured the tea into a cup.

"Da-vinda could we see you in here, Mr. Sharif would like to discuss an offer with you."

I smiled casually "Of course!"

I gave Ahmed his tea and Fatima her cold water.

Ahmed pulled a chair out as an invitation for me to sit down at my own table.

"Mr. Purewal you have a lovely house. I would like to know if you are able to vacate within, say, 14 days?"

I tried my best not to get what Anisha called all "teethy."

She always says that I smile like a horse when I get good news and give away how I feel.

To stop this from happening I kept my top lip over my teeth and looked like an idiot and made talking a little tough "That depends on what sort of offer you're going to make. We are able to move in with my mother and father in law. They live down the street at number 33."

Fatima joined the conversation "That's great."

Dave suddenly stopped smiling "Do you need your wife here before we negotiate?"

I shook my head "No, I think we're OK. So Mr. Sharif what's your offer?"

I sat there for what seemed an eternity and then he said "Mr. Purewal I would like to offer you" then he paused for dramatic effect "£200,000, **CASH!**"

It was like my record had been scratched!!

"Mr. Sharif you do know the asking price don't you?"

Ahmed placed his arms across his chest "I am aware of your asking price but I am also aware of the fact that this is a buyer's market and I am the buyer."

I looked at Dave who had a stupid smile on his face and was nodding like an idiot. "Mr. Sharif, Can I ask you a question?" he nodded "But of course."

I leaned across the table "Mr. Sharif. How exactly are you related to me?" he looked surprised with my random question "Excuse me?"

I changed my question "I'm just wondering why you would expect to get a £65,000 discount unless we're related real closely?!"

Ahmed looked incredulous at my aggression

"Mr. Purewal I don't think you understand, my offer is for £200,000, CASH. I have no house to sell. Dave has told me that you are in a hurry to move."

I glared at Dave who avoided my gaze.

Ahmed carried on "This offer is valid for 24 hours. I will leave you to discuss this with your wife. By the way that offer would also include all your furniture and electrical goods too."

I tapped my forefinger on the side of my head "Mr. Sharif, I don't need 24 hours, I don't even need 24 minutes, in fact I don't even need 24 seconds! I am respectfully declining your offer. Please contact Dave when you come up with a more accurate price."

Rather than being annoyed, Ahmed smiled in a knowing way and as he walked towards the front door he said "I know you will call me. Have a good evening."

As they left I said "Please don't hold your breath! In fact have a great life!"

The Sharif's left my house and spoke to Dave for a moment before they drove off.

After they'd driven off, Dave came back into the house.

He joined me at the dining table "Da-vinda I think you're being a little hasty"

I snarled at him "Hasty? We've only had the house on the market for a few days! Do you honestly expect me to drop my asking price by £65,000 and include all my furniture and electricals? If I did that I would resemble John Wayne Bobbitt!!"

I stood up and started walking to the door "I'm just saying it's the first offer and we should keep him warm just in case nothing else pans out."

I walked Dave to the front door "Dave you're not really inspiring much confidence right now! And please don't tell people that we're emigrating. It makes us look like we're desperate."

Dave looked hurt "OK no problem. Should I tell them that you'll think about it?"

I looked at him with my best "you better get moving boy!" look and he scurried to his car. "Dave just go before I question if your parents were married when you were born!"

Dave opened his car door and gave me the "OK" signal with his hand as I closed the door and went into the kitchen to place the cups in the dishwasher.

I called Anisha from my mobile phone. "Hi Ani" she could hear the tone of my voice "Who died?"

I wasn't in a talkative mood "Our offer"

I could hear the disappointment in her voice "What happened?"

I sighed.

"What would you say if I told you I took an offer for £200,000?"

I heard Anisha pause for a moment as she sipped her drink "Two things: number one: where are you going to be staying so that I could forward on your mail and number two: I would advise you to call John Wayne Bobbitt to ask for the name of his surgeon!"

I forced a laugh "I thought so. The guy was really aggressive and wanted me to come back to him within 24 hours. I told him that he wouldn't be getting a call back from us as the answer was no"

I was failing to hide my disappointment so Ani tried to reassure me.

"Don't worry Divind. It'll happen when the time is right. I should be finished here in about 20 minutes. I'll see you when I get home."

I hit the off button on the phone and sat down to watch some TV.

Just as I put the TV on, the doorbell rang.

I was still angry and assumed that Ahmed had come back so when I answered the door I just screamed "I told you, NO means NO!!"

The poor Indian man on the door step wasn't Mr. Sharif!

He jumped back at my aggressive approach.

I immediately calmed down and apologised "I am so sorry, I thought you were a different Indian man!"

The "new Indian man" on the doorstep looked like he was about to run away but then composed himself enough to speak "I'm very sorry to disturb you but I was driving past and saw your For Sale sign. Do I need to make an appointment with the Realtor or can I arrange something with you?"

I stepped into the house and ushered him in "Please, do come in. You're here now and it doesn't make sense to make you come back again."

He followed me in, took off his shoes and then extended his hand "Thank you. My name is Prakash"

I shook his hand, he had a firm grip but wasn't trying to break my hand.

I decided that this was a good sign.

I had always judged people by their hand shake and his was solid but not vice like.

"I'm Divinder. I promise I'm not always so aggressive! You'll have to excuse my outburst at the door, but I had just said goodbye to a couple who offered me £65,000 less than the asking price and then gave me 24 hours to respond!"

Prakash looked a little shocked "Having seen how you answered the door, I'll try not to annoy you!"

We both laughed.

Prakash had a loud laugh that ended abruptly, almost a "Ha!"

I liked Prakash with his firm hand shake and loud, weird laugh.

I walked over to the stairs "Please feel free to have a look around but I'd ask that you don't steal anything! I'll answer any questions you have when you come back"

Prakash laughed again "Thank you, I promise I won't steal anything!"

Prakash walked around the house as I tidied the kitchen.

Five minutes later Prakash returned to the living room, he grabbed his shoes and stood by the door. I was sure that a visit this short was negative "That bad eh?"

Prakash laughed again "On the contrary Divinder! I was merely sent on the reconnaissance mission by my wife. I really like your house and this area is very good. My in-laws live a few streets away and my wife is 5 months pregnant so we need to find a house soon."

I tried hard not to look excited so started making small talk, something that I'm really crap at "It's a lovely house and the area is so convenient for the City. We've been here for just under 10 years and we'll be sad to leave."

Prakash nodded and looked at his watch "I have to go but I have a quick question, why are you selling?"

I smiled "We're moving to Canada."

Prakash looked impressed "Wow! That's quite the move! Listen can I be cheeky and use your phone? I would like to call my wife and let her know where I am."

I pointed towards the home phone on the shelf "Of course you can, unless she's in India!"

Prakash laughed again and as he dialed he said "HA! You're a funny man!"

"Hello Pooja. I'm at that house in Denham Drive. Yes the white one. It is as nice inside as it looks. The owner is here with me. I'll ask him" he covered the handset. "Divinder, can I come back tomorrow with my wife?"

I nodded "Of course, what time?"

Prakash pulled a face "Would 8pm be too late?"

I gave him the thumbs up "That's no problem at all"

Prakash got back on his call "OK Pooja you'll see the house tomorrow. Bye" he handed me the phone

"Thank you, Divinder. How do you turn off the phone?" I pressed the off button and placed the phone on the table.

Prakash walked over to the door again "Divinder, could I trouble you for your phone number?"

I was so happy that I wanted to break dance!! "Of course, let me put that on a piece of paper for you"

I scribbled the number of a scrap of paper and handed it to Prakash.

As he left I shook his hand "Prakash, please do me a favor and call Dave Mistry on the number on the For Sale board. He'll need to know that you're interested."

Prakash nodded "Thank you Divinder, I look forward to seeing you tomorrow."

Prakash pulled off the driveway just as Ani walked down the street with the kids.

He smiled at Anisha and waved at Kamran and Sonya who waved back at him.

Anisha looked at the car as it drove off "Who's that?"

I smiled and kissed her cheek. "That, my dear, is Prakash and I think that he'll be the new owner of the house."

Anisha gave me a "whatcha-talkin' 'bout Willis" look. "You what?"

I walked into the house as she followed me in, nudging me in the back along for an answer. "Prakash drove past the house, saw the for sale sign, knocked on the door and he likes what he sees. He's bringing his wife over tomorrow evening at 8 to get the green light."

Anisha slumped down on the sofa "That's so weird that he drove past and knocked on the door. That's exactly what we did 10 years ago. That's fate that is." I joined her on the sofa "I hope so Ani, I really do."

Monday February 20th 2005.

Anisha and I were on the train traveling back home.

The phone started to buzz in my jacket pocket.

I answered the call "Hello Dave, Divinder speaking" it was Dave "Hi Da-Vinda, it's Dave. I've got Mr. Sharif with me in the office. He wants to know, if you've reconsidered his offer?"

"Dave, I thought I made myself very clear about his ridiculous offer two days ago."

I heard Dave say "It's no" to Mr. Sharif and then I heard Mr. Sharif say "Idiot! He'll be begging me in a month and then I'll offer him 50,000 less!"

I carried on "It's a huge no and tell him that I'd rather give the house away then sell to him! Also, just to let you know we have a couple coming over tonight for a second viewing. I'm doing YOUR job for YOU!!"

Dave was suddenly back on track "Is that Prakash and Pooja?"

I replied "Yes it is" and was just about to hang up when the idiot continued "OK I'll tell Mr. Sharif again that it's a no. Although I do think you're making a mistake

I stared at the phone and swore under my breath "Thanks for that Dave. Goodbye"

I hung up and gently slapped my forehead with my palm!

Ani laughed "I take it that was Dave?"

I made a face "Yup good old Dave."

Anisha put her head on my shoulder "Divind, I really hope that Prakash and Pooja are serious. I need some good news."

I agreed "I know." At 7:55pm, that evening we had just finished tidying the house for the third time.

Anisha was uncharacteristically nervous "OK Kamran, Sonya you get to stay up until after these people leave."

Kamran did a fist pump like Tom Cruise on Oprah's couch! "YES!! Result!"

Sonya was a little less enthusiastic "Mummy, when are they getting here?"

Anisha looked up at the clock "When the big hand points to the 12 and the little hand points to the 8."

Sonya gave her Mum a dirty look "You mean 8 o'clock?"

Anisha blushed "Sorry darling, I forgot you can tell the time."

Kamran grabbed Sonya's arm "OK Sonya let's go and play PlayStation. I'll even let you win!"

Sonya released herself from her brother's grip and ran to me "You better plug my controller in this time! Dad, tell him that he has to plug my controller in! Last week he made me think I was playing when my controller wasn't even connected!"

I fought the urge to laugh or high-five Kamran as he'd learnt these tricks from me but instead I said "Play nice Kamran!"

The kids ran upstairs.

Anisha was sitting at the dining table with a note pad that she was scribbling on.

"Divind, you know I told you not to count your chickens?"

I sat down next to her "Yeah" she turned her note pad towards me "Well I have!! Divind do you know how much £265,000 is in Canadian dollars?"

I pretended to do some calculations in my head but she knew that mathematics was my weakness.

"I have no idea, but I'm sure you're about to tell me."

She showed me an equation "OK there are 2.3 Canadian dollars to a pound. That means we would have over $609,500! We'd be half millionaires!! We could buy a lovely house with a small mortgage and even some college funds with that sort of money!"

I needed to rein her in, which was weird as I was the one who usually ran before I could walk.

"OK Einstein, you need to calm down a little" she seemed upset that I had rained on her parade.

"Why?" she asked, slightly hurt at my lack of shared enthusiasm at a plan that was essentially orchestrated by me.

I took her pen and started jotting a few words on her "First of all no one is going to pay us £265,000 for this house. That Stamp Duty malarkey is going to kill off that idea. Secondly we still have a massive mortgage on the house. Minus the mortgage from the house price, then minus Mr. Bean's commission check and whatever is left convert that into Canadian dollars." she looked like she was about to cry "Oh yeah." as she crumpled the paper and threw it at the display cabinet.

I took her hand in mine "Listen love, I suggest that if Prakash and Pooja offer us £250,000 we should take the offer and run." she pulled her hand away "Idiot! There you go again getting all giddy! Please do not settle for rubber car mats again!"

I didn't like being called an idiot, even when it was deserved "Let's just see what happens. But I think I'll be right and you'll be wrong."

Anisha stood up and walked over to the window and said something under her breath "That'll be the first time!" I didn't quite catch what she said so asked her to repeat herself "What did you say?" Anisha stopped mid-step and looked back at me with a smirk and said "I said...that would be just fine!"

Just as I was about to pick a fight, the doorbell rang and Anisha ran to the door.

I laughed and said "And I'm the giddy one!"

Anisha just poked her tongue out and said "Be quiet!"

Anisha composed herself before she opened the door and greeted the people we hoped would buy our house "Hi I'm Anisha, you must be Pooja." the woman at the door shook Anisha's hand "Hi Anisha, this is my husband Prakash."

Anisha nodded at Prakash "Hi Pooja, Prakash. Please come in."

Pooja and Prakash both walked in and took off their shoes.

I walked over to say hi "Please, there's no need to take off your shoes."

Prakash wagged his finger at me "We always take off our shoes." and then Pooja said ten words that made me smile like I'd won the lottery! "Besides which I would like to look after **MY** carpet!"

Anisha smiled and crossed her fingers behind her back.

Prakash pointed at the kitchen and spoke to Pooja in a South Indian language that neither of us understood.

He saw us trying to decipher what they were saying "Sorry. I was just telling my wife that we could turn the kitchen into a shower and utility room and make a large kitchen extension at the back of the house"

I nodded "I have already given Prakash the grand tour. Would you like to show Pooja around?"

Anisha walked over to Pooja "OK Pooja, let's start upstairs and work our way down."

Pooja followed Anisha up the stairs.

I turned to Prakash "Prakash can I get you a tea or a coffee?"

Prakash rubbed his hands "A tea would be great. Could I trouble you for Punjabi tea please?"

I patted him on the back "That would be no trouble at all. Please have a seat and I'll start on the chai."

I went into the kitchen and filled a saucepan from the tap and placed it on the stove.

As the water boiled, I threw in two tea bags and some tea masala.

When I went back into the living room Prakash was standing by the large photo frame from our wedding.

"Divinder, if you don't mind me saying, you looked like Borat on your wedding day!"

I laughed.

"Yeah, that was exactly the look I was aiming for!"

I pointed at the seats "Let's have a seat on the sofa Prakash, this tea is at least 10 minutes away from being ready."

Prakash sat in the armchair "By the way, where are your children?"

I pointed upstairs "We have locked them in the attic!"

Prakash looked like he didn't know if I was joking! "Really?"

I laughed heartily "No! But it was worth it just to see the look on your face! They are upstairs playing in the loft."

Prakash let out a little nervous laugh "You have a very - unique - sense of humor!"

We chatted for a few minutes and I found out that Prakash's in-laws had moved here a few years earlier and had now sponsored Pooja and Prakash to emigrate from India.

We were getting on like old friends and I wanted them to buy our house and enjoy it the way we had for the previous ten years.

A few minutes later, Anisha and Pooja returned with the kids in tow, just as I poured out the tea.

"And this is the kitchen and that is the lounge. That concludes the tour."

Pooja was smiling "It's all very nice. Prakash told me that the house was ready to move in and he was right."

Anisha looked like she was about to burst "If you don't mind me asking Pooja, is there anything you would change?"

Pooja looked around the room "We will change the color of the paint on the walls. I'm guessing that the walls were yellow when you moved in?"

Anisha blushed "No WE actually painted the house yellow a few years ago!"

Now Pooja blushed! "Oh I'm sorry! It's just a bit.....loud!"

Anisha agreed "Much like my husband!" they both laughed like old friends sharing an inside joke. "We, I mean Divinder, thought the yellow would make everyone cheerful."

Pooja laughed "It's definitely er, cheerful!"

The wives joined us on the couches.

Prakash put on his game face. "So Divinder, Anisha we obviously love the house. What sort of price are you looking for?"

We both replied at the exactly the same time. I said "£250,000" as Anisha said "£265,000!"

Pooja and Prakash looked at each other "OK so which price is it?" asked Pooja as Anisha glared at me "The asking price is £265,000" as I chimed in "But we would look at serious offers in excess of £250,000"

I could feel Anisha's stare and it was literally making my bladder feel a little queasy!!

Prakash spoke first "OK. Are you guys aware of the whole Stamp Duty issue?" we nodded.

"Yes, we are. Is that going to make this a deal breaker?"

Pooja took the baton "The truth is that we have already been pre-approved for a mortgage of £230,000 and we have a £15,000 deposit. So we're actually looking at an offer of £245,000"

Anisha bit her lip "We would really be looking for about £255,000"

Prakash and Pooja looked like they needed some time to think so we offered to go into the kitchen as they chatted.

As we walked into the kitchen and I closed the door and then Anisha punched me really hard on the right arm.

"What the...? What was that for?" then Anisha imitated me, badly "£250,000!" Have you learned nothing from that whole car mat incident? They love the house and I'm sure they'll pay £255,000. Just stop getting so bloody excited and teethy!"

I rubbed my arm which I was sure would have a bruise on it "Listen you violent muppet!! There is no way they're paying any more than £250,000. Think about it they either pay £2,500 in Stamp Duty by paying £250,000 or £7,000 in Stamp Duty on £265,000, which one would you choose?"

Anisha looked like she finally understood what I had been saying for the past few hours "OK maybe, for once in your life, you're right, but it would kill me if we didn't try to get as much as we could?"

I tried to pacify Anisha but the pain in my arm, was on my mind "Let's just see what they come back with. That punch really hurt! My arms killing me now! What if I punched you, how would that look?"

Our fight ended abruptly when Prakash tapped on the glass kitchen door.

I opened the door and Prakash and Pooja come into the kitchen.

Prakash took the lead with the negotiations.

"OK, guys, we have a compromise deal that I think, hope, you'll like. We would like to meet you half-way with an offer of £250,000 and then pay you an extra £2,000 for the washing machine, dishwasher, fridge, tumble dryer and TV."

Pooja added one more ask "One thing though. We would like to move in by May as I am due to give birth in July. Would that work for you?"

I extended my hand "Let's shake on it! You have a deal!" as Anisha screamed "Car mats!!"

Prakash look surprised by her random outburst "Car mats? Excuse me?" to which I replied "Don't worry about her Prakash, that's just what Anisha says when she's excited!!"

Pooja shook hands with Anisha as I did the same with Prakash.

And with that we'd sold our house, pending the exchanging of actual legal contracts!!

We waved Prakash and Pooja off as they drove away and then come back into the house.

I was half expecting another round of fighting with Anisha so attempted to hit first, metaphorically anyway! "Ani listen, before you start acting like Mike Tyson all over again there was no way they were going to pay any more than £250,000"

Anisha shrugged "I know. At least we're getting the extra £2,000 for all our stuff."

I relaxed my flight reflex "So what happens now?"

Anisha passed me the home phone "I suppose we contact Mr. Bean, Dave Mistry, and let him know WE'VE sold OUR house for HIM!"

I dialed Dave's cell number and got through to his voicemail.

"Hi, you've reached Dave Mistry with Realty Check. I'm not here at the moment but your call is important so please leave your message after the beep and I'll get back to you ASAP. Ciao!"

I was so tempted to say something rude like "Hey Mr. Bean, we did your job for you!", but chose to be classy instead "Hi Dave, it's Divinder. Good news, Prakash and Pooja made an offer, which we've accepted. Please call me and let me know what we do next."

We both slumped down on the couch, something we did a lot in the weeks leading up to us leaving.

Anisha tapped me on the head like she was knocking on a door "Do you think it's too early to pop the champagne?"

I looked a little perplexed "Maybe we ought to tell our folks first."

Anisha nodded "Oh yeah I forgot about our parents. Should we have them all over this weekend? Get it over in one hit?" it made sense "Let's do it." Anisha looked a little pensive.

"Do you feel a crazy sense of calm or is that just me?"

I nodded "Yeah, I know exactly what you mean, it's as if it's the most normal thing in the world to just sell your house, quit your job and then move yourself and your kids 5,000 miles away with no house to move into, no school for the kids to attend or a job to start in the hope that the new life is a better life."

We both laughed and she moved in closer to me "I'll be glad when we get to move out."

I looked at her, slightly surprised with just how practical she was being. "You'll be crying your eyes out when we hand the keys over, just you watch!"

She moved away "No I won't. A house is just bricks and mortar!" then it was my turn to move away "I disagree love! The fabric of this house holds onto all the memories that happened here. Ani this is the first house we bought after we got married. It's the house we brought the kids to when they were born. It's where they learned to walk and talk. We have had so many great times in this house. I'll be sad when we leave."

I saw her sort of hunch her shoulders in a resigned way "I suppose so" she dropped her gaze "We're going to be alright though aren't we?"

I looked at her and it was obvious that she just needed reassurance "Of course we are. Come here you soppy muppet."

I gave her a hug as a single tear trickled down her face.

Just then the cordless phone rang, it was Dave's cell number.

As I stood up to speak to him Anisha went upstairs to put the kids to bed.

"Hi Dave. How are you?"

Dave sounded out of breath "I'm great thanks. I just got your message, it's great news. What was the final offer price?"

I wanted to say three hundred thousand pounds just to shut him up but quickly realised that I would just be paying him a commission on money that I hadn't got!!

"We accepted £250,000. You were right Dave, that whole Stamp Duty threshold was the killer."

Dave laughed like he'd diagnosed a cancer when everyone else said it was a cold. "I don't want to say "I told you so" but I told you so!"

I soon stopped his laughter! "Dave if we're playing the "I-told-you-so" game then I could say I told you that I could do a lot better than the crappy offer that Mr. Sharif put on the table! The offer that YOU told me I would regret!"

I literally heard Dave gasp "Fair point."

Having beaten Dave up verbally, I went back into business mode "What do we do now?"

I heard Dave ruffle some paper "Well I'll need the name and contact details for your solicitor and then if everything goes according to plan we should complete in a couple of weeks. What date do they want to move in?"

I paused a little, just for effect.

"Prakash was looking at early May. That works for us as we'll just move in with Anisha's folks for a few weeks."

Dave couldn't contain his excitement "Sweet. There is the small matter of my commission that needs to be sorted out" the dreaded "C word"!!"Don't worry Dave we'll give you a cheque just as soon as the deal closes. I'll pop in on Saturday and fill out any forms that need completing"

I felt all grown up.

Dave sounded a little preoccupied "Great. In that case congratulations! I'll see you on Saturday afternoon. Ciao!"

I hung up the phone and looked around the room.

In flashback I saw Kamran taking his first steps on the carpet beside the stairs.

I looked over at the display cabinet and remembered when a toddling Sonya pulled the phone off the wall.

I turned and glanced at the front door and saw the first time that Ani and I walked through the doors as the owners of 12 Denham Drive almost 10 years earlier.

I ran my right hand through my thinning hair, the biggest reminder of the passage of time and then headed off to bed.

Sunday 27th March 2005

Anisha and I had just finished hosting a family gathering at our house for our parents.

Both sets of parents were now sitting around having enjoyed the dinner as Anisha brought in a tray full of cups of tea.

As she placed the tray on the table Anisha coughed as a cue for me to join them

"We have some news."

I walked over and sat on the side of the armchair that Anisha was sitting on "It's good news" my father-in-law, Mohan, looked over at me with a half-smile "You've sold the house haven't you?"

Anisha screamed "YES!"

Mohan got up and hugged Anisha and then shook my hand.

Anisha's mum, Rani, started to sniffle as my parents just looked at each other as if we'd spoken a foreign language.

I stood up to address all four parents "I thought we had this chat at Kamran's birthday party? We sold the house and will be out in early May."

My dad looked at me with a sad face, it made me want to cry and then he walked over to me "If you're happy, then we are happy for you. Come here!" he then gave me a huge bear hug that lifted me off the ground and slightly winded me!

My mum finally broke her vow of silence "When do you think you'll leave for Canada?"

I looked at Anisha, who had adopted the role of spokesperson "We were thinking sometime in early July. That way we can settle the kids into their new life before they start school in September."

Anisha gave me "the look" and I spoke "It just means we'll be living with Anisha's mum and dad for about 6 weeks" my dad gave me his "watcha-talkin`bout Willis" look "Why wouldn't you stay with us?"

I gave Anisha a quick glance, "Dad, you have a full house with Jarnail and his family with you at the moment. Anisha's parents have two spare bedrooms so it sort of made sense" my mum snarled "You can have our bedroom! We'll sleep on the floor!" she was pissed off!

I knew I had to pacify my mum as we had never really had the best mother-son relationship and I did not want our move being over shadowed by a random festering fight "Mum we'll come over and stay with you for a few days, I promise" just as I calmed my mum down Anisha's mum threw a fit!!

I wanted to leave the house!

We had just delivered the best news since we'd had the kids and our parents were upset!!

"This has happened so quickly. Won't you miss us?" this wasn't my battle so I let Anisha step in "Of course we will but it's something we have to do" then the waterworks started! "I feel like me and your dad failed to show you how much we love you!"

Anisha took her mum's hand

"Why.... else.....would.....you.....move....so....far....away?"

Anisha grasped her mum's hands tightly, looked her in the eyes and spoke very carefully "Mum did you love your parents?"

I knew what Anisha was about to do, having been on the wrong side of her "traps" many times in the previous 10 years so watched as her mum walked straight in! "Of course I did! What sort of stupid, bevcouf question is that?!" having got her mum's foot in the trap so to speak she sprung the trap! "Well you left them to come to Africa and then England didn't you?" her mum was open-mouthed!

She stuttered "Th-that's di-different and you know it!" Anisha folded her arms and said "How's it different Mum?"

Rani looked at her husband Mohan for moral support "We were leaving to have a better life."

Anisha clapped her hands "It's exactly the same for us Mum! Listen we need you all to be happy for us, your blessing would mean a lot to us."

Somewhat reluctantly all four parents got up and hugged us.

Just as the hugs came to an end Sonya and Kamran came down from the loft.

They saw the group hug and decided to head back upstairs again and I sort of wished I could have joined them!

Mohan sat down again and spoke quietly, slightly subdued by the news "Now that you've sold the house we need to get you a container for all your furniture and clothes. I have a friend who owns a freight forwarding company. I'll call him and get a quote."

Saturday 2nd April 2005.

My father in law, Mohan, and I were driving to a freight forwarder in deepest, darkest Barking in Essex.

As I pulled into a very rough looking industrial estate I pulled into a vacant spot, turned off the engine and took off my seat belt "So Dad, this guy, Amitabh, is a friend of a friend?"

Anisha's dad took off his seatbelt and leaned in "Well I've known him, Mr. Sharma, for a few years through my old friend Mr. Patel and the last time I saw him I mentioned that you were emigrating and he told me that he has an international haulage company."

I smiled, Anisha's dad was one of those well connected Uncle-ji's who knew everyone you ever needed to know. "If it's OK I'll let you do the talking Dad. I always feel like a little kid when I meet older Indian men and I end up calling them Uncle for no good reason!"

Mohan nodded "OK I'll do the talking but you'll need to let him know all the facts that I might miss."

Mohan got out of the car and walked across the car park with me close behind.

We walked into the lobby of the office and headed up one flight of stairs to be met by an older receptionist sat at a nice, expensive, mahogany desk.

The receptionist looked over her half-moon glasses that were perched on the end of her nose "Good morning gents, how can I help you?"

Mohan stepped forward "Good morning, my name is Mohan Bhojwani. We are here to see Mr. Sharma, he's expecting us."

The receptionist pressed a button on her intercom and let Mr. Sharma know that we were there.

She asked us to take a seat, which we did.

A few moments later a short, balding Indian man came out of a side office.

He was dressed in an expensive dark blue suit and had drenched himself in far too much aftershave.

He approached Mohan and gave him that two-handed hand shake that almost takes your hand off.

Then he turned to me, extended his hand and spoke "Mohan it's great to see you again. This must be your son-in-law Divinder. I've heard so much about you, Anisha and the kids. Please follow me."

We followed him into a large board room where Mr. Sharma took a seat and offered us seats either side of him.

Mr. Sharma looked like he was in his late 50's and had that big beer belly and skinny legs combo that a lot of Indian men seemed to favour.

He was bald expect for a "Laurel Wreath" of hair that was dyed jet black and just made it look like he was highlighting his shiny head.

To complete the look he had a "Magnum" moustache that was dyed the same as his hair.

"So Divinder, Mohan tells me you are off to Canada. I have a few cousins in Canada and absolutely love Vancouver. You are very lucky to be going there. Now I understand that you are looking to take a few bits and pieces with you to Canada. Can you tell me roughly what you're taking?"

I opened my mouth and became a teenager again "Well Uncle"

Mohan looked at me, sniggered at my uncle reference but then turned the laugh into a pretend cough.

I composed myself as I tried not to laugh "We have three beds, one double and two singles, a three piece suite, about ten pots and pans, the kid's toys and all our clothes."

Mr. Sharma nodded knowingly "I've got a guy called Brian, he's one of my best estimators and he'll come over to your house and check what size container you'll need."

I smiled, this guy was good and sounded like he knew what he was talking about.

"When can Brian come over? You see we're hoping to be packed in the next few weeks and out by the end of May."

Mr. Sharma took out a desk diary and thumbed through a few pages "I'll send Brian back with you and he can give you a quote today if that's fast enough. In fact once we have the quote I would suggest that it might be worth us getting all the boxes packed quickly and then have them stored here. That way we can pack the container closer to when you're leaving. What do you think?"

I wanted to high-five Mr. Sharma!!

He was making things happen. "That sounds great! Could you let me know who much a container would cost? I just want to work out how much we need to budget."

Mr. Sharma sat back in his seat with an enigmatic smile "We'll chat about that after we have your business! Now Mohan tell me how is that lovely wife of yours?"

I shook Mr. Sharma's hand "If it's OK I'll just give Anisha a quick call from the car. Uncle....Mr. Sharma, it was great to meet you."

Mr. Sharma tried to break my fingers with his hand shake but I flexed my hand. "No problem Divinder. I'll just keep your dad a few more minutes."

I walked back to the car and called Anisha on the cell. "Hi Ani, your dad is with the freight forwarding guy shooting the breeze so I thought I'd call you."

Anisha sounded anxious "What did he say? Can you speak up a little, there's a lot of background noise where you are."

I spoke louder and into the mic "He seems like a good bloke, he reckons that it shouldn't be a problem getting all the stuff packed up and stored at his warehouse."

I turned the volume up on the phone "That's great! When can he give you a quote?"

I told her "He's sending one of his guys over with us today."

Anisha was as impressed as I was

"Wow! There's no messing with this guy! When do you think you'll be back?" just as I about to tell her about Mr. Sharma's bone crushing hand shake I looked up "I have no idea, your dad is in full chat mode, hold on he's back with some white bloke. I'll catch you later."

Mohan walked back to the car with a middle-aged man named Brian in tow.

I stepped out of the car "Divinder, this is Brian. Brian this is my son-in-law – Divinder."

I shook Brian's shovel like hand "Hi Divinder. So Mr. Bhojwani, you lead the way I'll follow you in the van."

Mohan nodded as Brian walked over to his white van and Mohan started the engine and we pulled out slowly with Brian closely behind "So what did Mr. Sharma say after I left?"

Mohan laughed "Uncle" said that he would give you the family discount."

I laughed too "That's fantastic! I really have a good feeling about him."

Mohan continued "Mr. Sharma's a good man. Brian has been with him for 10 years and is one of the best estimators in the business. He'll tell you exactly what you need down to the last foot."

We arrived at my house and Mohan pulled up on our drive as Brian parked across the street.

Mohan remained in the car as I got out "Are you coming inside Dad? I'll make you a nice cup of tea."

Mohan shook his head "I'm off to the shops with your mum now, but do let me know how it goes with Brian."

I gave him the thumbs up "Thanks for all this Dad, we really appreciate all your support."

I walked to the front door and before I could get my key out the door was opened by a smiling Anisha. I was scared! Especially when she said "Ask me why I'm smiling" I stepped back thinking she'd found my secret stash "OK, why are you smiling?"

Anisha grabbed my arms "Dave just called, Prakash and Pooja's mortgage is all sorted and the building inspection came back without any concerns. They want to move in on May 27th!"

In the heat of the moment I kissed her on the lips! "Oh my god! It's all happening at once!"

Brian stepped out of his van armed with a digital camera and a measuring tape and crossed the street to our house.

I made the introductions "Anisha this is Brian, he works with Mr. Sharma. According to your dad he's one of Mr. Sharma's best estimators."

Anisha waved her hand at a blushing Brian "Hi Brian, do come in. I feel like I've said that phrase a million times since the house went on the market!"

Brian laughed and walked in.

He looked around the room and started taking photos from different angles.

"Can I start measuring upstairs? I find that the biggest furniture tends to be in the bedrooms."

I nodded "No problem" and I led Brian to the loft first and then into the bedrooms where Brian checked the beds and measured them.

He then looked in the wardrobes in each room and took a series of photos.

Then we came downstairs and he measured the couches and the dining table.

He finished in the kitchen and asked Ani which pots and pans she wanted to take with her.

Ten minutes after he'd arrived Brian was finished "OK guys, I'm all done. I reckon you'll only need a 100 square foot container, that's a ten by ten."

I looked at him and scratched my head "Just 100 square foot? That doesn't seem big enough."

Brian nodded "Yup. Believe me Divinder, 100 square foot container is more than enough space. If you go any bigger all your furniture will be rolling around and could get damaged in transit."

I looked at Anisha who had this expression on her face which seemed to say "Just listen to the man, you idiot! He's the expert."

I sat down and tapped Brian's note pad "How much would a 100 square foot cost?"

Brian looked at his notes "With all your stuff, I would say roughly £1800 plus tax."

I didn't like the idea that everything that we had amassed since we'd got married could fit in just 100 square feet!

This was one of those occasions where size mattered!

"So Brian, how much would a 200 square foot container cost?"

Brian looked annoyed at having his expertise questioned "About £2200 plus tax"

I bit my lip "In that case I'll take a 200 square foot container then."

Brian, who up until this point had been very calm, seemed to lose his temper "No offence, but that don't make any sense. Are you worried that all your worldly goods shouldn't fit into 100 square feet? Don't worry, a lot of customers feel a little weird about that."

I could feel my face redden a little and I looked at the ground. "No it's not that. I just think that we'll choose the bigger one to give us more space in case we buy anything else."

Brian got up, he realised that he was talking to an idiot so gave up trying to help me "OK, the customer's always right. I'll let Amitabh know what you want and I'll get him to contact you closer to the moving date. Have a good day Divinder. See you Anisha."

I walked Brian to the front door "Thanks Brian, see you later."

Anisha waved at Brian as he walked out towards his van as I closed the door.

I then joined Anisha in the kitchen where she was preparing lunch.

Anisha was holding up a knife and asked me a question, the two events were unrelated but she had a history of being a little impetuous so I stepped a little bit away from her. "That went well. Why are you so insistent on having a 200 square foot container? If Brian is saying that 100 square feet will do then why wouldn't you listen to him?"

I sat on the counter opposite her "Ani do you know how big 100 square feet is?" she rolled her eyes "I would guess it's 100 feet squared!"

I gave her the reverse V sign.

"Alright Einstein let me rephrase my question. How can we squeeze all our stuff into that small a space? It's only 10 feet by 10 feet."

Anisha seemed to feel my anxiety and placed the knife on the counter "Divind we're paying extra money out when we really need to save it."

I shook my head "Just you watch, you'll thank me when we get to Canada and all our stuff is intact."

Anisha turned her back on me and returned to lunch prep "You're obviously in one of those argumentative moods so I'll leave you alone."

"No I'm not!" I said jokingly but she didn't take my bait!

I hopped off the counter with a smile, feeling that I'd won a huge victory "Where are the kids?" Anisha pointed at our neighbour's house "They're next door at Paddy and Lisa's. Could you go over and call them back for lunch? It'll be ready in about 5 minutes. Please don't get into a long winded chat with Paddy."

I gave Anisha a sarcastic salute "OK, I'll be back before you're ready."

Rather than going through the front door I went into our garden and through the gap in the fence that Paddy and I created a few years earlier.

I looked in and tapped on the glass to get the attention of Paddy who was sat in an armchair reading the newspaper.

He saw me, waved and then walked over and opened the door. "Hi Divind, come in. The kids are killing each other upstairs somewhere!"

I laughed as I walked into their conservatory "Hi Paddy. Where's Lisa?"

Paddy pulled a face "She's gone shopping to the West End with her sister. I'd rather stay at home with the kids than face the horror of West End shopping on the weekend!"

I agreed "Nice one!" and we high-fived "Paddy, can I ask you a question?"

Paddy put his paper on the dining room table and put on his fake-serious face "Of course you can, as long as you're not asking me for money!"

I laughed as his face always looked more constipated than serious "No, it's not about money, although if you have any spare money I'd happily take it off your hands!"

Paddy reached into his pockets and turned them inside-out and produced a chewing gum wrapper and a train ticket "You can have half a wrapper and an old train ticket if you like." we both laughed "What's on your mind Divind?"

I sat down "Paddy would you do what me and Ani are doing?"

Paddy sat down too "What emigrate?"

I nodded "Yeah" Paddy shook his head so much that his jowls wobbled "No, never."

"Why not?" I asked Paddy, who took a deep breathe.

"It's a massive decision you guys have made. You're leaving behind all your family, friends and everything you have ever known to gamble that moving 5,000 odd miles away will make you happier."

I smiled nervously "But what if going 5,000 miles away allowed you to slow down the pace of life and have a little more money in the bank and spend more time with the kids? Would you go then?"

Paddy raised his hands and waved around the room "I already have that life here. Divind, for as long as I've known you, you've always said that you wanted to write a book but never had the time to do it here between being a husband, work commitments and being a dad. Maybe this move to Canada will give you the chance to do just that. It might make you happy. Lisa and I were talking about you guys the other night at a dinner party we went to. There were three other couples there and two of them were looking at leaving Britain for either Australia or Canada. You might be right and I might be on that sinking ship while the band plays on!! Are you having second thoughts?"

I involuntarily gulped and Paddy noticed "It's way too late for that. I think I loved the whole idea of telling people that I was moving to Canada and it became something to talk about. Now here we are, just over a year later and we've been accepted, we've sold the house and are looking at packing our stuff up to ship over to Canada."

Paddy placed his hand on my shoulder "It's happened too quickly hasn't it?"

I nodded slowly "Tell me about it! I'm suddenly hit by the massive tsunami that I started and I am ever so slightly scared that I'll become an 8 year old again and start crying any minute because it's too hard to do!!"

Paddy frowned a little and then smiled as if he'd thought of the perfect line to help me "You'll be fine Divind. After all what's the worst thing that could happen?"

I laughed "Funny you ask, because I had a nightmare where we got out there and everyone hated me, no one could understand a word I said so I couldn't get a job, we ate up into our savings and then ended up homeless!"

Paddy forced a laugh "That's pretty bad! OK Divind let me get your kids cos to tell the truth you're depressing me a little now!" he stood up "Thanks Paddy"

Paddy walked to the stairs and called Kamran and Sonya down "Kamran, Sonya your dad's here. It's time to go home and have lunch."

From upstairs Kamran shouted down "Paddy can you ask my dad if we can we have 5 more minutes please?"

I shook my head "Sorry kids, your dad says it's time to go."

The kids came downstairs with sad faces.

"Paddy look at their faces, you'd think I'm beating them at home!"

Paddy laughed "Mine are the same. I suppose I better start our lunch. Will you let yourself out?" I nodded and we walked through the back door as Paddy lit a cigarette and then popped his head into his freezer.

We walked through the gap in the fence and onto the patio. Kamran looked up at me "What's for lunch Dad?"

I patted my stomach "Mum's made kebabs!"

Kamran looked like he was going to throw up "Indian food?"

I laughed "Son, we just call it food because we are Indian!"

Kamran wasn't buying my sales pitch "But Dad, I hate Indian food?"

Sonya joined in the food revolt "So do I! Why can't we have chicken nuggets instead?"

I stopped in my tracks, lowered my voice for fear that Anisha might hear "That's a bit of a problem seeing as you are both in fact Indian!

Now just get in there, wash your hands and don't fight with each other. Mum has a very sharp knife and a very short temper!"

The kids walked into the kitchen and washed their hands as I took out the plates and cutlery.

Anisha was on the phone in the living room.

"OK Dad we'll come over tonight before we go out with Bo & Jane. Bye."

I placed the plates on the dining table "What's up Ani?"

Anisha put the 'phone back on the shelf "Nothing much, Dad just reminded me that Sunil Mahraj, the priest, is over tonight and he wanted to know if we wanted a reading done."

Our family priest Sunil Mahraj was coming over for dinner and doing a final reading of our birth charts.

I'm not a religious person, but Ani and her family had a lot of respect for Sunil Mahraj and over the years that I'd been married he had created my birth chart and his predictions had been ridiculously accurate to the point where he'd pointed out key life events and so when he spoke I listened.

The truth was that Ani wanted that extra affirmation, validation that what we were about to do was going to be successful.

I winced "Yes and no."

Anisha looked perplexed "What do you mean, yes and no? That doesn't make any sense!"

I carefully put the cutlery down "I mean yes, I do want to know if it's good news and no I don't want to hear him say that we're making a huge mistake moving to Canada!"

Anisha slapped me on the arm "Don't be silly. I think we should get the reading so we're ready for whatever comes our way"

I wasn't convinced "OK but if he tells us bad news it's all your fault!"

Anisha laughed but had a weird look on her face.

Later that evening at Anisha's parents' house the weird mood hadn't lifted.

We'd just finished dinner and Sunil Mahraj, was looking carefully at my birth chart.

Sunil Mahraj was an astrologer and placed huge importance on birth charts as indicators of what fate held in store.

Sunil Mahraj was a one of those rare people whose intrinsic good nature seemed to shine out of him "Divinder, please take a seat next to me."

I walked across the living room and took a seat by Sunil Mahraj "Mahraj-ji if it's bad news please break it to me gently!"

Mahraj laughed loudly and squeezed my arm "Divinder, you can relax, you really have nothing to worry about. Your stars show that this big move is a very auspicious one and that you'll be very happy, very quickly."

I breathed a huge sigh of relief as Anisha tried to calm me down "See Divind you were worried for nothing. Mahraj-ji, Divinder was concerned that you were going to tell us bad news. I told you we had nothing to worry about."

Mahraj raised his forefinger and beckoned Anisha over too "Well actually Anisha, your stars on your chart are very different from Divinder's chart."

Anisha almost started crying as she walked over and sat next to me "What?!"

Sunil took out the birth charts unrolled them on the table "Anisha, your birth chart shows that you're going to find it hard to settle in Canada from July 2005 through to July 2006" Anisha held my hand, hard, under the table "Does it say why?"

Mahraj looked at the various data points on the birth chart and started writing notes on his book "It indicates a huge upheaval in July which I guess is when you leave."

Anisha nodded "We have bought tickets to fly out on July 10th"

Mahraj continued "In late 2005, December, you will have a very big conflict that will change a key relationship with a male figure and will make you question your decision to emigrate."

Anisha looked completely sick "Does it say who the conflict will be with?"

Mahraj looked for the answer to her question but shook his head "Unfortunately it doesn't indicate anything other than it will be a male figure."

Anisha looked at me and her face was completely sorrowful in a way that I hadn't seen in many years.

She composed herself "Mahraj, what happens after July 2006?"

Mahraj pointed at a few dots on the chart "At that time you seem to make a major decision that lets you settle down."

I squeezed Anisha's hand but her face said it all "Thanks Mahraj-ji"

Sunil smiled and walked into the kitchen as I spoke to Anisha.

"Anisha, can I just say something?"

She looked at me with tears welling in her eyes "If it's "I told you so!" then no you can't! I really wish Mahraj-ji hadn't told me that it's going to take me a year to settle down!"

I brushed a tear off her cheek that was quickly replaced by another "I wasn't going to say that, well not just that! What I was going to say is that Sunil Mahraj-ji pointed out that you would get through it in 12 months."

Anisha took a deep breath before she spoke "I know but I'm now worried that the key relationship Sunil pointed out is me and you. What if we end up fighting each other? What if we end up hating each other?"

I honestly hadn't thought about that "We're going to be fine, just you see."

Anisha placed her head on my shoulder and whispered "I hope you're right Divind, I really do"

Looking back I think that moment was the closest we came to calling the whole move off.

Monday April 4th 2005.

I was sat at his desk writing out an email to my manager Marion.

It was only Terrence and I at the office before 8am.

I slowly re-read my email:

From: Divinder.Purewal@Jonathan.Hawk.co.uk
Sent: April 4th, 2005 7:58 AM
To: Marion.Sorrell Marion.Sorrell@Jonathan.Hawk.co.uk
Subject: Important email

Dear Marion,

I hereby tender my resignation. I will of course honour my 3 month notice period so my last day will be July 5th 2005.

Regards,
Divinder Purewal

Senior Consultant, Investment Management and Hedge Funds/ Jonathan Hawk/ Moorgate, London

I called Terrence over to my desk.

"Hey Terrence do me a favor and read this email, I need to know if it's enough information."

Terrence quickly read the email. "Divind, you haven't written down why you're leaving. Marion might think you're still upset about missing out on that promotion"

I agreed "You're right, should I tell her about emigrating to Canada?"

Terrence nodded "You've no reason to hide it now"

I started re-writing my email.

From: Divinder.Purewal@Jonathan.Hawk.co.uk
Sent: April 4th, 2005 8:01 AM
To: Marion.Sorrell Marion.Sorrell@Jonathan.Hawk.co.uk
Subject: Important email

Dear Marion,

I hereby tender my resignation. My family and I applied to
emigrate to Canada and our paperwork has finally come through.
We intend to leave in mid-July. I will of course honour my 3 month
notice period so my last day will be July 5th 2005.

Regards,
Divinder Purewal

Senior Consultant, Investment Management and Hedge Funds/
Jonathan Hawk/ Moorgate, London

Terrence quickly re-read the email and once he gave me the thumbs up, I hit the send button.

Terrence shook my hand "Congratulations! Now you've lit the firework stand back and watch the explosions!"

I laughed nervously and this wasn't missed by Terrence "Why are you worried Divind? You should be excited! This is the start of your new life."

I frowned "There's something about Marion that scares me!"

Terrence laughed out loud "Is it the fact that she stares right through you when she's talking to you? Like she can see how scared your very soul might be. That always gives me goose pimples!"

I nodded "That's part of it"

Terrence carried on "How about the fact that she never seems to blink! That always freaks me out!"

I nodded again "That doesn't help! I think it's just the idea that she might say go now and then what would I do for three months before we go to Canada?"

Terrence smiled like the Mona Lisa, the sly old dog had something up his sleeve!

He patted me on the back and said "I can guarantee that she won't do that mate!"

I probed "What makes so you sure?"

Terrence handed me a piece of paper from his jacket pocket "Let's just say that she's definitely going to need you for the next few months"

I read the letter "You got in didn't you?"

Terrence smiled broadly. "Yup! Phil and the board emailed me last night to tell me that they have approved the transfer to the Sydney office effective in 8 weeks! All signed, sealed and delivered mate!"

I jumped up and shook Terrence's hand "Congratulations mate! That is fantastic news!! Now, let's grab a coffee to celebrate OUR good news!"

Terrence smiled again "You mean let's not be in the office when Marion reads your email?!"

I laughed "Whatever! Two birds, one stone! Quick before she gets here! Let's go out through the reception, Marion never uses that route! I saw her calendar and she has a meeting with Phil from 8am to 10am."

We left through the back door just as Marion came through the other door.

We stepped out into the cold London air "Starbucks Divind?"

I shook my head "Only if you're buying, Terrence!" he took out his wallet "In that case let's go to the greasy spoon café around the corner!"

In the greasy spoon café I grabbed a table as Terrence brought over two very large mugs of tea.

I gave a round of applause "Now that's a cup of tea, sir!" he immediately looked disgusted when he saw bright red lipstick marks on the rim of his cup. "That's nasty!"

I looked at my cup before replying "Terrence what did you expect when you spend fifty pence on a litre of tea?!"

Terrence stood up "Fifty pence or fifty quid I don't want to be sipping from an unwashed cup with lipstick on it! I'm taking it back!"

He stomped off back to the counter and a few minutes later he returned with a fresh cup of tea and a small pack of biscuits.

He raised his cup triumphantly "See? I complained and got a new cup of tea, without lipstick AND a free pack of biscuits!"

I clapped and then sipped my tea. "So Terrence if we're both leaving what's going to happen to Arnold?"

Terrence took a big glug of tea "Don't know, don't care! Annoying Arnold can have the whole thing to himself as far as I'm concerned."

I bit into one of the stale biscuits "Arnold isn't all that bad once you get to know him"

Terrence almost spat his tea out "Hold on, are we talking about the same Arnold? Have you forgotten that it was YOU, who gave Arnold the nickname Annoying Arnold?"

I placed my hands above my head "Let's just say that he's got his redeeming features. I think he just tried too hard to be one of the boys."

Terrence shook his head "He can be your best friend then! Any more news on the move?"

I nodded "Well, we move to the in-laws house on May 28th and then we leave for Canada on July 10th."

Terrence raised his cup in a cheer "Well Divind, it's going to be the end of an error mate. The Investment Management team that was Divinder and Terrence is no more."

I looked a little quizzical "Surely you mean the end of an era don't you Terrence?"

Terrence laughed and said "No, we made a huge error when we recruited you!"

I punched Terrence on the arm "By the way I'll need your email address before you leave for Oz."

Terrence rubbed his arm "Why would I give you my email address? I'm leaving because I want to escape annoying gits like you!"

I punched Terrence on the arm again "That's funny because I'm only leaving to get away from you!"

Terrence rubbed his arm again and pushed his chair back, taking me out of his reach. "Enough with the punching already! Oh yeah one thing, when Marion mentions that I'm leaving please look surprised"

I nodded "Of course! You do the same if they announce my news in the next few weeks."

We raised our cups and toasted one another.

Terrence spoke first "To new adventures in the colonies!"

I agreed "Here-here! Here's to not falling flat on our faces in Oz and Canada!"

Back at the office Terrence went to the washroom as I tried to skulk through the reception in an attempt to avoid Marion.

I walked past the board room and stupidly looked in and caught Marion's eye.

I then even more stupidly tried to speed walk up the stairs but Marion called after me.

"Divinder! Can I see you for a moment?"

I looked back "Sure, no problem."

My bowels fluttered involuntarily.

I walked back to the board room where Marion was stood with a piece of paper in her hand.

It was my resignation email.

Marion asked me to take a seat "I got your email this morning. I'm going to need a signed copy to make it official."

I think I actually gasped out loud "Oh OK. Is there anything else?"

Marion looked a little scared "Actually there is. Phil just told me that the board has agreed to let Terrence get a transfer to the Australian office in Sydney. He leaves at the start of June."

I went into soap-actor mode "Wow! That's great for Terrence."

Marion bit her bottom lip "It is great for Terrence but with your news it puts me in a real predicament, I'll be losing my two most senior Investment Management consultants. Arnold will suddenly become my wing-man!"

I thought I'd feel elated at this moment – leaving the company and Marion a little high and dry - but I didn't. I felt sorry that she was left short-handed "I'm sorry I didn't know about Terrence before I sent my email. I'll happily stay for the three months, at least that way I can do a handover with Arnold."

Marion looked a little reassured that I would staying for the whole notice period. "I have to ask this, did your decision to resign have anything to do with you not being promoted?"

I was very careful not to show that I was pissed with her over-looking me for a promotion "No, I'm long over that. We applied to emigrate to Canada over a year ago and we got the green light a few weeks ago so we've started the whole process of selling our house and quitting our jobs."

"Why didn't you tell me you'd applied?"

Marion stared at me with those unblinking eyes and I was careful not to let her extract my soul!!

I looked at her face but stopped short of making eye-contact "I didn't want to jinx myself, no- one knows, not even Terrence."

Marion stared at me intently as if sizing up what I was saying was a sack of shit "Well, do me a favour, keep both bits of news under your hat for now. Phil will be making an official announcement at the team meeting on Friday." with that she opened her laptop "I'll see you later."

I stood up "OK, my lips are sealed. See you later."

I walked back to my desk and prayed that my legs wouldn't buckle underneath me and that my pants weren't brown!

Saturday May 14th 2005.

Brian knocked on the door.

He had unloaded his van of 100 flat packing boxes of various sizes onto our drive.

I opened the door with Kamran and Sonya behind me. "Hi Divinder. Here's the boxes for you to start your packing. There's a hundred boxes for now and if you need any more just give me a call on the office number. We'll be back on May 26th, that's a Thursday, to pick up all your stuff."

I looked at the mountain of flat cardboard boxes on the floor "100 boxes? I don't think we'll need half that number! Thanks Brian, I'll see you in a couple of weeks."

I opened the double doors and got Kamran and Sonya to help me get the boxes into the house. Kamran pulled at my shirt "Dad can we start packing our stuff up by ourselves?"

I wanted to think that he was being helpful but part of me knew that this was probably some scam "Why?" I asked Kamran looked at me with sincerity "Because we want to feel involved in the process."

I felt proud that my kids were being helpful "Wow! That's really mature of you Kamran. Mum should be back from the hairdressers any minute and she'll be able to tell us what we'll need for the next few weeks."

Just as Brian pulled away Anisha turned into the street.

She pulled into the drive, applied the brakes and turned off the engine.

She stepped out of the car and swept her hair to draw attention to her new style. "So what do you think hey Divind?" I gave her a cursory look "I think we have a lot of packing to do!"

Anisha looked deflated "Let me rephrase that, what do you think of my new hairstyle?"

I gave her a 5 second look "Very Rachel from Friends! Now grab a few boxes we have a VERY long night ahead!" she tutted and walked in.

Later that evening we were making a list of all the items we were packing for the inventory list I was losing the will to live! "Do we seriously have to list everything down to the last knife, fork and spoon?"

Anisha nodded slowly and deliberately "Yup, it says here that everything going into the container has to be listed in case our shipment is subject to a search by customs."

I looked around the room "We should have started last week! This is a huge job and I am getting sick just thinking about it!"

Anisha laughed "Come on, this is the easy part, we still have to unpack all this stuff at the other end. Look I'll make us some tea and you start making a list of all the stuff in the bathroom."

I nodded my head and took a pad of paper and a pen with me upstairs.

I walked slowly into the bathroom and looked at all the things that we were taking with us "Hey Ani, I don't think we're taking anything from the bathroom."

Anisha shouted from downstairs "What did you say?"

I shouted back "I said, I don't think we're taking anything from the bathroom. Unless you were planning on ripping out the bath, basin and toilet!"

Anisha laughed, "That's great! Now move onto the bedroom" I went into the bedroom and started to open the wardrobes and started to make a list.

Sunday May 15th 2005.

I looked at the clock radio, it was 2:15am.

We were both lying on our bed with pages of lists all around us.

Anisha turned to me "I can't believe we did so much in one day! I think we should start to pack away some of the winter clothes and stuff like plates and cutlery tomorrow."

I groaned as much out of tiredness as from the idea that we would be going back to packing hell tomorrow!

"If we pack away all our plates, what are we going to eat off of?"

Anisha tapped my forehead with her forefinger "Ever heard of paper plates?"

I looked over towards our bathroom "OK, I'm too tired to argue. Can you go to the toilet for me please?"

Anisha laughed and kissed my forehead "I was hoping you would go for me!"

We both fell asleep without getting changed.

Sunday May 15th 2005.

According to the clock radio at 9:11am I was woken up by Sonya prodding me in the eye and whispering in my ear. "Daddy wake up! Wake up! Are you up?"

I opened both eyes and looked at her "I am now! Sonya, darling why are you poking my eye?"

She put her hands on her hips like an old lady "We are hungry, starving. Can you wake up and give us some breakfast please?! "

I looked over at a snoring Anisha and then at the clock radio which now showed that it was 9:12

I beckoned Sonya closer and whispered "Don't tell Mum, but I give you and Kamran permission to eat anything you like for breakfast this one time! Just let me sleep, please!"

Sonya smiled like she'd just won the lottery. "Can we have a chocolate bar?"

I nodded "Yes" she had a mischievous look on her face "How about jelly?"

I was suddenly rethinking my offer as I was certain she was about to ask every possible permutation of what she could eat!

I tried to stifle a yawn "Yes! Anything! Please just leave quietly and close the door please. And don't put the volume up too high on the TV!"

Sonya came in close and then had second thoughts "Yes! I would kiss you, Daddy, but your mouth really smells!"

Sonya tiptoed out of the room and carefully closed the door.

I spent the next few minutes trying to go back to sleep but between the sound of Anisha's snoring, the kids banging cabinet doors and the sound of the TV that wasn't going to happen.

So I woke up, went to the bathroom and brushed my teeth as I showered.

Having changed into my "weekend uniform" of sweat pants and a tee-shirt I went downstairs where Sonya and Kamran were sat on the couch watching cartoons eating quickly from bowls of uncooked jelly, chocolate chip cookies, crisps and cakes.

They saw me and tried to eat faster.

I just laughed and shook my head as the kids stared hypnotically at the TV screen.

I went into the kitchen and opened the cutlery drawer.

I took out four knives, four forks and four spoons and packed the rest into a small box on the counter.

I then did the same with the plates, glasses and cups.

30 minutes later there were empty drawers and cupboards and five very full boxes labelled with their contents.

Kamran came into the kitchen and placed four bowls carefully into the sink.

I took four bowls that were in the plate cabinet and put them into the kitchen box.

I pointed at the various boxes and showed Kamran what was happening "Kamran we now only have four of everything. Four knives, four spoons, four forks, four glasses and four cups. Please put some water in those bowls."

Kamran looked sad "Are we poor, Dad?"

I laughed loudly "No, just emigrating. We've started packing and to make things easier we are putting away all the stuff that we don't need so that it can go into a container"

Kamran sighed. "Oh. Are you going to pack away that fitness stuff in your room in the container too?"

I shook my head "Not yet. Why do you ask?" Kamran ran past me and poked me in my stomach "Well you're fat so you probably don't use the fitness stuff so you might as well pack it up now!"

He ran off laughing as I breathed in.

Just then Anisha came down in a dressing gown and stood by the kitchen door "Have you been up all night Divind?"

I made myself look even more tired than I was "Yes Ani, I'm that sad that I couldn't sleep so spent the whole night packing!! Course I didn't! I did all this in about thirty minutes. I think it'll take us a few hours to get everything packed up so if we do a little every evening we should be done by next Friday. I really don't want to do anymore today so let's go out"

Anisha waved her hand in my face "Are you nuts?"

I shook my head "No, I just want a life other than packing boxes."

Anisha had that look on her face that indicated that she was in no mood to be messed around with "NO! I think we should send the kids to my mum and dad's house and then we'll finish the packing today. That way we can relax next week."

I wanted to cry!! "But, I am so bloody tired! Sonya came in this morning and woke me up by poking me in the eye. Can't we just chill today and start tomorrow?"

Anisha was in full Beyoncé mode and was practically snapping her fingers in my face "If you want to be lazy then I'll pack and you can chill! Kids, have you guys had breakfast yet?"

Kamran took this as his cue to throw his "fat Dad" under the proverbial bus and shouted out "Yes Mum! Dad said we had to have chocolate, jelly and biscuits for breakfast!"

I looked at Anisha and closed my eyes to avoid seeing the disappointment in her eyes "Did he now?"

"Thanks Kamran!" I shouted back ironically "Thanks a lot!"

The rest of that day was spent making inventories and packing away everything we were going to take to Canada.

By 8pm we were finished, in every sense of that phrase.

The kids had been with their grandparents all day as we knew that there was no way we could have packed the whole house, ready for the move, with them under our feet.

Mohan walked towards our house with Sonya holding one hand and Kamran the other hand

They reached the house and Mohan pressed the doorbell.

We didn't answer immediately as we had managed to stack the boxes in front of the door, so he pressed the bell harder and longer.

Kamran looked up at his Nana "Mum and Dad could be wrestling."

Mohan looked at Kamran "Excuse me? Wrestling?" Kamran nodded "Yup, every Sunday morning Mum and Dad wrestle in their bed. They tell me and Sonya to watch TV until they finish their fight!"

Mohan's face went red and he was just about to walk away when I opened the door with my sweaty-face "Hi Dad sorry about that, we were just wrestling with the packing boxes. Come in."

Mohan walked into the living room where the couches have been moved to the left hand wall and the dining table had been moved to one side. There were a number of large boxes placed all over the room with room names written on them in large black scribble.

The kids saw the boxes and rushed upstairs to get ready for bed in case we asked them to help us.

Mohan whistled "My god! You two don't waste any time!"

I rubbed my neck "I wanted to do a little packing every day over the next few evenings but Ani insisted that we finish today"

Anisha came over and gave her dad a hug "Just admit it Divind, you're glad you listened to me aren't you?"

I shook my head like a chimp "Why would I admit that working all weekend is what I wanted to do? Somewhat depressingly I'm going to be at my desk in 12 hours! Thanks Ani!"

Anisha came over to kiss me and I pushed her face away with my hand "You're welcome Divind!"

Mohan stepped into the kitchen and opened and closed the cupboard doors "What's still to pack?" Anisha followed him in "So far we've packed away all the stuff from the kitchen, the kids' bedroom and the loft. Brian gave us 6 portable wardrobes so we've hung up all our winter clothes too."

I joined in the chat "We'll pack the beds up closer to the actual move time" Mohan patted me on the back "You've done well. This makes it seem so much more real. Seeing all these boxes makes it so final."

I looked at my watch, it was 8:05 "Please excuse me Dad, I have a pile of ironing that needs my attention because your daughter seems to be allergic to ironing."

Mohan pulled a face and then quickly made his way to the front door "I am off anyway, good luck with the rest of the packing."

Anisha gave me a dirty look, as I smiled at Mohan and then stomped off upstairs as Mohan left.

I set up the ironing board and plugged in the iron.

While I waited for the iron to heat up I knocked on Kamran's bedroom door "Come in" I opened the door and took a seat on the end of the bed as Kamran put on his pyjamas.

His room looked really bare "Dad where's all my stuff gone?"

I pointed at the floor "It's in a box in the living room labeled 'Kamran's stuff' which should be right underneath us" Kamran smiled and then looked a little surprised "All my stuff fits into ONE box?"

I laughed "Yes, it's pretty cool isn't it?"

Kamran shook his head "No Dad, it's pretty sad"

I tucked Kamran into his bed "Dad, can I get a new bed when we go to Canada?" I bounced on his bed with my bum.

"Why? What's wrong with this bed?"

Kamran pulled face "There's nothing wrong with it but I need a double bed"

I raised my eyebrows "A double bed eh? Why would you NEED a double bed?"

Kamran sat up in his bed and slapped his duvet cover, like I'd fallen into his trap! "Well, you have one!"

I stood up and replied "I also have a wife, a mortgage and a pile of ironing do you want those too?!"

Kamran lay down again "NO WAY! But like you always say Dad, if you don't ask you don't get!! Can I ask you a real question?"

I pulled his duvet up to his chin and ruffled his hair "Of course you can" he suddenly looked a few years younger than eight "Dad, are you worried about leaving all your friends and family in England?"

I stuck my tongue out to the side of my open mouth "If I'm honest, a little bit. Why, are you worried?" he nodded "Yeah, I'm a little bit scared that I won't make good friends like I have here. What if people don't understand me or don't like me?"

I looked shocked that he could even suggest that any kid of mine would suggest they wouldn't be popular! "What's not to like about you? You're clever, funny, good looking - like me and a great football player too, also just like me" Kamran seemed reassured "Do you really think I look like you?"

I smiled broadly, feeling proud that my kid was a little version of me but without the hang ups that I had "Yeah I do."

I did not see the sucker punch!

"Dad, what's the youngest age I can get plastic surgery?!"

I tickled him until he begged for forgiveness "You cheeky little sod!"

I gave Kamran a gentle tap on his head then leaned in and kissed Kamran on the right cheek "Good night darling, I love you lots have sweet dreams and I'll see you in the morning, you cheeky git!"

Kamran looked over at his cupboard door "Good night Dad, I love you lots, have sweet dreams and I'll see you in the morning. Will you check my cupboard for you-know-who?"

I walked over to his cupboard and suddenly thought of revenge for his plastic surgery comment!

I opened the right hand door with my right hand and with my left hand, which was out of Kamran's vision, I grabbed my own head and in a deep American accent I said "Come here you!" and pulled myself into the cupboard, looking like Andre the giant had pulled me into the cupboard!!

All Kamran saw was his dad being dragged into the cupboard by what he thought was the ghost of Andre the giant and he screamed hysterically as I stepped out laughing like a mad man "Plastic surgery eh?"

Anisha ran upstairs and into Kamran's room.

She grabbed a crying Kamran "What did you do to him?"

I felt sick.

It was only meant to be a joke. "I pretended that A the G was pulling me into the cupboard. You know that thing I do when I use my other arm" and then I demonstrated my technique to a very unimpressed Anisha.

"What part of scaring Kamran was funny? The part where your kid thinks A the G really lives in the cupboard? Or the fact that A the G is dragging his dad into the cupboard?"

I wanted to say "both" but fought that urge for fear that she would punch my testicles which were dangerously close to where she was sitting on Kamran's bed.

I took a step back, to get out of her reach.

"I didn't really think about that."

Kamran's was literally shaking and rocking in Anisha's arms. The only thing he wasn't doing was sucking his thumb in the fetal position. "That's your problem Divind, you don't think! Get out and let me calm our son down."

I approached the bed to apologize to Kamran but he turned away and was literally hyper- ventilating.

"I'll be in there, ironing. Sorry Kamran darling"

I left Kamran's room and popped into Sonya's room before starting my weekly ironing marathon.

Sonya was sitting up in her bed with an evil grin on her face "Daddy, what was all the screaming and shouting about?"

I sat on her bed "Sorry about that Sonya. I was being silly and pretended that A the G was pulling me into Kamran's cupboard."

Sonya laughed maniacally and then put her arm in her mouth to muffle the sound! "I love it when you do that! He's such a wimp!"

I let myself smile. "OK darling you need to go bed now before Mum comes in. Good night darling, I love you lots, have sweet dreams and I'll see you in the morning."

Sonya hugged me and gave me a big wet kiss on my forehead. She whispered "I wish I had seen it! I love you Dad!"

I turned her light off and went into my room to tackle the ironing.

I started ironing at 8:08pm and by 9:15 the pile of creased clothes quickly disappeared from a crumpled heap on the bed to various hangers in the room.

Anisha finally walked into our bedroom just as I finished the last shirt.

Anisha grabbed her bathrobe from behind the door and went into the bathroom for a shower without saying a word to me.

She came back into our room at 9:30pm when I took my turn in the bathroom.

I took my time, secretly hoping that she'd be asleep when I went back into the bedroom.

I stepped back into our bedroom at 10:15.

Bugger, she wasn't asleep.

In fact she was in bed reading a book.

She still hadn't spoken a word to me since 8 o'clock that evening.

I took the bull by the horns "Are you going to ignore me all night?"

Anisha looked at me sideways and put her book face- down on the bed. "You know how sensitive Kamran is. It took me more than an hour to settle him down."

I raised my arm like I was asking for permission to speak "I just didn't engage my brain. It won't happen again."

Anisha gave me a half-smile "Don't you remember what it was like being an 8 year old?"

I smiled "When I was 8, I shared a bed with my two younger, sweaty brothers! I think I would happily have taken my chances in a cupboard with Andre the giant!"

Anisha tried really hard not to laugh but sniggered despite her best efforts. "Don't make me laugh I still want to be angry with you!"

I had her on the ropes so went for the killer punch!! "If you want, I'll become Mr. Serious. I'll start to part my hair on one side, I'll smoke a pipe and might even start to wear a smoking jacket like Hugh Hefner!"

Anisha playfully slapped me on my chest.

"You don't need to go that far but just promise me that you'll think before you act. Deal?"

She put her hand out for me to shake.

I took her hand and kissed it instead which made her laugh.

She kissed me on the lips. "Good night" I gave her my best 'watcha talkin' bout Willis' face "Any chance of a wrestling match?"

Anisha brushed me off "Not now, they're ain't, it's too late. If you hadn't made me spend an hour with Kamran we would have had time to wrestle."

I punched the duvet and managed to hit my own leg!

"You're just saying that! There's no way to prove it!" she smiled "You'll never know! Now turn off your light before A the G sees it!"

I crossed my arms across my chest.

"I'm not tired" she smiled "In that case do you want to get all sweaty?"

I sat up in bed excitedly "But I thought you were tired?" then she lowered the hammer! "Well if you're not tired you could finish off the packing!"

I pulled the duvet off her side of the bed turned off the light and said "GOODNIGHT, YOU GIT!"

"We are the champions!"

Wednesday May 25th 2005:

Today was the Champion's (soccer) League final between my beloved Liverpool and AC Milan of Italy.

It was taking place in Istanbul, Turkey and this was a game that Kieran and I had waited our whole lives to watch.

You see, I am a lifelong Liverpool and as with all sporting traditions I had indoctrinated my kids from a very young age to also be Liverpool fans.

Unlike her brother, who would have a bad day if Liverpool lost their match, Sonya wasn't that bothered and would occasionally wear the Liverpool shirt I gave her but she never bothered to watch a game with us and she would have struggled to name the whole of the 1977 squad!

From time to time Kamran would ask me to tell him about the glory days of the 1970's and 1980's when as he put it "Liverpool used to be good!"

So there were, just Kamran and I, in the almost empty house.

Ani and Sonya had decided to go to her parents' house because, and I quote Anisha "We would rather pull our fingernails out with pliers than watch football!"

Kamran and I were sitting on the futon that usually lived in the attic room watching the TV about 20 feet away.

Kamran had his yellow sponge football at his feet and as there was still thirty minutes before the game was due to start he gently kicked the ball over to me.

I picked it up and threw it back at him and it hit him directly in the face!

He looked up trying to work out if he wanted to cry or laugh, when he chose to laugh he grabbed the ball, placed it under his right arm and then ran at me, head down, full speed screaming "It's on, fat man, IT'S ON!" and with that we were rolling around on the floor with me attempting not to get hit anywhere near my genitals!

After a few minutes of this mad father-son fight I tapped out, before I had a heart attack and conceded that he had in fact beaten "the fat man"

Kamran brushed imaginary crumbs off his shoulder like his favourite WWE fighter and I laughed as he started kicking the ball against the radiator covers.

I was just about to tell him to stop when I remembered that his mum, who hated noise and things being broken, was a few houses away.

I asked him to pass the ball to me and we started playing a game in the house, using the radiator covers as goals.

The next twenty minutes went by in a blur of crazy shots, many of which knocked the telephone off its cradle and one which actually snapped a light off in the fixture above where the dining table used to be.

We each grabbed a glass of cold water and sat on the futon with our faces all red and sweaty.

Kamran looked up "Dad, who's going to win this game?"

I smiled "Liverpool of course!" he had a look on his face that gave away the fact that he wasn't buying what I was selling.

"Kamran, we have to believe that Liverpool are going to win or there's no point in watching the game or being a fan."

Kamran nodded and took a sip of his water "But Dad, AC Milan has Shevchenko and Crespo up front and Dida in goal. How are we going to beat that sort of team?"

I knew what he meant but really didn't want to think about how terrible a thrashing Liverpool were about to get.

At 7:45pm Liverpool kicked off and Kamran was smiling from ear to ear, wearing his Liverpool shirt with pride.

1 minute into the game, Liverpool gave away a free kick from a position on the right side of their goal area.

Kamran literally moved to the edge of the seat and watched as Milan's Paolo Maldini smashed a volley into the Liverpool goal past the outstretched arms of the Liverpool goalkeeper Dudek after getting the ball from a free-kick from Andrea Pirlo.

AC MILAN 1   **LIVERPOOL 0**
1 minute, Paolo Maldini

Kamran looked at me with tears in his eyes and I had to turn away as I had tears in **MY** eyes too!

I made an excuse and took the glasses into the kitchen to refill them and wipe my tear streaked face.

The next few minutes were all Liverpool attacking AC Milan's goal and Hyppia and Riise both took great shots but nothing was going in the back of the Milan goal.

Thankfully the game settled and Kamran and I were both getting into the back and forth of these two great teams.

15 minutes in and Milan's Crespo headed the ball towards Liverpool's goal and Liverpool's Luis Garcia cleared the ball off the line, we both jumped off the futon and cheered when the ball headed away from our goal.

I swear the last time I'd been this anxious had been the day Sonya had been born!

The game ebbed and flowed for the next 20 minutes and when Liverpool weren't given a penalty Kamran and I started screaming at the TV but in the counterattack Milan scored again through Hernan Crespo.

AC MILAN 2   **LIVERPOOL 0**
1 minute, Paolo Maldini
39 minutes, Hernan Crespo

I avoided eye contact with Kamran who was getting a puffy face he as he tried hard not to cry and I didn't want him to see that I wasn't that far from crying too!.

I stood up and tried to think of something motivational to say.

I was just about to say "This is a marathon and not a sprint" when Crespo scored his second and Milan's third goal at the 44th minute just before half time.

AC MILAN 3   LIVERPOOL 0

1 minute, Paolo Maldini
39 minutes, Hernan Crespo
44 minutes, Hernan Crespo

I think I swore!

Kamran walked over to the TV and turned it off.

He then threw the remote control across the room and thankfully it landed on the futon and then turned on me!!

"I thought **YOU** said **WE** were going to win, eh Dad!"

I moved closer to him but Kamran ran upstairs and a few seconds later he angrily threw his Liverpool shirt down the stairs and then slammed his bedroom door.

I thought about going to see him but thought it better to let him calm down.

Instead I sat down on the futon again and waited for him to come down again.

Ten minutes later, I heard Kamran's door open and he came downstairs wearing a hoodie.

He stepped over his Liverpool shirt and sat down on the futon.

He grabbed the TV remote and turned the TV off.

I was about to protest but Kamran rolled the ball to me.

"Dad, we're going to show Liverpool how to play!"

I nodded and we started kicking the ball around and Kamran was hammering the ball with a venom I had never seen before.

"Six crazy minutes!"

After 10 minutes of our own version of the game Kamran suddenly turned the TV on just as a slow motion highlight of Liverpool captain Steven Gerrard scoring a header came across the screen over and over again!

AC MILAN 3	LIVERPOOL 1
1 minute, Paolo Maldini	52 minutes, Steve Gerrard
39 minutes, Hernan Crespo	
44 minutes, Hernan Crespo	

We looked at each other and then started screaming and jumping around the room, loudly, so loud in fact that our elderly neighbour David started banging on the wall that divided our houses.

"Oi" he shouted "some people are trying to watch TV! Keep the noise down!"

We stopped screaming and sat back down on the futon.

The game started again and we were literally holding our breath, as if our ability not to breathe was making Liverpool play better!

120 seconds later, Vladimir Smicer scored a brilliant goal that brought Liverpool within one goal of a tied game!

AC MILAN 3	LIVERPOOL 2
1 minute, Paolo Maldini	52 minutes, Steve Gerrard
39 minutes, Hernan Crespo	55 minutes, Vladimir Smicer
44 minutes, Hernan Crespo	

Kamran and I both ran at the TV and Kamran grabbed his shirt, kissed the badge and then placed it over his hoodie!

We started screaming again and right on cue, our neighbour, David started banging on the wall again.

"Oi, I will call the police if you don't calm down over there! Do you understand?"

I shouted "Sorry!" grabbed a cushion and then covered my mouth with the cushion and screamed into it!

We sat down again and dared to think that Liverpool would tie the game.

Kamran's heart was beating so loudly that I could hear it!

And then Liverpool were awarded a penalty when Steven Gerrard was fouled in the area by Milan's Gennaro Gattuso.

A single, salty tear sneaked out of my left eye, rolled down my left cheek and landed in my moustache.

WE WERE JUST ABOUT TO GET BACK IN THE GAME!

Xabi Alonso, Liverpool's accomplished penalty taker calmly stepped up and smacked the ball with some power and we watched as the Milan goalkeeper Dida guessed the right direction and managed to save the shot but the ball bounced back to Alonso who made sure of a goal the second time of asking.

AC MILAN 3	LIVERPOOL 3
1 minute, Paolo Maldini	52 minutes, Steve Gerrard
39 minutes, Hernan Crespo	55 minutes, Vladimir Smicer
44 minutes, Hernan Crespo	59 minutes, Xabi Alonso

Kamran and I started screaming out loud and then hugged as we jumped around the room and then we were both crying as David pounded on the walls screaming "That's it! I'm calling the police now!" and Kam and I both screamed back "Do it!"

Liverpool went onto to win that game on penalties and when their captain Steven Gerrard held the cup over his head we sat in silence and the weirdest thing happened, Kamran looked at me like he would trust me forever because I had said Liverpool were going to win against all the odds. It was a proper Kodak moment and we didn't need a camera because the memory would be etched into our brains forever.

Moving day

I'd taken the day off to supervise the moving process.

Brian and two of his colleagues were taking the beds apart as I brought my electric tools down from the loft.

Brian saw the tool box and his eyes lit up "Are you taking those with you?"

I placed the box down "No, they won't work out there. I'm selling them at a car boot sale at the school on Saturday."

Brian stepped over to where I was standing "Anything decent in there?"

I opened the tool boxes for him to have a look "Here, have a look."

Brian looked at the tool boxes "They look pretty new, have you even used them?"

I shrugged "I have, but I bought them for a project I did a few years ago and after I finished, having nearly chopped my fingers off, Anisha made me promise never to use them again."

Brian looked a little puzzled "Why, what happened?"

I looked a little embarrassed "Let's just say that I nearly lost body parts that were used instead of a clamp!"

Brain winced "How much so you want for the lot?"

I went into sales mode "Seeing as they are practically unused, what about £75?"

Brian pulled a face "I'll give you £25."

193

I closed the lid of the tool boxes "Are you having a laugh Brian mate?! That jigsaw alone was £45, the rip saw was about £40 and I only bought that planer last year for £65. That's £150 worth of stuff. Make it £50 and you have a deal."

Brian looked like he was about to walk away "I'll give you £40, final offer."

I shook my head "£45 is the least I'll take."

Brian thought about it for a moment then took his wallet out and gave me two £20 notes and a £5 note that looked like it had been through a washing machine.

Then he called one of his colleagues over and handed him the three boxes "Hey Raj do me a favour, put these in the van."

Raj took the boxes out to the van.

I felt my cell phone buzzing in my pocket.

I looked at the screen, it was Ani.

"Hi Ani" she was at work so whispered "How's it going Divind?"

I looked at Brian and his crew rapidly clearing our house "Brian and his guys have just loaded the last of the boxes so we should be out of here by about 2 o'clock"

I felt an inner sadness at seeing all our stuff carted off "That's great! What time are Prakash and Pooja coming over?"

I instinctively looked over at the circular spot on the wall where the clock used to be and saw the one part of the wall that was more vibrantly yellow than the rest of the house "They should be here at 3:00pm. I told Dave that I'd have the house all ready when they get here."

Anisha seemed rushed "So what are you going to do now?" I wanted to say something smart but nothing came to mind "Well I thought I'd get the stuff over to your mum and dad's place and start to move some of our clothes in. Brian's happy to drop the boxes off before he heads back to the warehouse"

Anisha made an agreeable 'ah ha', "Do me a favour and pick up some shopping for mum and dad."

I hadn't planned on doing anything other than sleeping on my in-laws' couch.

"Sure, what do they need?" there was a pause as Anisha answered a question from one of her colleagues "Sorry about that, go ask mum when you see her later. Love ya!"

Anisha hung up and I watched Brian and his crew bring down the beds and cabinets.

We now had an empty house.

I looked at my phone, it was 1:57pm Brian was 3 minutes ahead of schedule.

I grabbed the last box and took it out to Brian who loaded it into the van.

"That's the last box Brian. If you turn the van around I'll show you where Anisha's Mum and Dad live."

Brian nodded and started the engine as I walked the 100 or so yards to my in-laws' house.

I rung the bell at my in-laws house as Brian pulled up outside the house.

A few minutes later he'd taken out the three large portable wardrobes and placed them on the drive.

Rani finally appeared at the door and opened it slowly "Hello son. I'm just going to have a shower so please put the boxes in the front room for now and we'll sort them out later."

I brought the first box over with Brian's help and after a few minutes we had put all three boxes in the hallway. Once they finished I stepped out again with Brian. "Thanks for all your help Brian. I'll let Mr. Sharma know how helpful you and your crew were today."

Brian smiled and his crew smiled too "So you would say that you're happy with all the work me, Bob and Raj put in today?"

I felt a little ganged-up on with Brian and his crew standing in front of me "Yeah completely."

Brian cleared his throat "What about showing a little royal appreciation?"

I had no clue what Brian was talking about! "Sorry mate, what exactly does royal appreciation mean?"

Brian winked at Raj and the other guy whose name I hadn't bothered knowing "A piece of paper with the queen's face on it!" I decided to play dumb, something that came very easily to me! "You want a stamp?"

Brian reacted to my stupidity somewhat aggressively "NO! Not a stamp! A bank note.....or two!"

I realised they weren't leaving without some beer money "Oh a tip? OK"

I took my wallet out and picked out the £20 note that Brian had given me a few minutes earlier "Here's £20."

Brian took the note "Thanks Divinder. That'll do for me. What about Raj? He took apart that big heavy table of yours?"

I looked at Raj who suddenly looked like a sad puppy "I suppose you're right. Here's another £20 for Raj."

I handed over another of Brian's notes over "And what about Bob?"

I looked at the fat guy with the wandering eye and bum cleavage "What about Bob? HIM?! He just sat in the van the whole time!! He didn't even pick up one box!"

Brian seemed to have anticipated this question.

He came over and placed his arm around my shoulder.

"Divinder, he may, as you say, have just sat in the van but without him we wouldn't be able to get your stuff from here to the warehouse! Come on, be a mate, sort him out!"

I looked in my wallet and gave Bob the £5 note that Brian had given me a few minutes ago.

Bob accepted it hungrily.

Brian shook my hand and I checked to make sure he hadn't taken my wedding ring off and then he headed back to his van "As they say in America. You have a great day now!"

I corrected him "We're going to Canada" and he drove off shouting "Same difference!" with the sound of my furniture clattering in the back of the van.

I walked back into the house and closed the door behind me.

I went through the kitchen and decided to have a seat in the garden.

As I stepped out I noticed that Beena, my in-laws neighbour was weeding in the garden as her two young kids played in their sand pit nearby.

She stopped weeding to come speak with me "Hello stranger! You moving in or what?!"

I laughed knowing that Beena, who went by the name Bee, knew we were moving in aibeit temporarily "Hi Bee, we're here now for the next 6 weeks so I apologize in advance for the noise and possibly smell!"

Bee laughed and placed her hands on her hips "Well, there goes the neighbourhood! Uncle Mohan was saying that you guys were moving in today. Are you sad to have left your house?"

I thought about her question for a few seconds before I answered "I was a little sad as we packed up the boxes but the truth is we had outgrown the house so it's time for a fresh new start."

Bee nodded like she knew what I meant.

She walked over to the fence "Yogesh and I were wondering if that was your first house?"

I stepped closer so that I didn't feel like I was shouting "It is, I mean it was. It's funny because this is the first house that Anisha and I ever lived in together. It's where we bought our kids back to from the hospital and it's where the kids learned to walk and talk."

Bee looked a teary eyed.

She had two little kids, Dylan who was about 4 and her toddler Amber "Wow! You don't really think about it like that do you? How's Ani taking it?"

I smiled "She's excited and a little anxious at the same time."

Bee nodded "I can understand the excitement but where does the anxiety come from?" I wanted to say "from not knowing if we've just made the biggest mistake we're ever likely to make!" but instead I said "Well we've been used to having our own place for almost 10 years now which means we've been able to come and go as we please. Now we're going to be living under different rules"

Beena looked a little confused "You've got nothing to worry about, your in- laws are cool. You watch, the next 6 weeks are going to fly by."

I sighed and then looked over Bee's shoulder

"Bee, do you let your kids eat sand?"

Bee shook her head "No, why?"

I pointed towards her kids "That's what I thought. You might want to turn around."

Bee turned around just as her son, Dylan, was about to feed his 2 year old sister, Amber, some more sand.

She ran across the garden "Dylan Patel you put the sand down **RIGHT NOW!**"

Dylan dropped the sand and ran to the kitchen door as Amber started to cry and spat out sand.

Bee excused herself "Divind I'll have to catch you later, I have a princess I need to pacify and a prince who needs the naughty seat!"

I saluted as Bee ran into her house, carrying a crying and sand covered Amber under her arm "No problem Bee, I'll see you later."

I looked at my watch: 2:04pm

I came back into the house and put on the TV, the news was on.

From the TV:

"Police today made a statement that London is still a prime target for a terrorist attack as we approach the fourth anniversary of the 9/11 attacks...

I decided to grab some lunch and looked in the fridge and it was like Old Mother Hubbard's cupboard!.

I shouted upstairs "Mum, I'm just going out to the supermarket, do you need anything?"

After a few seconds my mother-in-law shouted back "No, we don't need anything. Will you pick the kids up or do you want me to do it?"

I shouted back "I'll pick them up Mum. I'll see you later with the kids."

Rani sounded relieved with my reply "Thank you, bye."

I left the house walked to my car which was still parked on my driveway.

I unlocked the door, got into the driver's seat and started the engine as I put on my seatbelt.

I looked in my rear-view mirror and reversed off the driveway slowly.

This was going to be the last time it would be "my drive" and that felt weird.

A few minutes later I was heading along Cranbrook Road to Barkingside to a kebab shop where I was something of a regular customer.

As I walked in, the owner Yusef waved at me "Mr. Divinder how are you my friend? Long-time no see! Where you been?"

I waved back "I've been busy with stuff that my wife keeps throwing at me. You know what it's like."

Yusef waved his kebab knife at me "As my dear old dad used to say about women, you can't live with them and you can't kill them!"

He laughed, as if he'd heard the best joke ever and I suddenly wondered what sort of meat the kebab was actually made from.....

"Your dad must have been much loved by the ladies!"

Yusef smiled a gap-toothed smile "Yes, he was a real lady-killer...now Mr. Divinder what I can do you for?"

I pointed at the menu board behind Yusef "I would like one of your heart attack specials."

Yusef looked very confused with my request "You what?"

I suddenly realised that this was what Anisha called this order!! "Give me one of your large doner kebabs with chips please."

Yusef nodded "No problem. You have a seat Mr. Divinder. So what's new in your life?"

I took a seat at the table a few feet away from the counter "Well since I last came here I quit my job, we sold the house and in 6 weeks we all leave for a new life in Canada!"

Yusef looked a little shocked "Bloody hell Mr. Divinder! Most people get asked "what's new?" and they say not much! You, you give me a speech! Why you leaving England Mr. Divinder? This is the best place in the world innit."

I laughed at his honesty "England's been very good to us Yusef, but Anisha and I think that our future is in Canada."

Yusef looked visibly distraught "Mr. Divinder, I'm not going to lie, your news has really upset me!"

I felt bad that someone who served me bad meat and chips on a weekly basis was sad that I was emigrating "Why are you upset Yusef?"

Yusef joined me at my table "Mr. Divinder you are one of my favorite regular customers. You have come here every Friday for the past 4 years. In fact, you helped to pay for that new grill plate over there!"

I looked over at the shiny new grill and felt bad that I had spent THAT much of my hard earned money at his restaurant!

"It's good to know that my future ill health has a silver lining for you!!"

Yusef stood up and walked back to the counter and threw a handful of chips into the fryer "Why didn't you tell me before? I thought we were mates?"

I wanted to say "Mates? You serve me bad food once a week – for money, what part of that makes us friends?" but I didn't "Sorry about that Yusef but I didn't want to jinx the application. I hope you understand."

Yusef nodded reluctantly as he wrapped up a huge doner kebab with enough chips to feed five people into a massive paper bag "I suppose so Mr. Divinder. Here's your kebab and chips."

I handed him the money and he rejected it.

"It's on the house, my friend."

I reached over the counter and shook Yusef's meaty and very sweaty hand.

"Thanks Yusef, that's really kind of you mate. I'll see you next week."

Yusef waved his kebab knife which came dangerously close to my face "I expect to see you 6 more times before you go OK Mr. Divinder?!"

As I sat down to eat my lunch a fat Indian man walked in and Yusef greeted him like a long lost friend.

"Mr. Sanjeev my favorite REGULAR customer! How are you? Not leaving the country are you?"

I laughed and thought "The kebab king is dead, long live the king!"

20 minutes later and I had finished my huge lunch and said goodbye to Yusef as I rubbed my distended belly.

I then got back into my car and drove the short distance to the car park of the local supermarket.

I parked up, stepped out of the car and grabbed a shopping trolley and headed straight for the sweet aisle.

As I reached the chocolate section, I stopped, two hoodie-wearing teenagers had parked their shopping trolley sideways across the aisle making it hard for me to get past.

One teenager, a skinny kid was pushing the trolley while the other one, a fatter kid, was sat in the trolley.

My spider-senses were tingling, it was a school day and these two were up to no good.

I decided that I needed to kill them with kindness "Excuse me boys, can I get past?" the teenager pushing the cart, a red-faced boy with a skinny rat face turned around and laughed as the fat teenager in the cart spat near my feet.

The rat-faced kid spoke "Did you hear anything John?" the fat boy laughed "No. I didn't hear anything but I can definitely smell a Paki!"

They both laughed and high-fived one another.

I remained calm, these kids were just that – kids. "OK ha-ha you've had your laugh, can I get past now?" unfortunately these two idiots have decided that today was the day to pick a fight with a middle-aged brown man.

The fat boy spoke and spat his words out along with some cheesy crisps that he was eating "No you can't, you smelly Paki!"

I looked at the teenagers in front of him and tried to guess their ages.

I could already see the headline on tomorrow's news, "Middle aged man beats up two spotty twelve year olds in Sainsbury's! Banned from Canada! Wife says 'he was always an idiot!'"

"Listen, I don't want any trouble" rat-face gave me a sideways glance "What if WE do, hey Paki- man?"

I tried to get past them and they jammed my trolley in.

I stared at them with my 'Dad face'

"Do you want me to call security?" rat-face imitated my voice "Do you want me to call security? Can't you fight your own battles Paki man?"

I was close to losing my temper but kept seeing the headline "Violent middle aged man heard saying 'I wouldn't want to waste my time on a couple of teenage chavs like you!'"

I moved back, pulling my trolley with me.

Rat face and Fat boy grabbed the cart and started to pull it towards themselves. "Where you going Mr. Paki man? We're not finished yet."

I pulled my trolley hard and when they resisted I quickly let my trolley go and they both crashed to the ground.

The fat boy hit his head on the shelf and was rubbing the purple bruise that appeared almost immediately on his forehead.

The noise of them falling brought the security guard over.

The guard, a huge black guy, quickly assessed what had gone down, grabbed both boys by their hoodies and dragged them out of the store.

As they were being pulled away, rat face shouted back "We'll be waiting outside for you Mr. Paki man!" and fat boy joined in "Yeah, you wait Mr. Paki man!"

I watched as the security guard pushed them out and then he came back in and found me. "I'm sorry about that sir, they are a couple of trouble makers who think it's OK to pick fights with our customers."

I smiled awkwardly "Thanks for coming when you did. I don't know if a man my age is allowed to slap kids who are that young!" he nodded "That's the thing sir, they know that we can't touch them because they are only 13. Are you OK?"

I smiled "I'm fine thanks. I'll just get my stuff and leave."

I finished off my shopping and when I left I have to admit I looked both ways but saw no sign of the two hooded hooligans.

I headed towards the kid's school and found a parking spot a few hundred yards away.

I walked slowly to the school and turned right into the nursery that finished five minutes before the rest of the school did.

I was just about to take a seat on the bench outside Sonya's class when Sonya's teacher, Miss Carter, tapped on the window to get my attention.

She pointed to the classroom door and I nodded and walked towards the locked door.

Miss Carter unlocked the door and beckoned me into the small hallway.

Miss Carter was one of those lovely, middle-class, willowy, "English Roses" who had chosen to teach at an inner-city school much like a missionary in Victorian times would have gone to Africa.

"Hi Mr. Purewal, I hope you're well."

I smiled "I'm great thanks, how are you?" she looked surprised that a parent was asking how she was "I'm well but a little concerned about Sonya. Can I have a quick word before Sonya leaves?"

I nodded "Of course you can, is everything alright?"

Miss Carter stepped forward and gently took a hold of my right hand.

I tried to hide the shock of her holding my hand "I know I've only been Sonya's teacher for a few months but I have become really attached to her. She told me something today that had me worried."

I looked in the class and wondered what my daughter had said! "What did she say now?"

You see, Sonya had a made it a habit of making things look worse than they actually were!

Like the time she'd told her teacher she was from a 'broken home' when we were having some home renovations done and a few spindles in the staircase had been snapped in the process.

"Well, Mr. Purewal we were having a chat about family life and when I asked her about her family she said my Daddy has been packing boxes for the past few days and is leaving home soon – forever."

I couldn't help it, I laughed like a maniac and Miss Carter immediately let go of my hand.

Miss. Carter was not impressed.

"Mr. Purewal, I don't think divorce is a laughing matter!"

I waved my hands and composed myself, "I'm sorry Miss Carter I'm not laughing at you or at divorce. Sonya probably hasn't told you but we're emigrating to Canada in about 6 weeks' time. I've been packing all our stuff into boxes for the container that's being sent out in 5 weeks' time."

Miss Carter's face started to redden with embarrassment. "I am so very sorry Mr. Purewal. I feel such a fool. Can you ever forgive me?"

I nodded "Don't worry about it, there's nothing to forgive! I have to tell you that she told her last teacher that she was from a broken home once because we were having some building work done at the time and our banister was being rebuilt!"

The bell sounded and I saw Sonya grab her back-pack and run towards me.

I bent down and scooped her up.

"Have a good weekend Miss Carter."

Miss. Carter avoided making eye contact with me "You too Mr. Purewal and you too Sonya."

Sonya piped up with a "Bye Miss!"

"So my dear Soniya how are you?"

Sonya grimaced "I'm good Daddy, please don't call me Soniya, my name is Sonya!"

I put on my fake serious face "Sorry SONYA!" she smiled and then carried on "That's OK Daddy, just don't do it again!"

We walked off hand-in-hand towards the infant's school with Sonya telling me all about her day.

After a few minutes, a stream of kids came pouring of the main doors and after all the kids have left, Kamran came out looking like he'd done a few rounds with Mike Tyson!

His shirt was un- tucked and one leg of his trousers was folded up and the other wasn't.

I looked him up and down "I hope you won that fight!"

Kamran looked at me with a funny expression on his little face "What fight Dad?"

I shook my head "You mean you weren't in a fight?"

Kamran shook his head "No! Why would you think that I was? Did Mr. Drew call you?"

I was interested in what he might have done that required the head teacher to call me, but left it alone.

Meanwhile Sonya gave him a dirty look about his well dirty look "You look all messy! Boys are so...yuck!"

I grabbed Kamran's back pack and placed it on my shoulder and we all walked to the car.

Kamran tried to engage in small talk as he knew that I was sure to ask him why Mr. Drew would have been calling me.

"Dad, did you pack up all the boxes?"

I nodded "Yup. Brian came over earlier and all the boxes are now in a container waiting to be shipped off to Canada. I even gave the keys to Mr. and Mrs. Wijayaratna. They are the new owners of our house."

Kamran stopped mid-step "Hold on Dad, so if we don't live at 12 Denham Drive anymore, are we homeless now?"

I laughed loudly, making a few parents look back at me "I suppose we are but don't tell your teacher that we're homeless Sonya! She already thinks your mum and I are getting divorced! If she thought we were also homeless too she'd be contacting the authorities!"

Kamran joined in with my laughter as Sonya gave us both a dirty look, let go of my hand angrily, stuck her tongue out and then punched Kamran's arm as a final act of defiance.

Sonya sat on her seat with her face screwed up in a scowl and her arms folded tight across her chest.

I'd seen that look many times only on her mum's face!!

She refused – point blank - to speak to either Kamran or me all the way home.

Even when we arrived at her grandparent's house she jumped out of the car and slammed the door and ran to the door and tried to ring the bell that was just out of her reach.

I put my key into the lock and opened the door that Sonya pushed wider allowing her to run straight upstairs.

Kamran tapped my shoulder "Women eh Dad!! Dad why is she so moody?"

I looked down at him, at aged 8 and half he knew what had taken me 35 years to realise, "You know Kamran I have thought about that and I have come to the conclusion that you are like me, a good looking, athletic dude with a great sense of humor and Sonya, well she's a little moody like your mum can be sometimes!"

We both laughed and I thought I saw the curtain in the front bedroom window twitch.

We both started to walk into the house, Kamran ran to the conservatory "Dad will you play in the garden with me?"

I walked over to the glass door and pointed at all the lovely flowers that my in-laws had planted and tended over the year "That might be tough, Nani's a little fussy and she likes her flowers with their heads on and if we play football they'll just be stalks left after a few of your mad shots!"

Kamran punched me really hard in my kebab-filled belly and I almost puked in my mouth! "My mad shots? You're the one who shoots like your shoes are on the wrong feet!"

I tried hard to not vomit so sat down "Now we're definitely not playing!" and then I tapped Kamran on the chin and we had a play fight in the kitchen.

Later that evening, after I'd picked Anisha up from the station we were all finishing having dinner around the dining table.

Sonya was still picking at the chicken curry on her plate whilst Kamran had resorted to trying to hide some food in his napkin to throw away when the adults weren't looking.

Anisha saw him as he was as subtle as Mr. Bean "Kamran, darling, your napkin isn't hungry, you should be, please stop feeding it!"

Kamran looked up like a deer in headlights and stopped his little plan.

Sonya stopped dissecting her food for a moment "Mummy, where are we sleeping tonight?"

Anisha turned to her and replied "You and Kamran are going to share the box-room and Daddy and I are taking the second bedroom..."

Sonya dropped her fork!

She pointed at her brother "You mean I have to share a bed with **HIM**?"

Kamran stared his sister down "Calm down Sonya, you don't see me break dancing about that idea do you?!"

Sonya wasn't having it. "Why can't I sleep on the sofa instead?"

Anisha lowered her voice, something she did as a last resort before she went to shouting mode "No. I am sure that you and Kamran can sleep in the same bed for 6 short weeks."

Sonya didn't tune in to her mum's tone and kept pushing "But Mummy he was being really rude to me today and so was Daddy."

Ani turned towards me, with accusing eyes and asked "What happened Divind?"

I looked at Sonya and shrugged my shoulders as if to say, "You started this!"

I cleared my throat "It was nothing really, Sonya told Miss. Carter that I was packing boxes and leaving the home soon and the poor thing thought we were getting divorced!"

Anisha tried hard not to spit her food out laughing and almost choked in the process.

Sonya gave me a really great dirty look accompanied with the best stink eye she's ever perfected "That wasn't it! Mummy, what does moody mean?"

Anisha looked at Sonya sternly and then turned her gaze to me "Where did you hear that horrible phrase Sonya?"

Sonya immediately pointed at me! "Daddy said it earlier today! He told Kamran that I was a little moody, just like **YOU**!"

Anisha turned her stern look to me again and I swear I felt a bit of my soul leave my body, either that of some of that greasy lunchtime kebab was departing!

"Moody eh?" she looked around the table and picked up the ladle in the chicken curry "Do you want to explain now or after I beat you across the head with this ladle?"

I slowly and very carefully disarmed Anisha of the ladle and placed it on an empty plate, out of her reach.

I smiled "Ani, before you give me serious brain damage, with that very heavy looking ladle, please hear me out" she folded her arms across her chest just like Sonya had done earlier "Go for it, this better be good."

I shuffled my chair closer to hers "OK this is what happened, Kamran asked me why he was like me, and Sonya was so different. I told him that he's like me and Sonya is like you."

Anisha had a crazy look on her face "So you think I'm a little moody do you?"

The truth was I was caught by a 5 year old spy and had no way out without lying and that's something that Anisha and I had said we wouldn't tolerate from our kids "That's not what I meant."

Anisha didn't blink "It doesn't matter what you meant, is it what you said?"

I felt that I was being cross-examined by one of those high-powered lawyers!

I wanted to ask for a recess to change my underpants!

"Yes, but...no..."

Anisha stopped her unblinking-stare-off "Kamran, Sonya go help Nana and Nani with the washing up. Kamran please close the door when you leave and maybe cover your ears too."

Sonya walked out with a huge smirk on her face.

Kamran left, loudly attempting his version of the Catholic cross.

"Spectacles, Testicles, Wallet, Watch!"

Anisha moved her seat next to mine and took my hand in hers "Divind, in time, I will find it in my heart to forgive you for calling me a little moody." this was going a lot better than I imagined as the ladle wasn't anywhere near my head and my testicles were still where they were meant to be and were intact!

I decided to be apologetic "OK Ani, I'm sorry" Anisha leaned in and squeezed my hand a little "Be honest are you sorry for calling me a moody or for being caught calling me moody?"

I flexed my hand a little to kick start the blood flow I said "Both!" and then kissed her nose.

Anisha laughed "Please be serious for a moment and realise that we are going be pretty intense for the next six weeks living in each other's pockets. So we, actually you, need to do all you can to make the next month and a half as stress-free as possible."

I extracted my hand from her vice-like grip and crossed my heart "Ani it's going to be fun. It'll be like staying at a really nice Bed & Breakfast that your parents happen to own!"

Anisha laughed "I don't know Divind, we've been used to having our own space for nearly ten years. I think it's going to be tough to get on with my folk's little ways" in air quotes with her fingers.

I dismissed her fears "What do you mean? It's going to be a barrel of laughs."

Anisha stood up, she was in a serious mood, "Think about it, mum and dad are older, so they're set in their ways. They do things in a certain way and might struggle to cope with the extra work that the four of us will bring to their house."

I stood up and placed my hands on her hips to reassure her "It's not like we're not going to help. I think you're worrying for no reason. Just you watch it's going to fly by in a blur of smiles and hugs!"

Saturday May 28th 2005.

I was woken suddenly from my fitful sleep by the sound of what I thought was a lawn mower.

I squinted my eyes and looked over at the clock radio as it changed from 5:56 to 5:57am and then I turned to a snoring Anisha and nudged her.

"Ani, can you hear that annoying sound?"

Anisha tried to ignore me by pulling the duvet over her head and covering her ears.

I nudged her in the small of her back and whispered in her ear "Ani, Ani can you hear that annoying sound?"

She turned towards me and opened one sleepy eye "The only annoying sound I can hear is you asking me if I can hear an annoying sound! Now shut up and go back to sleep!" she looked at the clock radio, punched me on the arm and rolled over saying "it's not even 6 o'clock yet!" angrily under her breath as she took most of the duvet with her.

I got up and put on my track-pants.

Hearing me shuffling around Anisha turned around "Where are you going?"

I pointed in the general direction of the door "Downstairs. I need to know what that noise is! If it's a lawn mower you may hear the sounds of someone being strangled with my bare hands!"

Anisha yawned and stretched her arm and legs and her right foot popped out the side of the bed "Seeing as you've woken me up and are going to be downstairs anyway any chance you could make me a cup of tea?"

I nodded "OK but the tea might have to wait a few minutes while I do some killing."

After going to the bathroom, I tiptoed downstairs.

The annoying seemed to be coming from INSIDE the house.

As I walked towards the kitchen, the sound got even louder.

I started thinking that some crazy burglar was using a chain saw in the house and got slightly scared and grabbed the tiny metal cup that held the incense and thought about using this as a terribly weak weapon.

As I walked towards the conservatory I saw my father in law lying face down on the floor chanting "Om, Om" over and over again loudly.

At first, I thought he'd fallen so walked over to him "Dad what exactly are you doing?" he looked up from the floor, his glasses perched on the end of his nose "Good morning. I am doing my breathing yoga."

I looked at the clock.

"But Dad, it's not even 6am yet. We were sleeping and I heard what I thought was a lawn mower so came down to investigate."

Mohan smiled and moved into a crossed legged pose "Oh I'm sorry, I completely forgot that you were sleeping here."

I smiled as if to say "it's OK" and then wanted some clarification "Is this something you do every Saturday?" he shook his head and for a spilt second I was reassured "No"

I blew out a theatrical sigh of relief "Thank god for that!" and then he added "I do it every day!"

I could feel my face drop "What? Dad, we don't get up until after 8am on the weekends. It's the one time we get to have a lie-in" he looked a little worried in that way that old men do where they look all sad and forlorn "Oh. You see I have been doing yoga for two hours every day my whole life and if I don't start my day this way I get a headache."

I was just about to say, "and if you do this at 6am every day, then the rest of the family will get a headache?" but thought better of it, instead I said, "Here's a suggestion could you maybe do it after 8am?" he looked even more concerned "But I wake up at 4am, what would I do for 4 hours?"

I was incredulous "4 hours? Why do you get up so early? When I'm retired I'm going to go to bed at 2am every morning and wake up at about 2pm just in time for breakfast!"

Mohan laughed as he rocked back and forth into his cross-legged pose.

"Divinder I used to think that I would sleep all day when I retired but the truth is that when you get to this age you just need less sleep. I could go to sleep at midnight and I would still wake up at 4am."

I shook my head "That's messed up! Seeing as I'm awake, would you like a cup of tea?"

Mohan nodded his head in that sideways motion that Indian people do. I never knew if this meant yes, no or maybe so asked again "Is that a yes?" he gave me the thumbs up "Yes please, I'll have half a cup thanks."

I filled the kettle and hit the on button.

While I waited for the water to boil I watched my father-in-law finish off his yoga routine.

It was impressive seeing a man in his mid-60's move his body with such finesse.

He had 30 years on me and I got a bad back if I coughed awkwardly!

I made the tea and gave my father-in-law his half a cup and took a tray loaded with two cups, a pack of biscuits and a tea kettle upstairs to Anisha.

I pushed the door open with my foot and placed the tray on the chair "Oi mistress! Your tea is here!"

Anisha woke up and sat up on her side of the bed.

She took my pillow and used it to prop herself as I handed her a steaming hot cup of tea.

Anisha had always been able to drink boiling hot tea whilst I waited for mine to cool down to what Anisha called "orange juice temperature."

She took the tea "Thanks Spartacus!" she then blew across the top of the cup as she sipped the hot tea that had been in a metal teapot a few seconds earlier.

I took the tray off the chair and placed it carefully on the floor.

I then sat down in the chair

"Have a guess what the noise was Ani?"

Anisha shrugged her shoulder "Wasn't it a lawn mower?"

I laughed "No, it wasn't a lawn mower. It was your dad!" she looked at me with a little disbelief then fear "My dad? Is he in pain?"

I shook my head "No pain, just yoga."

Anisha nodded "Oh yeah, mum said he does that every morning from 4am to 6am."

I stared at her "Is there anything else you might suddenly remember your mum telling you about?"

Anisha made like she was thinking really hard and even stuck her tongue out the side of her mouth "No, that's it. I lowered my voice and joined her on the bed "Are you sure your folks aren't nudists or devil worshipers? I think I'd take Satan worshipping over seeing them nude!"

Anisha slapped me across my back "Oi! That's my mum and dad you're talking about! What if I said the same thing about your parents?"

I shuddered.

"Whoa! Time out lady, that's a visual I could do without! So what are our plans for today?"

Anisha sat up and pulled the duvet higher "Mum likes to clean the house for four hours every Saturday so we could help her"

I winced "How the hell can she clean this house for four hours? Does she scrub the skirting boards with a tooth brush or what?!"

Anisha took a deep breath "My mum likes to make sure that she gets everything good enough to eat off of. It's like her hobby."

I made the 'loose screw' circular hand gesture against my head "Did it skip a generation with you, love?"

Anisha slapped my back again "She needs a new hobby, besides which I don't think we clean up to her exacting standards, she'd only re-do whatever we'd cleaned."

Anisha agreed "In that case we could go shopping at the Freeport mall" now usually the idea of shopping on a Saturday morning with the millions of people doing the same thing would be up there with putting pins in my eyes, but the alternative was listening to her dad chanting "OM" whilst he mum cleaned her "OME"!

"That sounds like a great way to kill a few hours. But what are we going to do for the next few hours until the shops open?"

I edged towards Anisha on the bed.

Anisha made the time-out sign "Before you get any funny ideas Mr. Purewal I must remind you that my parents are in the next room and the kids are five feet away and the bedroom door has no lock. There will be no wrestling happening in this ring for the next six weeks!"

I lay face-down on the bed, bit down on the duvet and punched the mattress.

Friday June 3rd 2005, Terrence's last day at Jonathan Hawk.

The whole company had been asked to attend an after work event at "The George" pub in Moorgate.

The Managing Director, Phil Marks, stood in front of the team with a microphone in hand "OK guys if I could get your attention for a few moments" the room quickly silenced "Thanks guys I promise I won't keep you too long from your drinks!"

Everyone laughed.

"I've called this meeting for two reasons. Firstly we've had a great second quarter so I thought I would let everyone let down their hair, no offence Divind."

I raised my glass as laughter filled the air again.

Phil waited for the laughter to end "Secondly we have a couple of people who have decided to leave the Jonathan Hawk family."

People started to look at each other and shrug their shoulders whilst a few managers started to whisper to each other. "If I could ask Terrence and Divinder to come up to the front please."

Terrence got up and I followed.

As I passed Maurice he tugged on my suit jacket. "You getting the sack Abdul?"

I smiled "Let's see eh Hymie."

As we got to the front, Phil resumed his role as the host "It's with a heavy heart that I announce that today is Terrence's last day with Jonathan Hawk in London. Terrence has been approved for a transfer to our Sydney office, in Australia, and starts with them on June 13th."

The whole room went into a stunned silence.

Phil spoke again "I'll hand over to Terrence now to say a few words."

He handed the microphone to a shell-shocked Terrence. "I'm sorry but I didn't know that I would have a leaving party so didn't prepare anything. OK, here goes, I started at J Hawk when I was 27 and I have just celebrated my 40th birthday so I feel like I have seen the company grow over the past 13 years. I am looking forward to my new life in Australia but I will also miss some people at JW. I won't name check you because you know who you are. Have a great life!"

Terrence raised his glass and everyone shouted cheers back at him.

A red faced Terrence quickly moved to one side as Phil took the microphone back. "Thanks Terrence, we all appreciate your time with J Hawk and wish you all the best. Here's a small token of our esteem."

Phil handed Terrence an England football shirt with the words "Tezza" emblazoned across the back.

Terrence looked genuinely shocked at getting such a great send-off "Thanks Phil, thanks guys" he stood back admiring his shirt "Moving on, literally in this case! Divinder is also leaving these green and pleasant shores but he's going in the opposite direction to Terrence. England's gain is truly Canada's loss!"

Again the room filled with applause and laughter as I shook my head slowly and smiled.

I took the microphone from Phil without it being offered to me, "Thanks for that great...whatever it was that you just did Phil! It's true, my family and I are off to Vancouver sometime in early summer to start our new life. I haven't been here for 13 years like Terrence but."

I didn't get a chance to finish because Maurice heckled me "It just feels like 13 bloody years for the rest of us!"

The room once again erupted with applause and laughter as the news sank in.

I took to the mic again "Cheers Maurice I'll miss you too, you bastard! As I was saying, before I was so rudely interrupted by that peasant Maurice, we are off in about a month's time. It's been great working with most people here and I hope that people will keep in touch when I am in the frozen North. Thanks guys. Here's the microphone back Phil."

Phil placed the microphone down on the table and led the applause. "Don't worry Divind we'll have an Indian cricket shirt for you too closer to when you leave. It'll take us that long to save the money to get your whole name across the back! OK guys, it's now 6:15ish and the free bar is open for the next two hours. Enjoy yourselves!"

Phil shook our hands and then Terrence and I made our way to the bar.

Terrence still looked shell-shocked "If I was constipated before, I'm all good now!"

I laughed "I know the feeling! Wow Terrence, 13 years eh? You started here when I was 5!"

We both laughed as we took our stools at the bar as people started to mill around us and patted us on the back and shook our hands.

8:25pm.

I was sat on a train headed back to Ilford.

At Stratford station, I took out my cell phone and called Anisha at home. "Hi, I've just got on the 8:32 so I should be at Ilford in about 8 minutes. Can you pick me up?"

Anisha paused for a second as she told the kids to be quiet "Of course. Have you eaten yet?"

I was hungry "I've had a few shrimps and crisps but I could murder some junk food."

Anisha shushed the kids again "Great let's grab some KFC on the way home. See you at about 8:45. Bye."

ILFORD STATION, EVENING
8:48pm.

I was stood outside Ilford train station waiting for Anisha, I was approached by an Indian teenager with an unlit cigarette in his mouth.

The teenager looked and smelled like a junkie with his bad skin, rotten teeth, damp smell and shaking hands.

He approached me "Hey mister, you got a light?"

I clutched my briefcase a little firmer.

I made eye contact, then stood slightly bigger than I usually did, as I didn't want him to think I was scared, which I was, "Sorry son, I don't smoke."

He looked me up and down.

He seemed to be sizing me up so I edged back, towards a few other people waiting for their rides, they in turn scurried away from me sensing the potential trouble I brought with me.

The teenager couldn't quite work out if I was stocky or just wearing a big coat.

He stepped forward aggressively as I stepped back taking him into the station with me where I knew there were video cameras.

Just as the teenager was about to make his move Anisha pulled up and pressed the car horn loudly.

The teenager was distracted by the sound of the car horn long enough for me to make a move for the car.

I quickly got into the car and locked the doors.

Anisha could see that I was a little anxious as I kept looking back as she drove off "Who's your new friend?"

I smiled in the safety of the car "No one I'd want to introduce to you, love. Let's get out of here and grab some food."

As the car moved along into traffic I looked back as the spotty faced thug who had moved onto the other commuters.

London wasn't the place I wanted my kids to call home.

MOHAN AND RANI'S HOUSE, DAYTIME
Saturday 18th June 2005. School Garage Sale
11:30am

Kamran and Sonya were playing in the back room with their grandparents as Anisha and I were unloading the weekly shop.

"I've been thinking more about having a leaving party, you know what we were talking about a few weeks ago?"

Anisha put the box of cereal in the cupboard and then faced me "Hold on, didn't you say – and I quote - 'that a leaving party smacked of desperation?'"

I blushed "Yes I did but..." she wasn't finished! "And didn't you also say that only sad people would see how many of their friends would turn up?"

She was smacking me all over the kitchen.

"Yes I did, but can I say something?" she was on a roll "In fact I think you actually said something like, a leaving party was like being at your own funeral! If I remember correctly you said it was like that episode of 'Friends' when Ross faked his own death!"

She was right, I had said all those things but I had changed my mind.

"What I actually said was that a leaving party was like being a guest at your own funeral and seeing who would cry!"

Anisha chalked up an imaginary number 1 in the air with her finger "One nil, team Anisha!"

I laughed as she asked, "What's made you change your mind ROSS?"

I shrugged "I just had a change of heart. Is that illegal now?"

Anisha shook her head and pushed further, "No, I'm not buying it! What's the real reason? Come on fess up!"

I shook my head but she tickled me "OK, we have given out hundreds, possibly thousands, of pounds in gifts over the years and I want some love back!"

Anisha laughed out loud and snorted too "That is really sad, I love it, but it is sad! How big a party do you want?"

I looked at my feet "I was thinking about 40 people. We could maybe have the party here, at your mum and dad's place?"

Anisha immediately killed that idea "40's fine, but not here. There ain't enough room to swing a cat with all of us living in the same space. Why don't we book the banquet room at Gourmet Buffet?"

I raised my hand for a high five "I love it! That way everyone can pay for themselves and we still get presents!"

Anisha slapped my hand "I wasn't thinking about that, but good call!"

We finished the unpacking and then walked into the living room and each took a seat at the table.

Anisha took out a piece of paper and a pen from the cabinet. "Let's make a list and see who we agree on. First there's our folks, 4 down 36 to go."

I thought for a moment "OK, you have to put Bo, Jane and Amber on the list."

Anisha agreed

"OK we're doing well. That's only 33 people left."

Anisha scratched her head as I said "My brother's and their families."

Anisha added their names to the list "That's another 12 people on the list. We're already up to 16 people. You know we may need to increase the numbers. How about Naya and Kamaljeet?" I shook my head "No way! I still haven't forgiven them for what their son said to Kamran as his birthday party"

Anisha waved her finger at me "Let me remind you Divind, he's a Vet and she's a successful financial planner. They will bring a good present!"

I thought about it for a few seconds "That's a good point. Put them on the list. Is that 20 people so far?"

Anisha counted the people on the list "Yup. We must know more than 20 people! Come on, throw some names at me!"

I looked at the contact list on the 'phone "What about Sandra and Dominic?"

Anisha screwed up her face and shuddered "No way! He's a complete creep! He always tries to grope me when he says hello!"

I dismissed Anisha's character assassination of Dominic "Don't flatter yourself Ani, he even tries to kiss me! He's just a little, you know, touchy-feely!"

Ani indicated that this wasn't going to happen by saying "Next!"

I scrolled down the list and smiled "Liz and Alan from football?"

Anisha returned my smile "Good. Talking of football how about Tracy and Alan and David and Cathie?"

I nodded "Definitely! What are we up to?"

Anisha counted down the list "That's 32 including all the kids."

We looked at each other with some disappointment as we pondered the list.

In sheer desperation, I suggested we widen the net "Are there any work people you want to invite?"

Anisha thought for a second "I would probably only invite Kaye and Susie. How about you?"

I scratched my head "I would invite Terrence but the trip from Sydney might be a lot to ask! I think we should come to the list later. We're already up to 34 people. Besides which it's nearly 11:45 and we need to set up our table for noon."

Anisha folded the list in half and placed it back in the cabinet with the pen. We both walked over to the front door.

Anisha looked back and made one last check with me "Have you packed all the stuff into the car?"

I nodded "The boot's full but we have a couple of boxes left to go onto the back seat."

I opened the front door, picked up the two small boxes, in the porch, and stepped onto the drive and unlocked the car.

I opened the back door and carefully placed the two small boxes onto the back seat.

I then opened the boot and made sure that the boxes were all in place.

Having locked the car again, I walked back into the house.

Anisha was stood by the front door "Divind, mum wants to know if you want to take a cup of tea with us or just buy one there?"

I shook my head, time was against us and I wanted to get a good spot "We'll get one there. Let's leave now and we'll be able to get a good table. Kamran, Sonya let's go."

Kamran strolled over from the kitchen, with ketchup all over his face "Where are we going?"

I tried to sound excited about selling off our junk "To the school. It's the school fair and garage sale today, it's going to be a lot of fun."

Kamran looked at me and could tell that standing at a table in the blazing midday sun sounded like the opposite of fun, "Do we have to go? Sonya and I wanted to spend the day with Nani and Nana. We only have three weeks with them before we go to Canada."

I leaned down to Kamran and whispered "It's up to you guys, but there's going to be candy floss, a popcorn machine, hamburgers, hot dogs and a bouncy castle....

Kamran's eyes literally lit up "See you later Nana, Nani!" he grabbed Sonya's hand "Bye Nana, Nani! We'll see you when we come back yeah? Remember, we still have three whole weeks together!"

Mohan and Rani both laughed as Sonya and Kamran stood by the car singing "Hamburgers! Hot Dogs and bouncy castle! Hamburgers! Hot Dogs and bouncy castle!"

Seeing me saying goodbye to his grandparents, Kamran started getting a little anxious "Come on Dad, what are we waiting for?!" his sister joined in "Yeah come on, old man! The hamburgers are waiting!" and they both laughed.

Gearies school playground

Anisha and I pulled up in the staff car park.

The kids undid their seatbelts, opened their doors and jumped out and ran towards the bouncy castle that was being inflated in the middle of the school yard.

Anisha screamed after Kamran "Kamran darling, keep an eye on Sonya!"

Kamran turned back and gave Anisha the thumbs up.

I started to take the various boxes out of the car "OK Ani lets unload the boot. I think we're still early enough to get a good table."

Anisha came over "Divind, you start unloading the boxes and I'll see if I can get a cart or something for all our stuff."

I nodded and started to take the larger boxes out of the trunk.

Anisha returned a few minutes later with a shopping cart "I bumped into Mr. Drew and he said that as we are the first here we get to use the much-prized school shopping cart and we get to choose the site of our table."

I did a fist pump "Perfect! I'll load these into the cart if you push it over to a spot by the bouncy castle. I'll grab a folding table for us to set up."

Anisha looked a little surprised by my idea "Why would you want to be next to the noisy bouncy castle?"

I smiled knowingly "I've given this a lot of thought Ani and I'll happily explain why it's the ideal spot. Every kid will want to go on the bouncy castle and while the parents are waiting we'll have their undivided attention!" for once, Anisha didn't fight me or make an alternate suggestion.

"OK let's do it."

Anisha pushed the cart over to the bouncy castle and started to unload the boxes as I struggled with the heavy wooden table that weighed a great deal more than it looked. Anisha saw me man- handling the table "Ani help me with this table! It weighs more than I do!"

Anisha rushed over, grabbed the other end of the table and helped me set the table down.

We unfolded the table legs and pushed the table about 10 feet away from the bouncy castle generator.

After a few seconds the generator started to make a really loud noise so we shook our heads and moved to the other side of the bouncy castle.

Placing the table down I said "This'll do Ani." we started to place our objects on the table just as other sellers started to arrive.

A few minutes later Chris, a teacher at the school, set his table next to ours. "Hi Chris, how you doing mate?" Chris shook my hand "I'm good thanks Divind. How are you and Ani?"

I rubbed my hands together "Hopefully after today we'll be a few hundred pounds better off! This is all going towards our Canada fund."

Chris laughed "Oh yeah, Kamran was saying that you guys are off to Canada soon."

I nodded "Yup we leave on the 10th of July."

Chris looked impressed "Can I ask you a question?"

I liked Chris he was a straight-talking Yorkshireman who always asked good questions "Of course you can Chris" Chris pulled up his jeans over his big belly "Why Canada? Why not America? If I was going across the pond I would go to America."

I smiled, it was a question that I'd heard many times before "Three reasons Chris. 1, I have a younger brother who lives in Vancouver so we'll have somewhere to stay until we get our own place. 2, Canada is just like a diet version of the US, similar fizz with less of that annoying gas! And 3, since 9/11 it's become really, really hard to get a green card. Some people think that being brown equates to being a terrorist out there!"

Chris laughed "But Divind, isn't Canada just like a boring version of America, like New Zealand is snoresville compared to the exciting Australia?"

I laughed, I'd heard the same thing asked a few times before when we'd said we were looking at Canada rather than America and people would say "Oh! Canada?"

"You know what Chris, after 35 years of living in Britain I've had all the excitement I need. I want to be in a place where people still say hello to each other and where smiling isn't just what crazy people do!"

Chris nodded "Put like that, I can see why that would be appealing. I better get unloading all my stuff before the hordes arrive. I'll catch you later."

I finished off arranging our table as Ani stood by the bouncy castle where Sonya and Kamran were bouncing around. I looked at her and smiled.

I had what I called my "Life is good" smile on my face.

12:00pm

Bob Drew, the head teacher came out with a megaphone in his hand.

The school yard was now full of people looking at the various tables.

Bob stood by the candy floss machine and brought the megaphone to his mouth "Good afternoon everyone. Welcome to the first Annual Gearies

School Fair and Garage Sale. It's now 12 noon and I declare the fair open! Have a great day!"

The kids in the crowd cheered loudly in reply as Bob covered his ears and took the megaphone and ran back to his office.

Anisha looked over at me with a nervous look on her face "Divind, ask Kamran to get his friends over to check out his PlayStation games. Once people see that we've got some good stuff we'll be swarmed"

I looked over at Kamran who was holding court with his merry little gang "That's a good idea."

I raised my hand in his general direction and Kamran looked over "Hey, Kamran, come here mate, you're not in trouble....yet."

Kamran walked over with a huge, pink candy floss in his right hand. He stood in front of me with as much candy floss on his face as on the stick that he held "Yes Dad?"

I pointed at him and said "Two questions, number one, where's Sonya? And number two, where did you get that candy floss?"

Kamran pointed over at Jane and Bo who were stood with Sonya and their daughter Amber by the candy floss machine.

Bo waved at me and reading my mind pointed at Sonya who was devouring a candy floss like her life depended on it.

I gave Bo a thumbs-up and turned my attention back to Kamran "Kamran I need you to get all your mates to come to our table."

Kamran looked a little surprised "Why Dad?"

I crouched down, something that I did when I wanted to tell him a secret "Because I want them to check out the detail on the wooden table top! You muppet! I need them to see what we have to offer so that they can annoy their parents into buying it off of us."

Kamran nodded in a knowing way "What's in it for me, old man?" and then he made the universal hand sign for money by rubbing his forefinger and thumb. It took all my effort not to laugh at the fact that my 8 year old son was hustling his old man!

"Excuse me Kamran?"

Kamran smiled and made the hand sign again "I said what's in it for me?" and then he did a really bad and loud impersonation of Tom Cruise as Jerry McGuire that made everyone look over "Show me the money Dad!"

I resisted the urge to laugh, instead choosing some haggling myself "How about Mum, Sonya and I all go to Canada and I leave you here with Nana and Nani?"

Kamran winked and placed his hand on mine "Dad you always say if you don't ask you don't get. What if you pay me 10 percent for every game I sell to one of my friends?"

I looked at the huge pile of games on the table and did some quick maths in my head "Kamran, there's about 50 games for sale! I would be bankrupt if I took that deal!"

Kamran started walking away slowly and looked back "That's the deal old man. Take it or leave it!"

I jokingly gave Kamran "the look" but he just laughed as he stood holding his ground. "OK you have a deal. I can't believe that you're stealing from your own dad! You're cold, you hear me? Cold!"

Kamran walked back with a distinct swagger in his step.

He extended his little right hand "No offence Dad, but we need to shake on it. Make it all legal."

I looked at his candy floss covered hand and then shook it and gave it a gentle bone squeeze.

He winced a little but didn't want to scream in front of his school friends "How did I end up with such a cold blooded kid?"

Kamran rubbed his hands and winked at me "You got lucky I suppose Dad!"

I watched as he ran off to his circle of friends and pointed towards the direction of our table. After a few minutes he came back to the table with fifteen of his classmates in tow.

His friend Mike was the first to speak. Mike was that fat, pink-faced kid that every class had who wore shorts and a tee-shirt all year round as if he doesn't feel the cold.

"Kamran do you have Killer Pigs part 3?"

Kamran nodded "Brilliant? How much do you want for that?" Kamran replied before I had a chance to speak "That's only £10 to you" Mike looked upset "But I only have £7.50."

Kamran turned around, covering the table and pointed at the £2.50 price sticker on the front of the game.

I quickly took it off and started doing that with the other boxes too before the boys got their sticky hands on the games. Kamran picked the game up and handed it to Mike "OK Mike, because you're a mate I'll take that. Here's the game."

Mike had a huge smile on his face "Thanks Kamran! Thanks a lot!" as he handed over his money and ran off excitedly with the game towards his Mum.

Kamran wrote down the name of the game on a piece of paper with a "7.50" in the corner. I saw that Kamran was a man on a mission "I'll leave the games to you eh?" I don't think that Kamran even heard me as he started his patter "Roll up! Roll up! PS2 games for sale! Dirt cheap!"

I walked over and handed Anisha the £7.50 from the game sale.

She smiled "Have you already sold 3 games?"

I laughed "Not exactly. Kamran has cut a deal with me where he gets 10% of every game he sells to his mates."

Anisha smiled "You mean he sold one game for £7.50?"

I nodded "Yup! What can I say he's a real wheeler-dealer! Little Donald Trump!"

Anisha looked genuinely shocked.

Taking a table at the school fair had been my idea and she'd thought we'd barely break even.

"Bloody hell! We might make a few quid from this!"

I laughed, as if I knew we'd make a small fortune if Kamran kept bringing his friends over "I hope so."

The afternoon flew by and by 2pm the school yard was emptying quickly.

The only games left were the ones that everyone considered too babyish.

Kamran spotted his friend Peter coming off the bouncy castle and placed the last of the PS 2 games into a shoe box and put them under our table.

"Hey Peter" said Kamran to a red faced Peter "check out these last PS 2 games!"

Peter ran over with his puffy faced parents in close pursuit.

Kamran carefully took the box out and looked around like he was on a secret mission. "Pete, I've kept these games back for you" he then placed the box on the table.

Peter looked at the games and then looked at Kamran with a "so what" look on his face. "But Kamran, these are all the kiddy games like Toy Story and Shrek. Why would I want these?"

Kamran looked like he knew exactly what Peter would say "Are you joking Pete? These are the best games I have! They're classics! The Toy Story game is wicked. I'm prepared to give you all 4 games for only £10.00. What do you say?"

Peter didn't seem certain so walked over to his mum and whispered in her ear and pointed at our table, I waved at her.

His mum, Maureen, walked over to the games and rummaged through them "They're a bit kiddy aren't they Kamran?"

Kamran smiled and made puppy-dog eyes and then loudly said "Mrs. Riley if you love Peter you'll buy him these games!"

Peter looked at her with anxious eyes and Maureen looked at Kamran with angry eyes and I just looked at the ground and bit my lip because I was scared I was going to laugh out loud.

After about twenty seconds, in which time Peter looked more and more likely to cry at the thought that his mum's reluctance to buy four crappy PlayStation games indicated how little she truly loved him.

Maureen reached into her bag, took out her purse and from it carefully extracted a £10 note and angrily thrust this into Kamran's waiting hand as she took the games and the box and stomped off swearing under her breath.

Kamran handed me the note and I shook my head "No son, that's all yours. You've earned that one!" he ran off like he'd won the lottery and headed off towards his friends and bought them the equivalent of a round of candy floss!

With only enough stuff to put into a shoe box I started to put things away. Anisha was standing with Bo and Jane counting the takings. She walked over to me "Divind I think I may have miscounted because we seem to have made £826 and 25 pence!!"

I did a double-take like that old Scottish fella from the Laurel and Hardy movies.

"How much?!" Anisha showed me a sheet of paper with a bunch of numbers on it "£826 and 25 pence!!"

I stared at the paper, Anisha had broken down all the takings into different columns "How much of that was PS 2 games?" Just as I said that Kamran appeared at my side as if he was a genie! "Yeah Mum, how much was from the sale of MY games?"

Anisha smiled and showed Kamran the paper and he said "£300??!!" he stood there with candy floss in his hair and some on the end of his nose and he was trying to work out his share "That's 3, carry the 1...£30 PLEASE!"

I looked at him and said "How is it that you usually have to take your shoes and socks off to count past ten unless it's to do with money that you're owed and then you're suddenly good at maths hey? OK here's your £30 share, as agreed."

I jokingly held onto the three £10 notes tightly as Kamran tried to prize them from my fingers.

Kamran was scared that he'd rip the notes in half "Come on Dad release the cash, a deal's a deal!"

I released the money and he almost fell over "You're cold blooded, man! Cold blooded!"

He jokily stuck his tongue out and rejoined his friends with his wad of cash in his hand.

JONATHAN HAWK OFFICE, DAYTIME

Friday 1st July 2005. my last day at work.
Almost 5pm

I got an email just as I was logging off for the very last time.

From: Marion.Sorrell@JonathanHawk.co.uk

Sent: July 1st 2005 4:59 PM

To: Divinder Purewal Divinder.Purewal@JonathanHawk.co.uk

Subject: Important email

Divinder, please come down to the boardroom before you leave.
Arnold and I need to complete the final handover.

Cheers,
Marion

Marion Sorrell,
Manager – Investment Management and Hedge Funds/ Jonathan
Hawk/ Moorgate/ London

I replied with a simple "No problem" and then switched my PC off and felt a little sad that this was it, the last time I'd ever sit at this desk. I looked around and noticed that I was alone. As I walked through the other offices I noticed that no-one was sat at their desks.

I walked towards the boardroom and heard the sound of voices that suddenly stopped when I approached.

I opened the door and was hit with a wall of sound.

"SURPRISE!!"

Marion guided me into the board room and gave me a seat at the head of the table.

The whole team was there to see me off.

I smiled at Maurice and Arnold who were holding pieces of paper in their hands.

Marion smiled at me "So Divinder, as you've probably realised this isn't a handover!"

I smiled back, feeling a little like I was about to cry so I made a joke "That's just typical, the poor Indian gets ambushed by a bunch of cowboys!"

The room exploded with laughter.

Marion placed a small gift wrapped box and a white envelope in front of me "Here's a gift from the whole team. We thought about getting you a plaid shirt but we decided that you'd probably need the cash instead. I am going to miss you and hope that you'll keep in touch. Now give me a hug to show there's no hard feelings!"

I stood up and hugged Marion and then sat down and opened the gift. It was joke book entitled "The 1,000 best jokes ever" I opened the front cover and read that everyone had written a comment as a farewell card.

I felt genuinely shocked "Thanks guys. I really didn't expect a gift. Thanks."

Marion could see that I was close to tears, "Anyway, let's move on with the afternoons proceedings before Divinder starts crying! Now Divinder we didn't want to let your last day go by without a little trip down memory lane. In the absence of Terrence, we thought that Arnold and Maurice could guide you along your four years at Jonathan Hawk. So everyone grab a glass of wine as I hand over to Maurice."

Maurice stepped forward waving his paper over his head. A few people applauded.

He cleared his throat in a theatrical way "Thank you fans! Divinder, my old mate, I sat down last night and worked out that I've only known you for about three years but it feels like so much longer and that ain't a good thing!"

The team laughed again and I joined in too as Maurice continued his roast "When Marion asked me, well told me really, to say a few nice words about you I tried to get out of it as my religion frowns on lying! But seriously it's been an emotional roller coaster working with someone intelligent, witty, blessed with good looks and a great human being too, but that's enough about me let's talk about you eh?! I have never met anyone like you who could make a room laugh.....just by leaving it!"

I laughed as a few other people groaned and a few others giggled as the wine kicked in.

Maurice took his applause with a huge smug smile on his face "No, but seriously, it's been great working with you Divind. You have an infectious sense of humour and your ability to laugh at yourself is refreshing in the stressful world we live in. I'm going to miss you and hope that you'll come back and visit us or better still let me and my family come visit you when we go skiing next year so I'm booking my room now! I'll now hand over to Arnold."

I shook Maurice's hand as Arnold stood up "Lords, ladies and germs! I have known Divinder for the shortest amount of time but in a weird way I feel like I know him better than most people. I spent the past few days contacting a few of Divinder's clients asking them what they'll miss about him. Here's a few comments. Peter Lockwood from Goldman Sachs said, "Who the hell's Divinder?""

His jokes met with scattered laughter in the room but Arnold carried on regardless "Mary at JP Morgan said, "I have no idea what he does at Jonathan Hawk but he seems like a nice enough chap when he calls me every few months." Chris at Barclays Global was a little more helpful when she said "Divinder has been a real asset to the company. Is she the little Indian girl on reception with the slight hump on her right shoulder?""

The room rippled with slow clapping and a few giggles and even a random fart.

"Divinder what we're trying to say is that none of us exactly know what it is that you do but we're going to miss you doing it anyway! Now over to you. Speech! Speech!"

I shook Arnold's hand, stood up and took a piece of paper out of my pocket as the team started to shout "Speech! Speech!" at me.

I took a few steps towards the door so that I could see the whole team "Thanks guys. I know most people don't actually do speeches when they leave but I wanted to say a few words. Firstly, I have loved working at Jonathan Hawk...well when I say I loved, I actually mean I love the part from 4pm onwards every Friday! The team here really are the best people to have come out of the care in the community program! I would like to make special mention to a couple of people. Maurice, having you around makes me realise that I'm not THAT fat!"

The team laughed as Maurice raised his glass, smiled as he gave me the V sign and then winked and breathed in.

I turned towards Arnold, "Arnold, you have been a pleasure to work with."

Arnold waved his hand in the air. "Arnold, seeing you deal with clients has been a master-class in how NOT to be a recruiter! I will miss you guys, and hope that you'll keep in touch with me. For those who want my email address please get a pen and paper out now."

A few people grabbed their diaries or scraps of paper as I took a sip of water from my bottle "Everyone ready? My email address is getstuffedyougreedysods@hotmail.com!"

Phil, the MD, laughed and in doing so spat his wine out over Arnold's head!

Phil apologized "Sorry Arnold, get stuffed you greedy sods! Classic Divinder, classic!"

Arnold wiped his head with his sleeve "That's alright Phil."

I said one last toast "Thanks again guys. This means a lot to me." as people gave me hugs, back slaps and even a few kisses.

I texted Anisha and let her know that I'd be on the 6:15 train home.

Saturday July 2nd 2005, the big leaving party.

It was 6:40pm and we'd booked the banquet hall at the Gourmet Buffet restaurant for our leaving party starting at 7:00pm.

We were getting ready to leave when my mobile phone rang.

I looked at the screen and picked up the phone "Hi Carla how are you?"

Carla sounded a little annoyed "I'm great Divind but his lordship is sick. We're going to have to bail out of tonight's bash. Sorry but we'll try to catch up with you guys before you all leave."

Now Carla was one of a rare group of people as she was able to wind me up and I always assumed that she was up to no good "Is Doug really sick or are you winding me up again?"

Carla sounded sincere enough "I wouldn't joke about Doug, you know that."

I was disappointed as Carla was not only a great friend but she was also an unofficial Godmother to Sonya "It's just that you do have a history of being a windup. Give Doug my best wishes."

Carla seemed to be laughing but turned it into a cough "Will do. See you soon love.....I mean before you guys leave."

I hung up and Anisha looked over at me, "That was Carla. Doug's sick. They can't make it."

Anisha knew how much I wanted to see Carla "That's a shame. Oh well let's get ready for the other guests."

I nodded as my mobile phone rang again. This time it was my friend Dave.

"Dave mate, how are you?"

Dave sounded a little distressed "I'm good mate, but Rea has just started puking. Cathie thinks she might have food poisoning. We're going to see how she does for the next few hours so will probably miss your leaving party. I'm really gutted mate, please give my love to Anisha and the kids"

I tried really hard to hide my disappointment "OK Dave, please give our love to Cathie and wish Rea well."

I hit the off button and threw the 'phone on the bed "This evening is turning into a washout. First Carla and Doug and now Dave, Cathie and Rea. If that phone rings again I'm not answering it!"

Just then the mobile buzzed into life again!

I just stared at the 'phone, then at Anisha and then back at the phone. Anisha got the hint and picked up the phone. "Hi Al. I'm good, how are you, Trace and the kids?"

Anisha bite her lip and nodded occasionally as she listened to our friend Al. "No, Al that's fine. There seems to be a lot of it going around at the moment. In fact you guys are the third lot of people to pull out for the same reason. No don't worry about it. See you later. Give my love to Trace."

Anisha folded the phone shut and placed it slowly on the bed.

She looked at me and I was in a full on sulk.

"Hey mister, turn that frown upside down!"

I looked at her and pointed an accusing finger "This is why I didn't want a leaving party! People just can't be bothered anymore! Let's cancel the restaurant. I'm in no mood to socialize tonight."

I got up, and stomped off to the bathroom and closed the door with a huge slam.

Anisha followed me and knocked on the door.

I ignored her first five knocks so she opened the door and popped her head in to see me sitting on the side of the bath.

"I come in peace!"

I was very emotional "Ani why are people so quick to let us down? I would never pull out of a party on the actual day. You know the worst thing is that I was actually thinking that I was leaving so much behind and now I realise that there's nothing keeping us here!"

Anisha carefully walked closer to me, not quite sure which version of me she was going to get "Divind, don't you think you're being a little overdramatic?"

I stood up, to make my point "No I don't!! We have known some of our friends for about ten years and that doesn't seem to count for anything when we're about to move 5,000 miles away!"

Anisha tried to hold my hand in an effort to calm me down "But that's the thing Divind, life does go on. Do you honestly think that people are going to cry for the rest of their lives when we emigrate? Some people will be upset for a few days even a few weeks but life has to carry on."

I don't know why I was so upset but I was, "I know that Ani, but it would have been nice if people pulled out a few stops to show us that we are important to them. Do me a favor Ani leave me alone for a minute I need a little time to myself."

Anisha saw that I was a little edgy so backed off "OK but we need to leave in about 5 minutes. You know how hard it is to get parking in Ilford on a Saturday night."

I didn't turn around but nodded.

Anisha left the room and I closed my eyes.

At 6:47pm I came downstairs.

I was in a better mood.

"OK guys, let's get this show on the road."

Anisha smiled at me "You OK?"

I smiled back "I'm great. You're right Ani, life does go on. Let's have our leaving party."

Anisha clapped her hands "Come on, you heard your Dad, let's go guys"

We left the house as Anisha's dad turned the alarm on and locked the front door.

GOURMET BUFFET CHINESE RESTAURANT, EVENING.

It was 7:05 and we were the only people scattered around the large banquet table.

The tall, skinny Chinese waiter stared at his shoes and was sucking food loudly off his teeth with his tongue.

I was so angry that his sucking sound was amplified in my ears!

I looked at the rest of the table and everyone looked bored.

This was going to be the worst leaving party ever!

At 7:10 my older brother Sarbjit arrived with his wife Ranjvir.

Sarbjit took a seat beside me as Ranjvir took a seat between Anisha and her mum.

Like me, Sarbjit was a talker "So Divind this is it eh? Are you getting nervous yet bro?"

I thought about it for a moment before I replied "Funnily enough, I'm not nervous at all really. I guess I'll get nervous at the airport"

Sarbjit nodded "I think you're brave, making this big move. Good luck to you both but I don't think I could do it."

Ranjvir looked like she was sucking a lemon "I agree, especially as you haven't even got a house or jobs to go to. And you are taking your young kids so far away from all their family." this was typical Ranjvir, she always wanted to keep people down and was the ultimate pessimist.

Anisha glared at Ranjvir "We're actually moving to give the kids a better life"

Ranjvir turned to Anisha with an angry look "How would moving from London give your kids a better life? This is the best place in the world innit!"

I pushed my chair back because I knew that Ranjvir had just lit Anisha's fuse!!

"What's so great about it? The drive-by shootings? The people selling drugs on the street corners? Or the fact that we can't afford to live where we live? You can have London we'll try our chances in Canada thank you very much!"

I wanted to applaud but then I saw Carla, Doug, Cathie, Dave, Alan, Tracy and their kids all arrive together.

I looked over at Anisha who smiled knowingly at me.

"You evil wind up merchant! Whose idea was it? I bet it was her idea wasn't it"

Anisha laughed and pointed at Carla who quickly grabbed both my hands before I could slap her.

Carla cackled "Did you believe me darling?"

I shook my head, way too quickly, like a five year kid caught with his hands covered in chocolate.

"No, I knew you'd be here."

Anisha immediately blew my cover! "LIAR!! Carla, you should have seen him! He was drowning in his own tears!"

I stared at Anisha and begged her with my eyes to stop but she was on a roll!

"Oh Carla you'd have died laughing at the incredible sulk over there!! At one stage, he even said – and I quote –"

I reached over the table and tried to cover Anisha's mouth but Carla dragged me away "Go ahead Ani, I've got Divinder!"

Anisha blew me a kiss and carried on with her story "as I was saying he said 'it would have been nice if people pulled out a few stops to show us that we are important to them'!"

Everyone, except Ranjvir, laughed loudly as Carla released me and kissed me on the forehead "I got you again Divind! That's two nil to team Carla!"

I went into full denial mode, US Congressman style "No you didn't! I knew you were winding me up. That's why I asked you if Doug was really sick."

Carla raised her hand and placed her palm in my face "Speak to the hand cos the face ain't listening, you muppet! Divind just admit it, you have met your match in me!"

I shook my head "Never! I am – and always will be - the undisputed king of the wind-ups!"

Carla stopped laughing.

"Oh really Divind? Shall I tell everyone here about the deli incident?" this was my worst nightmare coming true, Carla not coming was better than Carla being here and telling my family how she's wound me up like a clock!!

I shook my head, which was looking at the ground "No it's OK, besides which, that was ages ago. So what's new with you guys? You look like you've lost some weight girl! Have you changed your hair style?"

Anisha tapped me on the hand. "What's the deli incident about Divind?"

Carla clapped her hands as the waiter hovered over with a tray of drinks that he was trying to place on our table "Hasn't he told you Ani?"

Anisha shook her head and Carla tutted "Divinder PureWaffle you really should learn to share!"

I could feel my face start to heat up and go red and I was grateful that my face was dark as it covered my shame at the story that Carla was about to tell.

She moved her seat to the head of the table and spoke to her captive audience. "As you all probably know, I used to work with Divinder a few years ago here in Ilford. In fact, he was my trainer. Well you can only imagine how much fun it was having Divinder as my trainer. Well one day he decided that it would be funny to get me to interview a very stern African Catholic nun as my first interview on Monday morning!"

Everyone laughed

"So there I was on my best behavior and watching every word I said for fear of going straight to hell! It was the longest hour of my life and all the time I could hear Divinder laughing in the other office as he told everyone in the London offices what he'd done. I must have said Jesus and God about twenty times in that interview and when I was done I swore that I would get revenge and I did that Friday!"

The waiter finally placed the drinks tray down as Carla continued with her story.

I sort of wished he'd tripped and dropped the tray all over Carla's head!

"Ani, what you probably don't know, is that Divinder is a terrible flirt! I don't mean he can't help flirting, just that he does it so badly! Every day we would have a breakfast bagel at a tiny deli that had opened next to Ilford train station. It was run by a youngish bleach, blonde Turkish woman and her teenage daughter. Divinder thought he was Joey Tribbiani from 'Friends' because he would go in and start chatting with the older woman saying stuff like "You don't look old enough to have a teenage daughter.""

As everyone laughed, I raised my hand and tried to stand up for myself "Listen, in my defence, it was all part of my plan to get an extra rasher of bacon or two!"

Carla slapped my hand down.

"Whatever! What was worse was that the woman would give me two rashers and he'd get about six rashers and he never shared! Anyway, it was so embarrassing listening to him attempt smooth talk but it gave me an idea. So as I said, that Friday I booked Divinder for an interview at 8am so that I could go get breakfast myself. I came back to the office at about 9am and I was laughing to myself. So – as you all know - his lordship over there can't stand to be left out so he goes "What's so funny?" so I just keep laughing like a nut-case!"

I knew the worst part of the story was still to come so tried to deflect "I think we should get our food now! Who wants Peking duck?"

Carla looked at me with a withering stare.

"Why don't you get us all some Peking duck and I'll carry on with my story! Anyway, back to my story. After a few minutes Divinder snaps and says "You better tell me what's so funny!" So I say, "I'll tell you on the condition that you won't hit me or get angry" Well by now he's almost frothing at the mouth! "OK, OK!" he says. "I promise I won't hit you or get angry. What happened?" So I tell him that the older woman at the deli place saw me ordering our breakfast so was asking where you were. So I said that it was very sad about what had happened to Divinder. So Divinder's getting red in the face, a lot like he is now!"

I had my hands in prayer and was begging Carla to stop but she was hell bent of sharing her victory!

"So I carry on. I told her that Divinder had had a nervous breakdown a few years earlier and as part of his care in the community program he was encouraged to carry on with his previous daily work routine, in order to get him ready for the real world. So I told her that he still came into work, unpaid, where his pc was unplugged and his phone line was dead!! Well the poor woman almost starts to cry thinking of Divinder chatting away to people on a dead phone line as a taps away on an unconnected keyboard."

I looked sick as Carla carried on.

"Well that's when Divinder flips out! He jumps out of his seat and drags me to the deli which is a good 500 yards from our office."

I took her pause to deflect again, "Spring rolls, anyone?"

Carla and Anisha both gave me "the look" and I sat in my chair with my arms folded across my chest as Carla continued "So picture the scene guys, he's pulling me along the street and I'm laughing away like a nutter with tears running down my face and my messed up mascara makes me look like a ginger Alice Cooper!"

I tried again to interrupt her story "Guys, this isn't as funny as she's making out."

Anisha brushed me off "We'll be the judge of that! Carry on Carla, I'll gag Mr. Interrupter over here!"

"Thanks Ani! Well, we finally get to the deli and we are the only people there. Remember he's still holding my hand tightly. The woman looks up at Divinder with his crazy look on his face and discretely grabs a small paring knife in her right hand. Do you want to carry on with the story or shall I carry on?"

I shrugged "You're almost done so please continue your character assassination!"

Carla was crying now as she retold the story and her mascara was running down her cheeks.

"OK love. Divinder is now red in the face and starts to shout, "Forget what she's told you, I am not crazy! I really am paid to come to work and my pc and telephones are both plugged in!" Well this poor woman is scared witless! Here's this crazy Indian fella screaming that he's not mad but looking very much like he might be!"

I stood up again "Please tell me people, what's funny about mental illness?!"

Carla was in full flow "After a few seconds Divinder realizes that I hadn't actually said anything at all to the woman and that he can never come back there again! We walked back to the office and he made me promise never to tell anyone about it!! That wasn't so bad was it?"

Everyone at the table, except Ranjvir and I, were laughing as I shrugged my shoulders.

Anisha leaned over and kissed me on the forehead.

Anisha held my hand and mockingly admonished Carla "Hey listen Carla, Divinder is a nut-job, but he's my nut-job OK?!"

Carla howled, "You can have him Ani, and so can Canada!"

More guests arrived throughout the evening and by 10pm the party was winding down.

All the family members had left hours earlier, Anisha's parents had taken the kids home so it was only me, Anisha, Jane, Bo, Cathie and Dave that stayed and chatted as the restaurant staff tidied up around us.

Bo looked a little puffy-eyed "I've got to be honest mate, this feels so weird. Just thinking about you guys not living in London anymore after July the 10th is going to take some getting used to."

Dave agreed "You're right Bo. You guys were the glue that held us all together. What will we do when we want a proper Indian dinner?"

I laughed, "That's easy. There are places called Indian restaurants that serve Indian food, in exchange for money!"

Dave pulled a funny face "Oh I've seen those places and always wondered what they were!"

Cathie was in a semi-serious mood "Can we come to the airport with you guys or do you have to be brown to do that?"

Anisha nodded "Of course you can come to the airport Cath, Jane and Bo just said they would be coming too."

I smiled at Cathie "That's a really nice gesture Cath, thanks."

Cathie took a swig of her wine and whispered loudly "I'm only going to the airport to make sure you get on that plane as I talk Anisha and the kids out of going with you!"

We all laughed and then a few seconds later I looked around the table and noticed that an air of somberness had suddenly entered the room.

It struck me, again, our good news was bad news for other people.

I tried to lighten the mood again "Come on guys smile, laugh, someone tell a joke! You all look like you're at a funeral! If I wanted to hang around with grumpy sods I would have asked my family to stay! We're only going 5,000 miles away!"

Dave replied "I know but that's a far distance mate, it might as well be five million miles!"

I knew what he meant, London was an expensive place to live and flights weren't exactly cheap "Listen guys, if you're true friends you'll sell one of your kids, buy a plane ticket and make that trip. If not then you can get stuffed and have a good life!"

Dave raised his glass of wine "Here's to having a good life wherever we are!" as Cathie said "I wouldn't get more than ten quid even if I sold all three of my kids!"

We all raised our glasses as the waiter started to stack chairs on the tables near us.

Being a tourist in your own city

Wednesday July 6th 2005
10am

Anisha had suggested the idea of us taking the kids out of school at the start of July so that we could spend some time with the family before we packed up and left London forever.

Kamran was supportive of any idea that avoided him having to work whereas Sonya wanted to know if she could take some homework on the plane to Canada!

That Wednesday Anisha had suggested that we go "explore London!" a city that I had lived in for all but four years of my life when I'd been studying at university in Birmingham.

"Divind, it'll be fun!" she said almost pre-empting my reluctance to fight off the hordes of commuters and real tourists who were heading to London. I shrugged my shoulders "But Ani, why would we need to check out a city that we've both lived in for most of our lives?"

She smiled as if she knew I'd say that.

She turned to the kids who were watching cartoon on TV and said "Would you like to go on a train to London and then go to London Zoo?" they looked up and nodded excitedly.

Damn, I thought, I was out voted.

I decided to play dirty "OK let's go but remember that today is the first Wednesday of the month and that's the day the zoo keepers do their regular clean out of the Gorilla's compound. I think it's forecast to be about 26 degrees today, that's going to be one stinky place today...

Anisha laughed at my lame attempt as the kids looked at her for confirmation or denial of what I'd just said. They had come to realise years ago that half of what I said was a lie and the other fifty percent was probably not the truth!

Anisha looked at the kids and spoke slowly "Kids, your Dad is lying. I told you both before that you can tell when he lies when... Sonya joined in "...Daddy's lips move!"

I grabbed my heart and faked looking hurt but sniggered after a few seconds at the fact that my kids knew me so well, so young!

"OK, if we are going to London Zoo then we need you guys to get ready quickly while Daddy and I make some sandwiches for lunch" the kids jumped up and ran past us.

Anisha tidied up the breakfast dishes while I opened up the fridge and took out some lunch meat, salad greens, a cucumber and a whole loaf of bread.

30 minutes later we were walking to the station.

Sonya held Anisha's hand and I had Kamran running a few feet ahead of me.

I had the backpack with all the food and drinks for the day and I was sure that Anisha had placed a few house bricks in there too.

"Hey Ani, why is this bag so heavy?"

Anisha smiled "I put the kids' fleece's in there too as it might be cold when we get back."

I looked at her with an incredulous expression "Fleece? Ani it's the middle of summer! What else is in there?"

She smiled again "I may have placed a few bottles of water in there too"

I stopped walking!

"Ani, you do know that they sell water in shops don't you?" she tapped the side of her head "Are you nuts? Why would we pay for something we have at home?"

I sighed and carried on walking.

We bought our tickets and waited on the train platform and waited for the Central Line Train to arrive.

I sat on the bench with the kids as Anisha stood by the large Underground map on the wall then traced our route with her finger. Gants Hill – Redbridge – Wanstead – Leytonstone – Leyton – Stratford – Liverpool Street.

It was like she was seeing the map for the first time or travelling it for the last time.

She had always loved the tube map and called it a piece of art.

After a few moments the train came rushing through the tunnel with a whoosh of cold air that made the kids jump and their reaction made me laugh.

I loved seeing their innocence at things I took for granted.

Kamran stared at the train with wide eyes, he's always been fascinated by trains and I had to keep hold of his hand tightly.

When the train stopped we entered the same carriage and sat down in a row of four seats.

Sonya sat by Anisha and I sat with Kamran as he stared out of the window.

We left the dark depths of Gants Hill station as the train trundled west towards Redbridge and then Wanstead where the station switched to the over-ground lines and we emerged from the tunnel to a bright summer's day.

The kids looked out of the windows at the row after row of terraced housing that lined the railway lines.

I can honestly say that this was the first time, in my life, that I had noticed the washing lines that filled many of the gardens.

On my daily commute I had usually been slammed up against some other passenger, who invariably was allergic to soap and deodorant, on a sweaty, hot and crammed train.

This was a different experience, I suddenly had the same sort of moment that Anisha had experienced at Gant's Hill station when she'd looked at the Tube map with new eyes.

I looked at the houses as they passed by and thought about the people that lived there, hearing the sound of the trains passing by every few minutes. I wondered if they ever got used to the constant noise.

I was suddenly reminded of my cousin Jaspal in Vancouver.

She lived directly under the flightpath of the airport and whenever we'd gone to see her in the past I had been deafened by the sound of the planes as they flew, what seemed like inches above us making our plates and glasses shake like the opening scene from Jurassic Park and she would shout "YOU GET USED TO THE PLANES AFTER A WHILE! IN FACT YOU HARDLY NOTICE THEM AT ALL!" as she held down her table cloth!

We arrived at Liverpool Street station and the kids looked like they had descended into the bowels of hell!

The mixture of all the sights, sounds and smells of the City of London hit them all at once.

I held onto Kamran's hand, rather he held my hand like he was trying to kill it whilst Anisha had Sonya clutching her leg as she walked.

We needed to leave the station and head for Moorgate station which was about 10 minute walk away.

We walked through the fairly busy station concourse and maneuvered our way through the throng of tourists and commuters who seemed to take great delight in just standing still in the middle of the station doing nothing important.

Arriving at Moorgate station I pointed my office out to the kids "Over there, just by that traffic light, is where I work, used to work." they gave the office a cursory look, nodded and then asked if it was "lunchtime yet" as they were apparently "starving"

Talk about not hiding their lack of interest!

We entered the station and made our way to the Northern Line platform as we needed to get on another train to Camden Town.

30 minutes later, a 15 minute train journey followed by a 15 mine walk, we arrived at The Zoological Society of London.

I have always felt very weird about zoos.

I've never quite known if they were a place where ordinary folk, who probably wouldn't ever see wild animals in their natural habitat, could see them up close and where scientists could do whatever research they wanted to do or if they were just a prison for animals.

We wandered around the zoo for a good two hours and I watched my kids and others "ooh" and "aah" as they saw ever more exotic animals from all around the world.

We ate our sandwiches as we walked around and, despite my initial reservations, I was sort of having a good time and then we reached the gorilla's enclosure.

The enclosure was protected by thick, heavy glass at the front and wire fencing above and when I looked in I saw a huge Silverback sitting on a tree stump by a rubber tyre that hung from a rope.

He looked really sad and all at once he looked straight at me and he seemed to be looking into my very soul and asking me if it was OK that he was sat there, for my amusement?

I literally shuddered because this gorilla was asking me a question that I didn't have an answer to.

I tried to look away in the hope that he would catch someone else's gaze and it worked for a second but when I looked he was still staring at me.

I felt so uneasy that I walked away but felt like I was nauseous.

I walked along until I found Anisha and the kids. I took her to one side "I need to leave."

Anisha looked at me with a weird concerned expression. She touched my forearm "What's wrong Divind? You look like you're going to be sick."

I pointed back to the gorilla's enclosure

"I've just had a really weird experience over there."

Anisha joked "Did you see a long, lost relative back there?" my expression gave away the fact that it was not a joke.

I told her what happened and she tried to make me see sense, and even used the classic Indian line "but we've paid now and it would be such a waste of money to leave before we see the whole zoo." in the end we agreed that would leave and take a walk in Regents Park and that she and the kids would meet me there in ninety minutes.

I walked out, avoiding any chance of seeing the Silverback again.

I felt really sad in that place.

Two hours later we were at Tower Hill station and on our way to see the Tower Of London and London Bridge.

As we stepped out of the station, I saw a hot dog stand and asked the kids if they were hungry.

This was actually code for "Dad's hungry but needs a smoke screen in case mum gets angry that he's eating junk food" the kids had just eaten sandwiches a few hours earlier so decided to share one hot dog.

I walked over to the hot dog stand and thought I'd play a little trick on the owner.

You see, I'd watched a TV show a few weeks earlier where an undercover reporter had shown that tourists, whose English wasn't so great, were being ripped by street vendors. I wanted to see if this was real so when I approached the hot dog stand I adopted a full-on Indian accent!

"Hullo!" I said in a cheerful voice to the swarthy-looking man with the unshaved fat face. Just for effect I nodded my head in that side-to-side way that many of my older relatives did when they meant yes or no.

The vendor smiled and his mouth had about eight teeth that were either yellow, brown or yellow and brown.

"Alwight mate" he said in a thick Cockney accent, with a glint in his eye, the game was on!

I looked at the hot dogs that were bobbing away in the hot water "How much for two hot dogs plis? £6?"

Now the price was listed as £3 but that wasn't going to stop "fat face" from trying to rip me off.

He smiled "If you just want the sausage it's £3 but if you want the bun, onions, ketchup and mustard that'll be £6 EACH" it was my turn to smile now. "OK, I will have two hot dogs please." he nodded and started to make the hot dog as I ushered the kids over.

"Fat face" quickly handed me the first hot dog, which I gave it to the kids and they quickly drowned it in ketchup and mustard. A few moments later he gave me mine and I took a bite, reached into my pocket, took out my wallet and handed him a crisp £5 note.

He took the note and said loudly "Yeah, that's five and you still owe me another £7 MATE! They're

£6 EACH!"

I leaned in close, and then wished I hadn't! This guy obviously hadn't seen a bar of soap or used toothpaste in many years.

I dropped the Indian accent "You're lucky I'm even giving you a fiver mate! I could have that policeman over here in two minutes!" and I pointed at a police officer stood by the station.

He bit his tongue and I smiled at him as I walked off with him swearing at me!

We don't need to see and do everything in one day do we?

We took dozens of photos at the Tower Of London, with Tower Bridge as our backdrop.

I was happy enough to play along because I thought we'd be back home before the evening rush hour began and then Anisha had the bright idea of checking out Parliament and Buckingham Palace!

Hours later, with my feet swollen from all the walking and having seen every tourist attraction in London it was 7:30pm.

We were in Leicester Square and decided to have dinner at Pizza Hut and then head home to avoid the crazy rush hour traffic.

I looked back and regret that I'd been in such a bad mood for most of that day but I just couldn't shrug off the gorilla experience at London Zoo.

As we sat in Pizza Hut, in Leicester Square, watching Kamran attempt his 8th slice of pizza I finally smiled.

I sat there in the hustle and bustle that took place around me and wondered if I would miss this, the fast pace of London life.

All at once I was struck by the fact that since we had been given the green light to move we had pretty much placed our lives on hold.

Our fridge door had stopped closing a few weeks ago so we'd gone to Ikea and bought a plastic strap-lock that would keep the door from staying open.

Then our washing machine had started to show signs of old age and the wash cycle lasted 2 and a half hours!! So we'd just prayed that it would hold out for another few weeks and had even started to wash our clothes at my in-laws' house!

I was also struck by the fact that this whole move was about me and how truly selfish I had become.

I had wanted to move just because I didn't like my life.

A wave of nausea started in the pit of my stomach.

Had I just convinced Anisha to hate her job and life as much as I hated mine?

Did I fan the fires when Karen took credit for her idea and used that to push Ani over the edge?

I felt a bead of cold sweat run down my forehead.

Anisha noticed it "Hey, are you getting sick Divind?" I gulped "No, it's just the lack of an air conditioning in here that's making me sweat" she fell for my white-lie as I brushed the sweat away.

Twenty minutes later and we were heading home.

I couldn't shift that sick feeling.

We walked onto the over ground platform at Liverpool Street and waited for the 9:07pm train to Shenfield.

As we sat down on the bench I looked around at the hundreds of people milling around the station.

There were the middle-aged "suits" heading home to the burbs, young people going to and from their part time jobs, the slick Yuppies in their smart clothes heading to the West End and a mix-bag of tourists, homeless people and other people just hanging around.

The train arrived at 9:02 and we made our way into the carriage with our tired kids practically dragged behind us.

I sat down on a seat opposite Anisha.

I had Kamran's head leaning on my shoulder while a sleepy Sonya was laying on Anisha's lap.

I loved looking at the kids when they slept, they always looked so peaceful, just a shame that peace left when their eyes opened!

Anisha looked a little sad "Hey Ani, what's up?"

Anisha suddenly smiled "Nothing."

I wasn't convinced

"OK Ani, what's going through your mind?"

Anisha laughed "I'm just thinking how ironic it is that we've lived in London all these years and it's only now that we're enjoying all that London has to offer, in one day, three days before we emigrate with our kids with us!"

I laughed too.

It was true, we'd always wanted to go to the theatre and concerts but had never had the chance what with the kids being so young and with us being so tired from working long hours and commuting home.

The train trundled along and I had flashbacks about me on the train over the past few years.

As a very spotty faced 18 year old travelling to Oxford Street for my Saturday job at a sports store.....heading to Hyde Park with Anisha when we were still dating, in secret from our parents, when we were still at school.... going to interviews after finishing university with hair and a moustache like Borat.

As we left the station I looked back with a weird sensation.

I had always worried about Liverpool Street station as it was the hub where so many train lines came into and I shuddered as I remembered the terrible times in the 1970's when the fear of an IRA attack on London had been very real.

I had no idea that London was about to be rocked again, only this time with home grown terrorists.

Seven/Seven, fade to black

Thursday July 7th 2005

It's amazing how quickly you get used to not having to get up early when you don't have to go to work.

Once we'd both left our jobs I'd got used to a routine where I was sleeping after midnight and waking up after 10am.

That was until that Thursday morning, July, Seventh, 2005.

I remember having a really fitful sleep that Wednesday night.

I woke up feeling very anxious at around 8:30am.

I went downstairs and had breakfast by myself as Anisha's parents were already out and the rest of the house was still asleep.

I put the TV on and kept the volume fairly low.

At about 9am breaking news came on about a series of bomb blasts on a London train near Liverpool Street station.

My blood ran cold.

I turned the volume up and listened as the newscaster explained about reports coming in about an explosion on an underground train in central London.

I picked up the phone and dialed my old office number.

The phone rang for a while before my friend Andrew Adams picked up "Good morning, Jonathan Hawk."

I sighed with relief "Andy, it's me Divinder."

Andy swore, "Shit! Where are you Divind?"

I tried to remain calm because I had a hundred questions in my head "Andy, I'm at home. Is everyone OK at the office? I mean, did the bomb affect you guys?"

Andy was usually Mr. Calm but he sounded nervous as he spoke "Yeah Divind, everyone's here and we're just about to head off to the boardroom to have an emergency meeting with Phil. I don't know what happened but I don't know how I'm going to get home tonight. There are armed police buzzing around and you can't hear yourself for the sound of police cars, helicopters and shop alarms blaring out."

I kept watching the news as I spoke with Andy and I wished him well as he had to go and then hung up.

I sat there watching the news as more and more details came up.

Anisha came down at about 9:45.

"Hey any danger of a cup of tea Divind?"

I looked up at her with a sick expression and she came and joined me on the sofa "What happened?"

I pointed at the TV screen "Some bombs went off at on a train near Liverpool Street station."

Suddenly, Anisha's expression suddenly matched mine

We sat there in stunned silence and then jumped in shock when another news headline came up about a bomb on a bus in the West End.

This was London's very own 9/11.

The last time I'd felt this sick was when we were in Vancouver in September 2011.

We were getting ready to travel to Seattle for the day and watched the 9/11 attacks happen live.

I remember watching the footage of the plane crashing into the WTC and thinking, "this is a little early in the day for such a graphic movie" before realizing I was watching the news.

We spent most of the morning watching the news and calling friends and family around the world finding out how they were and confirming that we were OK.

That day was somber to say the least and all our plans to visit friends were shelved as London was placed on lockdown.

Anisha, who was already close to tears at the prospect of leaving went every quiet "Divind, we were there, at that exact station twelve hours ago. That could have been us. Those poor people, just going about their business and now they're dead."

I sighed at the thought of those innocent people who wouldn't be coming home to loved ones and gave Anisha a tight hug which just made her tears flow.

Saturday July 9th 2005.
8:15pm

I was standing in my parent's kitchen chatting with my nineteen year old niece Amy.

She stacked the dishes that I had just washed.

Amy looked sad as she dried the dishes "Chacha you know that I'm going to miss you guys don't you?"

I stopped washing for a moment and replied with a smile "I was sort of hoping that would be the case!"

Amy leaned in close and gave me a hug.

She was a little weepy as she spoke "I know you've probably heard this a million times but it's going to be weird not having you guys around. I've always had you in my life."

I turned the tap off to give Amy my full attention. "I know, but we're only going to be 5,000 miles away. Wow! That suddenly sounds like such a huge distance. Amy, do you think we're doing the right thing?"

Amy looked astounded with my question "No offence Chacha but isn't the day before you emigrate a little late to be asking anyone that question?!"

I laughed.

"What I mean is, would you do what we're doing if you were in our shoes?"

Amy eased herself onto the kitchen counter before she answered.

"I do sort of understand why you're going but I don't know if I could take the risk that you and Chachi are taking."

I joined her on the counter "What do you mean by risk?"

Amy chose her words carefully "Well, you're both leaving stable jobs and a huge circle of family and friends to go to a place where you could fall flat on your faces!"

I laughed again "Thanks for the vote of confidence darling!"

Amy blushed and then realised that I was joking "You know what I mean Chacha! You might end up hating your life out there and then what would you do? You know that some people would love it if that happened don't you?"

I nodded.

"You're right Amy, we could crash and burn, but the truth is if we don't take this chance now we'll never do it. Besides which, your Chachi and I are both graduates, who speak English and have 14 years' experience in the world of work. We're taking a very calculated risk."

Amy smiled, as much for me as for herself "Well, for what it's worth, I hope you all get what you want."

I hugged her and then we raised our glasses and toasted one another.

"Here's to all of us getting all that we want!"

Just then, the kitchen door opened and Anisha came in with a tray full of empty glasses.

Anisha looked over and saw us chatting "Hey there dishwasher boy! Get these clean before the natives get restless!"

I jumped off the counter, saluted Anisha and took the tray off of her, as Amy laughed.

Anisha jumped up on the counter that I had just left "So Amy, are you coming to the airport tomorrow to see us off?" Amy stopped laughing.

"I'd be useless at the airport. I feel like crying now!" and with that she started to sniffle.

Anisha placed her arm around her.

"Come on Amy this is meant to be a party. You'll start me off in a minute."

Anisha and Amy were now both crying so I left the kitchen and went into the living room closing the kitchen door behind me.

My dad and father-in-law Mohan were seated on the sofa chatting about when they moved to England from India and Africa.

I stood opposite them and listened to their trip down memory lane.

Mohan spoke first.

"It was different back in the 1970's, you met a fellow brown person and treated them like a member of the family" my dad agreed, "I know what you mean Mohan. When I came to England, in February 1962, Heathrow Airport was a tiny little landing strip with a customs and immigration hut. When I got off the plane I thought I've made a huge mistake! I'd left the heat of India for freezing cold England! All the white people looked grumpy and I kept thinking they all looked so miserable and grey!"

I laughed but quickly realised that my dad was actually opening up, for the first time, about the harsh realities of being an immigrant.

He continued, "I remember there was a young Muslim man, I'll never forget him. His name was Ahmed Ali from Lahore. He sat next to me on the plane. He had a large letter B written on the palm of his right hand. He kept his hand ahead of his body for fear that the B might rub off. After a few hours of sitting next to him I asked him what it meant and he said that he had a cousin who lived in a 'city that started with the letter B'. It turned out that poor Ahmed was completely illiterate but knew that if he got to the city that began with that letter B that he had family there"

I nodded, having never heard this story before as my dad carried on.

"Well, we arrived at Heathrow and I was heading for the bus to go to Bradford so I walked with Ahmed who kept his right hand in front of his face like it was a map to hidden treasure. Oh, you should have seen his face when he saw the buses going to Bradford, Birmingham, Blackpool, Bolton and many other English cities that started with his beloved letter B!! The poor man he started crying! He said 'which bus should I get on?' I didn't know so said I guess 'Bradford is as good a place as any!' and he joined me on that 7 hour bus journey to Bradford!! I often wonder if he had a cousin stood at the coach station in Birmingham saying 'where the hell is bloody Ahmed?!'"

We all started laughing, including my dad.

I took a seat on a nearby armchair.

As I sat down my dad slapped me hard on my right thigh.

I wanted to scream the house down as my dad had hands likes catcher's mitts!

My dad laughed at my attempts to hold in a scream "It's different for this generation. They have no idea what hardship we went through to give them a better life."

I tried hard to ignore the hand-shaped pain that was coming from my thigh "That's not true Dad we know what you went through and I speak for my whole generation when I say thanks!"

My dad laughed and raised his hand and tried to slap my leg again but I had the sense to quickly edge away and stood behind my brother Ajit, Amy's dad.

"How's it going Ajit?" my brother Ajit, was a man of few words "Great Divind. So, this is it then, in a few hours you'll be heading for your new life in Canada. You'll do well out there."

I was surprised by Ajit's response as he was usually quiet a pessimist "What makes you say that?" he nodded towards the far end of the room.

I guessed he wanted to have a private chat.

Ajit walked over to the table and I followed him and took a seat next to him.

"Well you've never let people tell you that you couldn't do something. You never have. You went to Uni when mum and dad told you to get a job. Then after Uni you married a Hindu when the rest of us married Sikhs. You've always travelled on your own path. Good luck mate, listen I've got to go now, working the night shift."

And with that he stood up, put out his hand but I took the opportunity to hug him tightly instead.

I leaned in close "You look after yourself Ajit."

He replied in a whisper "You too Divind, you too. Maybe I'll see you in Vancouver one day eh?"

I stepped back and replied optimistically but knowing it was never going to happen "Anytime Ajit, anytime."

He walked away and said his goodbyes to the rest of the room and then left.

Just as the front door closed, Anisha came into the living room with Amy.

They both had puffy eyes

"I heard the door open and close. Who left?" she asked looking around the room.

"It was Ajit." I replied.

She looked a little disappointed "Hello! A goodbye Anisha would have been nice! Maybe even a 'Have a nice life'! I would even have taken a 'Hope you don't hate it there!'! Jeez it's like some people don't realise were going to move 5,000 miles away tomorrow!"

I looked at Amy as I spoke "You know what Ajit's like, Ani he's not the best at showing his emotions. In fact he just wanted to shake my hand goodbye! I had to hug him against his will!"

Amy joined in "Chacha's right, dad isn't great with showing how he feels. Chacha you should be glad he even offered you his hand!"

We all laughed.

The room was now suddenly quiet and the mood had become very dark.

My dad and father-in-law were looking at their feet trying to avoid everyone's gaze.

Our mums were looking through a pile of photo albums and the rest of the family were just trying to look cheerful.

I felt like I was at a funeral, my own!!

My mum finally broke the silence.

"We should let Divinder and Anisha go now so they can get some sleep, they have an early flight tomorrow."

I looked at the clock on the wall "It's OK Mum we'll leave at 8am tomorrow. We don't need to be at the airport until 10am."

Amy, her brother Jason and their mum Jas grabbed their coats.

Jas come over to say her goodbyes "We have to go now. Good luck tomorrow and please call us when you get to Amarjit's house."

I gave her a huge hug and then let her hug Anisha and the kids.

Amy and Jason were next and they moved along the line and hugged me first before giving Anisha, Kamran and Sonya tight embraces.

Amy's voice cracked as she spoke "Chacha you make sure you stay in touch OK?"

I nodded with puffy eyes as the first tears fell onto my cheeks.

They left and were quickly followed by Anisha's parents who took the kids with them.

It was now just Anisha, my parents and I left in my parent's house.

My dad had always been a very emotional man. He was the sort of man who cried watching bad Christmas movies and I had inherited his soft heart.

He was sat on the sofa with a glass of whiskey in his hand.

He patted the seat next to him and I walked over "OK Dad, but no slapping my thigh!! My leg is still burning from an hour ago!"

He laughed and I sat down as Ani went into the kitchen with my mum and busied themselves.

My dad looked at me and I saw an old man, far older than his mid-60's.

He looked so sad and I felt the worst guilt I'd ever felt in my life.

I was walking away, going 5,000 miles away and taking my kids - his grandkids - with me just because I somehow hoped I'd get a "better life".

I wanted to say something to reassure him that we would be OK but, for the first time in my life, words failed me.

I just looked at every crease in his face and tried to take a mental photo of how he looked at that exact moment.

It had one of those weird feelings when you look at someone who you see all the time as either your kid, your sibling or parent and suddenly see them as a human being rather then what they are to you.

I stared at my dad and saw his tough life as if it were etched on his face.

My dad was the middle child of a horde of kids and had lived in abject poverty like much of his generation in post-war Punjab. He'd lived through the partition of India and money had been very tight but he was bright and had decided that he wanted to get educated to give himself and his family to a better life.

He told us how he would wake up at some ungodly hour so that he could finish his farmyard chores off extra fast so that he could then sit outside the classroom in the blazing sun and listen to the lessons and follow along by "writing" in the sand that made up the floor of the school yard.

He was so poor that his family couldn't pay the school fees so he would have ended up as yet another illiterate farmer but he had a fire in his belly that pushed him along.

Amazingly, the teacher saw him sat outside, scribbling in the sand, for several weeks and one day tested him and when he aced her tests she allowed him in the class to take his lessons free of charge, much to the annoyance of the other village kids.

After he finished school, and against the wishes of his parents, my dad got a scholarship to Punjab University. His academic career was followed by a short stint as a truck driver in Calcutta and in 1962 he'd come to England.

He thought he'd come to heaven but it turned into a living hell.

The job that had been promised, never happened and the blatant racism he encountered made him doubt his decision to leave India but he had this crazy idea, a belief that his life would get better if he just kept on going.

Years passed by and he got married had his own horde of kids and had been successful in every measure of that word. But through it all was this fear that he'd be poor again so he and my mum never really lived, instead they merely existed.

They never ate at restaurants, never took a holiday and worse still they never took the time to enjoy all that they had.

I think I had an epiphany as I stared at my dad that he and I weren't that different, we were both financial immigrants wanting a better life for our kids only 43 years apart.

I stopped staring when he spoke, he did so with a slight croak "Son, it's a brave thing you and Anisha are doing. I know you have your degrees, speak English, will have some money in your pocket and will live with your brother Amarjit until you settle down, but trust me, starting again is never easy."

I simply nodded.

He carried on "I have heard you tell people over the past few weeks and months that if you somehow fail in Canada that you'd stay there because you feel some people would be happy you failed. That isn't going to happen. And that's because you have a drive that reminds me a lot of myself at your age and that will make you push yourself to keep going even when things seem really hard to overcome. Nothing that's worth having, comes easy."

I nodded because I felt that what he was saying needed to be acknowledged.

He carried on "If someone had told me when I was 20 years old that I would eventually have five boys and see all of them happily married I would never have believed them but here I am, 65 years old and the grandfather to eight grandkids. What I'm saying is, that you're going to have some hard times ahead. You are going to have situations where the easy way out would be to just jump on a plane and come home again. In those times remember why you left and push your way through. Now I know that your mum and I haven't always told you that we're proud of you and my god you made that easy when you were younger but we are proud of what you and Anisha have achieved."

I cried in front of my dad for the first time and he returned the favour.

Come fly with me!

Sunday July 10th 2005. The big day, today we were leaving England.
5:30am

I woke up early that morning.

Partly, because I wanted some peace and quiet but mostly to get the bathroom to myself, something that had eluded me over the previous 6 weeks.

I stood at the sink having a shave and stared at my face.

I saw the dark circles under my eyes and the "crow's feet" that seemed to have appeared over-night.

I looked at my rapidly receding hairline and sighed remembering the "Ace Ventura" quiff I'd had when I got married a few years earlier.

Man, I was old!

It didn't help that I'd woken up at 4am after another fitful sleep.

I washed the soap off my face and looked in the mirror again, for a moment I saw the 25 year version of myself and I smiled.

I realised that I was daydreaming when the house phone started ringing followed by a quick knock on the door.

"Yes?" I said as the knocking at the door almost guaranteed that the rest of the house would descend on the bathroom any second.

It was Kamran "Dad that was granny on the phone, she's coming over with granddad in a few minutes. And mum said can you hurry up because she would like to take a shower."

I dried my face with a warm towel and replied "OK Kamran, tell mum that I'm nearly finished."

I heard him step away from the door "OK dad I'll let her know."

I opened the bathroom door where Anisha was stood with her bath towel under her arm.

Her eyes were red and puffy.

I gave her a kiss on her forehead and tried to make her laugh by saying the lines from a Michael Jackson song that would usually have made her laugh "Hey Ani, are you OK? Are OK Ani? Ani, are you OK? Have you been crying?"

Anisha put her head down and walked into the bathroom, making me step out "I'm fine. I just need a shower. Do me a favour and get Sonya ready while I get myself sorted."

I nodded "No problem."

Anisha locked the door and I could hear her crying, even over the sound of the shower being turned on.

That was the first of many times that day when I doubted what I was about to do in taking my family so far from home.

I went into the second bedroom where Sonya was fast asleep and looked at her as she slept peacefully.

I always loved looking at my kids as they slept, they always looked like they didn't have a care in the world.

She had no idea that this would one of the toughest days of her young life.

I sat on the bed and gently brushed some hair off her face, I whispered "Sonya darling it's time to wake up."

Sonya opened her left eye, looked directly at me, gave me a dirty look and then turned over and pulled the duvet over her head just like her mum did!!

I gently tugged the duvet down and whispered "Sonya we're going to Canada today. If you don't get up and get ready you'll have to stay here!"

Sonya suddenly sprung into life and hugged me.

"What time do we get on the plane Daddy?"

I pushed her hair away from her eyes "Our flight is at 12 o'clock. But we need to be at the airport at 10 o'clock. Do me a favor and get yourself ready and I'll make you some breakfast. What would you like to eat?"

Sonya tapped her head, something she did when she wanted us to know that she was thinking hard. After a few seconds of hard thought she said, "Um. French toast please Daddy!"

I liked that idea as it was easy, "No problem. Mummy's taking a shower so you use the toilet in the meantime and by the time you've brushed your teeth your French toast will be ready."

Sonya stepped off the bed and walked over to the washroom as I went downstairs to the kitchen.

As I came downstairs I looked into the back room and saw my in-laws sitting on the sofa, a cup of tea in their hands.

I knew I had to say something, even though I kept feeling like I was a few seconds from crying every time I opened my mouth "Hi Mum, Dad how are you?"

Mohan looked up with blood-shot eyes.

My mother-in-law just stared at her feet.

This was the second time that day that I doubted the move.

Mohan cleared his throat "As good as expected. Your mum didn't sleep much last night. She was crying."

Now, I don't know why I said what I said next, I guess it just came out "Why?" this time it was Rani who responded and with an accusing tone "Why do you think eh?"

I have to admit that, somewhat selfishly, I had hoped that everyone would be positive about our adventure and that today would be a happy day for all of us "Mum, I thought we'd been through this already? This is the right move for us and the kids" but that ignored the obvious and Ani's mum finally said what I guess many people had been thinking.

She looked at me with red raw eyes and spat her words out "Divinder it seems to me that you're taking my only child and only grandchildren 5,000 miles away just so that you can have a bigger house!"

WOW!

I have to admit that I was a little shocked that it had taken anyone this long to say that.

I took her hand in mine and spoke softly "Mum, you know that isn't the reason we're going. I just feel that my life here in London is just a series of boring routines. I am going crazy and do not want to look back when I'm 65 and wonder "what if?"" she seemed to think that I'd given her a lifeline, "Then maybe, rather than going 5,000 miles away you should look at moving out of London if London is the problem."

I shook my head and even though I tried to get my words out, nothing came out.

She carried on "How am I going to get through my days without my heart and soul, Kamran and Sonya? Your generation are so damn selfish!! All you think about it yourself. You don't care about what this move is going to do to me and Anisha's dad!"

She started to sob between her words.

I felt like crap.

"Mum, I know you're upset, but this is the day we leave to start a new life. I really need your blessing so please find it in your heart to give us your best wishes"

Mohan stepped in as she sobbed uncontrollably "Of course you have our blessing, you have to forgive your mum she is seeing her baby leave the house a second time. Most parents of daughters cry when they see their child get married and you think that you can never cry that much again. Last night she cried again and I honestly thought she would dissolve away."

I felt a lump in my throat, so stepped over to the sofa and held my mother-in-law's hand.

"Listen Mum, you are going to love Vancouver. Once you come out there you'll want to stay with us, just you see" she looked up at me and from the angle she was sitting her eyes looked comically large through the lens of her glasses and it almost made me laugh which would have probably seen me murdered by my in-laws!

She blew her nose loudly and the sound almost made me laugh "I hope so, son."

I hugged her as the doorbell rang.

Kamran came running down the stairs "Dad shall I get the door? I think it's granny and granddad" before I could answer, I heard the front door open and then the sound of my parents greeting Kamran.

Rani looked at me with a look of panic, she wanted to appear strong in front of my parents "Divinder, I don't want your parents to see me like this. Please distract them so that I can go upstairs and wash my face and put on some make up."

I nodded and walked into the hallway and guided my parents into the front room as my mother- in-law used me as a human shield and walked upstairs.

My mum looked as stoic as ever.

In my 36 years, as her son, I had never seen her appear anything other than stern.

She was also terrible at coping with silences – a trait that Anisha would tell you I inherited!!

After a few seconds she started making really bad small talk "All packed?"

I was so tempted to say "Oh my god, I knew there was something that I forgot to do!" but decided that I didn't want a slap from my mum so just said "Yes Mum. Can I get you both a cup of tea?" my dad laughed "Can we get our coats off first?!"

I appreciated someone not crying so apologized "Sorry Dad! Would you like to take off your coat and then have a cup of tea?"

My dad shook his head "No tea for me, I've already had two cups. Where's Anisha and Sonya?"

I looked upstairs "Anisha's having a shower and the kids are upstairs. Sonya come down please, granny and granddad are here."

Sonya stood at the top of the stairs and shouted down "Coming Dad" my dad looked towards the back room and saw someone sat on the sofa. "Are Anisha's parents ready?"

I looked at the back room "Yup, her dad's in the back room and her mum's upstairs getting changed." my dad stood up, he didn't like it when women cried and he knew that tears were imminent.

"I'll go say hello to Anisha's dad." he walked through the kitchen to the back room and took a seat by Mohan.

Rani came down the stairs and hugged my mum and they both started crying.

I stood there awkwardly until they stepped into the living room and sat on the sofa.

The kids came downstairs and sat between their grandmothers in the living room.

I decided to head upstairs and carry out one last baggage check.

As I headed up the stairs I felt my mobile phone buzz in my shirt pocket.

I took the phone out, unfolded it and looked at the number.

It was Bo.

I sat down on the step and took the call "Hi Bo, how are you mate?"

Bo sounded a little upset "I'm good thanks. Just a quick call to confirm that we'll meet you at the South Terminal at Gatwick Airport for 10 o'clock."

I looked at my watch it was 6:40.

"Oh OK, but I thought you guys were coming here first?"

The plan had been that we would all leave together "So did I but Jane reckons she'd be a complete wreck. She thinks it's better to see you off at the airport and get her crying over and done with all at once!"

I nodded and then immediately realised that he obviously couldn't see me so said "That sort of makes sense in female logic! We'll see you there."

Bo replied "OK mate, bye for now."

I placed the phone back in my pocket and continued upstairs.

I heard the shower running so headed straight into the bedroom and started to count off the luggage and looked through the passports, immigration papers and airline tickets.

The cell phone buzzed into life again.

This time it was David and Cathie. "Hi David" I said as the female voice at the other end of the line tutted "NO Divinder, you muppet, it's not David, it's Cathie. Is Ani awake?"

I laughed at the well-deserved insult "She's just in the shower can I take a message or get her to call you back?"

Cathie thought for a moment and then said "Yeah, tell her...not to go to Canada!"

I laughed again "Is there a sensible message I can give her?"

Cathie sounded very unlike her usual chatty self "Nah, just ask her to call me. I want to hear her voice."

I spoke softly back into the phone "Will do Cathie. I'll see you later." suddenly the old Cathie was back "Not unless I come to Canada you won't!"

I laughed again, "You know what I mean!"

I put the phone back into my pocket, picked up the largest suitcase and tried to guess if it was overweight.

I decided to take the luggage downstairs in readiness for leaving.

When I had taken down the fourth and final suitcase I heard Anisha open the bathroom door.

She still seemed quite upset so I gave her the messages hoping that they'd take her mind off of what was ahead.

"Two messages while you were in the shower, Cathie said please call her back, Bo and Jane are going to meet us at the airport."

Anisha nodded and then quickly turned back into the bathroom and leaned over the sink "I feel sick!" she said and I did that thing that all men do and tried to brush it off in the hope that she wouldn't see that I was feeling exactly the same.

"Don't worry Ani, it's just nerves. It'll pass" she shook her head "No Divind it's not like being late for a job interview. This is one of those stomach churning feelings."

I stepped into the bathroom and rubbed her back "Would a cup of tea help Ani?"

Anisha gave me a dirty look, which made me think she must be feeling better "What is it with you Punjabis? You think everything can be sorted out with a cup of tea!"

I laughed, not knowing if she had just insulted my whole culture, my culture's love of tea or both!

"Is that a yes or a no to the tea?" she steadied herself "I'll try a cup of tea, in the meantime give me the phone and I'll call Cathie back."

I handed her my phone "By the way my folks are downstairs so please keep the chat brief yeah?"

Anisha nodded as I headed back downstairs.

And we're off!

7:35am

The luggage was now dispersed, between my dad and my father-in-law's cars.

I started the engine in my father-in-laws car as my dad started his engine too.

I reversed off the drive and as I looked in my rear view mirror I saw Mr. Patel, the man who lived three houses away from my in laws, he was out at this ungodly hour lovingly washing his VW Golf, like he did every Sunday morning.

Mr. Patel waved at us as we drove past.

I waved back.

I smiled at Anisha who sat in the passenger seat "I won't miss seeing Mr. Patel washing his car for three hours every Sunday! What a saddo!" I said and Anisha came back like she was his defence lawyer "What's more sad Divind, him washing his car for three hours or you noticing that he washes his car for three hours every Sunday?"

Everyone laughed in the car except Sonya who said "What's so funny? Someone tell me why you're laughing!"

9.15am

We finally arrived at Gatwick Airport.

Anisha and I grabbed two luggage carts as our dad's started to take the luggage out of their cars.

I looked at Anisha and she was smiling for the first time that day "This is it Ani. No going back now darling."

I held her hand as she bit her bottom lip "I know."

I needed to keep Anisha focused on the task in hand, getting us on that plane so kept her talking "So, how are you feeling Ani?" she looked at me and seemed to have become a 6 year old! "A mixture between real excitement and wanting to crap myself!"

I laughed as I felt exactly the same "Interesting combination!"

Anisha could tell that I was anxious too "How about you Divind? How are you feeling right now?"

I cleared my throat "There's a part of me that just wants to start our new life and another part that wishes I could be put into a coma and wake up in a year so as to miss out on any pain we might suffer when settling in."

Anisha smiled but her eyes gave away the fact that she was petrified.

When she spoke again it was in a low whisper, so low that I had to lean in to hear her "We're going to be alright aren't we Divind?"

I smiled and squeezed her hand tightly "Ani, do you remember what I said to you on our third date back in April or May, 1987, when I was 18 and you were 17?"

Ani smiled as she knew exactly what I was referencing.

"Yes I do." she replied with a laugh.

"You told me "I'm going to marry you, we're going to have two kids and we will live happily ever after in Canada' I should have run away then!"

I laughed and continued.

"Two of those three promises have already come true and now we are heading to the final challenge."

Ani looks reassured so I finished my pep talk with a flourish and holding her face in my hands I asked "Have I ever let you down?" she shook her head but didn't make eye contact.

Oh! Canada?

I thought I heard her say, "Not yet" but didn't want to that clarified so didn't ask her to repeat herself.

We came back to the cars, put the luggage onto the two carts and headed for the departure hall.

As we wheeled our cart into the airport I noticed Bo and Jane standing next to the Zoom check-in desk next to Cathie and Dave, who they'd met at our house a few times. "Ani look over there, it's all our white friends in one group!"

Anisha screamed "Oh my god! Cathie, you made it!"

I looked a little surprised as I thought Cathie was planning on seeing us off, well at least me anyway! Anisha read my mind "She said she wanted to but was worried she'd start crying like a "silly moo" as she put it!"

I tried to act all nonchalant, but had never been good at that, as it usually came off as me looking stupid.

I approached David and Bo and shook their hands as Jane, Cathie and Anisha formed a group hug between the three of them.

Anisha left the hug and spoke to the men "I am so glad you guys could make it!"

I just smiled, like an idiot,

I was lost for words, a fact that didn't go unnoticed by Bo who said "Cat got your tongue Divind?" I just felt that I was close to tears and didn't want to set Anisha and our parents off so just smiled again.

Thankfully, Jane noticed my awkwardness and saved me "I wish you weren't going but I wouldn't miss this for the world."

Cathie took Jane's cue and joined in by talking in a loud whisper "I just want to make sure that Divinder gets on that plane! I can't stand him!"

I played along with the running joke "Oi! I'm not deaf!" Cathie winked and replied "Sorry love, must remember my inside voice!"

We all laughed as I pushed my cart towards the check-in queue, behind three other passengers.

I looked over at Anisha and she was sharing a joke with Cathie and Jane.

It suddenly struck me that it might be years before we'd see these great friends again.

I let her finish laughing and then caught her eye "Ani can you get the kids over here please? I think we should just get the bags checked in and then we can relax a little."

Anisha nodded and guided her cart along with the kids to where I was standing in the queue.

Kamran and Sonya were full of nervous energy and it was like trying to keep them focused was looking trying to put a sweater on a cat.

Anisha put on her school teacher tone and spoke to the kids "OK Kamran, Sonya I need you both to be on your best behavior now. You understand?"

They both thought she was joking but then saw me shaking my head and quickly nodded in an exaggerated manner.

The queue moved along quickly and we were next.

The check-in woman ushered us over with a wave of her hand "Over here please sir, madam."

I quickly pushed my cart as Ani pushed hers straight into my heel.

I stopped myself from swearing and instead gave her a look "Shi...eesh! Could you be a little more careful Ani?!"

Anisha did that thing that wives do when they mess up, she made it seem like it was my fault! "I didn't do it on purpose! Besides which, you stopped too quick."

The check-in employee, Denise, looked seriously uncomfortable and tried to diffuse our tension "Can I see your passports please sir, madam?"

I nodded and said "Of course" as I handed over the four passports and then rubbed my heel as Anisha ignored me.

Denise looked at each passport and peered over the top of the counter to see Kamran and Sonya who both smiled at her.

Denise smiled back at the kids and then handed me back the passports.

She got off her seat and pointed at the luggage "Could you put your luggage onto the weighing scales, one at a time please?"

I carefully lifted the first of the suitcases, making it look lighter than it was and placed it onto the scales. The digital reading flashed up 34.8 kilograms!

Denise did a double take!

I smiled as I placed the next suitcase on the scales.

This was lighter than the first but was still 28 kilograms.

Denise looked a little worried and she blew out a breath of air when the last two registered at just over 27 kilograms each.

When all the suitcases had been weighed Denise took out her calculator and started tapping on the rubber keyboard "Sir, madam are you both aware of our airline's luggage allowance?"

I tried to act nonchalant again, and failed again as I said, "Sort of!" and smiled cheekily.

Denise adopted a less friendly tone when she spoke again "OK sir, let me educate you. Each passenger is allowed to take up to 23 kilograms in luggage. This would give your family of four a total allowance of 92 kilograms. Your luggage presently stands at 118 kilograms, that's 26 kilograms overweight."

She tapped the keys on her calculator again and showed me the bright green screen "Now at £10 per kilogram you owe us £260! Will that be cash or credit card?"

Anisha started to cry.

She stepped forward and addressed Denise woman to woman.

"Denise, sorry it is OK if I call you Denise, Denise?"

Denise nodded.

"See that old, tiny, skinny Indian woman over there?"

Anisha pointed in the general direction of her parents.

Denise nodded "You mean the old, tiny, skinny Indian woman whose crying uncontrollably?"

Anisha nodded "Yeah that's the one. That's my mum. You see, I'm an only child and we are emigrating today to Canada. All our money has been converted into dollars and is sitting in the Surrey branch of HSBC bank in Canada."

Denise looked sympathetic "Oh, I see. Couldn't your parents help?"

Anisha ramped up the tears like she was chopping 10 lbs of onions!!

"They would if they could but they are both retired so they can't even help us if they wanted to. Is there anything you can do to help us out, please Denise?"

Denise looked at Anisha crying and then at her blubbering mum.

She looked around and then started typing frantically on her keyboard.

A few seconds later four boarding passes came whizzing out "I guess that you're early enough for us to overlook the luggage issue. Especially as you are emigrating. Here's your boarding passes. Please head to gate 36. Your flight is on time so you'll be boarding at about 11am. Good luck with Canada."

Anisha squeezed Denise's hand "Thank you, thank you, thank you Denise!! I'll be writing to your supervisor!"

Denise waved over the next passengers "I'd rather you didn't actually madam, I could get fired if anyone ever finds out what I just did! Have a great day. Next! Over here miss, I can help you."

We walked back to our group with the kids.

I nudged Anisha "Hey Meryl Streep, where did the water works come from?"

Anisha nudged me back "Listen mate, when someone's trying to get £260 out of me I could have a kid on cue!"

I laughed "Good to know!" and high-fived her as our friends and family looked at us with surprised looks on their faces

Mohan approached us "What happened? Why was Anisha crying?"

I laughed and reassured her dad that we were alright, "Everything's great dad. Let's just say that your daughter could win the Oscar one day!"

Mohan looked perplexed with my answer, but having been my father-in-law for the past ten years he'd got used to not always understanding what I did, said or thought.

10.05am

We all headed off towards the departure gate across the airport.

Sonya and Kamran were busily chatting with Bo and Jane's daughter Amber as Anisha went with her dad to pick up coffee.

Mohan was his usual quiet self and I guessed that he wanted to spend some one on one time with his only child when he volunteered to go with Anisha "What time do you they start to board the passengers?"

Anisha looked at her watch "We should aim to get to immigration by about 10.45am. We have enough time to enjoy our last cup of coffee."

Anisha ordered their drinks and they took a seat as the drinks were made.

Mohan seemed to be looking at Anisha with a new-found admiration "You seem so calm Anisha. What's going through your mind?"

Anisha smiled "I'm just on auto pilot Dad. Ever since we got the green light to emigrate we have put our lives on hold. We didn't buy anything new for the house and anything that broke was just patched up or held together with duct tape."

Mohan smiled back reassured with her response "Aren't you a little nervous? You're moving 5,000 miles away. I remember feeling so scared when I moved here from Tanzania back in 1972. I was so frightened that I was making a huge mistake."

Anisha stopped smiled for a moment "Don't get me wrong Dad, Divinder and I have had so many, many late night chats about what if this happens and what if that happens. The truth is Divinder had been so unhappy for so long and he's convinced that a new life in Canada is what we both need. We can't afford to buy a better lifestyle here in England and our skills are in demand in Canada right now. What sort of wife would I be if I didn't support him? Besides which if it does fail we'll come back and live with you and mum and I can blame him for the rest of his miserable life!"

Mohan smiled weakly "You're not going to fail. Please realise that you are most welcome to come back whenever you like! The truth is that your mum and I are more worried about how you will settle without us."

Anisha looked very surprised with his question "Why me?"

Mohan spoke carefully "Anisha, you're an only child and we've always done everything together. Even when we bought our car a few years ago we asked you about the model and the colour!"

Anisha laughed at the memory of that chat when I had said, "I don't remember marrying your parents all those years ago!"

Anisha composed herself "I know. To be honest, Sunil Mahraj's words about me struggling to settle for the first year are stuck in my head. But I have to cut the umbilical cord. You and mum have done so much for us with Kamran and Sonya and now we need to take over the parent role."

Anisha put her hand on her dad's hand, reassuring herself, as much as her dad.

"We'll be OK Dad just you see" they carried their drinks back to where the rest of the group were sitting.

I was busily chatting with Bo as the kids played in the nearby amusement arcade.

My parents walked over to where we were standing. My dad approached me and put his arm on my shoulder.

Now, as I said before, my dad is a very emotional man in that he cries watching a Tom and Jerry cartoon but isn't someone who shows affection easily.

"So son, you've finally grown up eh?"

I involuntarily laughed "Finally? Dad you told me that I'd finally grown up on my wedding day and then again when both the kids were born!" my dad laughed too "Yeah, they were all big steps towards this day when you really have finally grown up!"

My mum was tagged into the verbal wrestling match that I had unwittingly joined in!

"Son, it's no secret that your dad and I were so worried that you would stay stupid forever!"

Bo laughed so much that he spat some coffee out! "You what Mum?"

My mum was on a roll "I remember every stupid thing you ever did and there were hundreds of them! Like that time when you threw that fire cracker into the neighbour's garden."

Bo laughed again but had the sense to put his coffee down. "Mrs. Purewal, I've never heard that story before, Divinder seems to have forgotten it. What happened?"

I looked at Bo with daggers in my eyes "It's a pretty rubbish story really and it was such a long time ago."

My mum glared at me, like it had just happened, "Rubbish story eh? Nearly burning the neighbour's house down is not a rubbish story!"

Bo rubbed his hands together "I've got to hear this!" with that he called the rest of the group over, including Kamran and Sonya.

"Cheers Bo!" I said sarcastically.

My mum waited for her audience and then started her story "Divinder was about 16 or 17 and he was classmates with Malika, our neighbour Mr. Mahmood's eldest daughter. Mr. Mahmood was a very suspicious man and didn't like the idea of her daughter being led astray by the crazy Sikh boy next door so one day he had a 12 foot high fence built across the gardens. His plan was that if the kids couldn't see each other then they wouldn't chat like they used to every evening."

I edged close to my mum and whispered in her ear "Mum please don't tell this story. Kamran and Sonya are listening and I'll never be able to tell them off after they realise how stupid I was as a kid!" my Mum brushed off my plea "They need to hear this story! If only to understand why I have so many grey hairs!"

She continued as they laughed.

"So, as I said, Mr. Mahmood built the 12 foot fence and Divinder wasn't happy! In fact he told his brothers that he was going to teach Mr. Mahmood a lesson."

Kamran, Sonya and Amber took a seat closer to my mum to catch every single detail.

I put my head in his hands.

Bo kept the story going "So what did he do?" my mum was in full flow and I suddenly appreciated that I got my story-telling from her!! "Well, let's just say that bonfire night came early that year! Divinder secretly bought some fire crackers and hid them under his bed"

Kamran stood up "Granny are you saying that **MY** dad did **THAT**?"

My mum nodded "Yes Kamran, and it gets worse!"

Kamran raised his hands in disbelief "He buys fire crackers but won't buy me a PS2!"

"So picture the scene, Divinder, Amarjit and Jarnail are all in his room as he tells them his plan, he's going to throw a fire cracker into the garden to show Mr. Mahmood that he is still in reach!"

I looked at my watch "Mum we have to go now! OK kids, say your goodbyes now... my mum slapped my hand "You have enough time to hear the rest of the story! Anyway, Divinder tells Amarjit that he's going to throw the fire cracker into the garden just to scare them a little. Amarjit looks out of the window and says "Divind, don't throw it. Mr. Mahmood's grease covered overalls are hanging on the line and knowing your luck, the fire cracker will land on his overalls and set the whole line on fire." Divinder, being Divinder, ignored Amarjit and said, "Just you watch!" He then opened the window, lit the fire cracker and launched the fire cracker as far as his skinny little arm would allow!"

Kamran was enraptured "What happened next granny?"

My mum laughed and said "Well Kamran, let's just say that your uncle Amarjit was right - again!"

I decided that I needed to laugh at myself as everyone else was about to "That bloody Amarjit, he was such a jinx!"

My mum carried on "The fire cracker landed in the pocket of the greasy overalls. It fizzled for a few seconds and then exploded. I was in the kitchen and after the loud bang all I saw was the overalls burning like an oily rag and then the rest of the plastic line caught alight dripping boiling plastic onto their clothes. Then I heard their garden door open and that's when I heard the kids come running down the stairs like a herd of elephants!"

Bo slapped me on the back "Divind, you arsonist you!"

I smiled sheepishly.

My mum wasn't quite finished.

"About five minutes later Mrs. Mahmood was at my door asking if we have also been attacked like they had. She was holding a pile of ruined clothes! Well I played dumb, closed the door on her and came back to the living room where Divinder and his brothers were sat watching TV. They could not have looked guiltier! Divinder's heart was visibly beating through his sweater, Amarjit couldn't stop sweating and Jarnail was already sniffling and crying. I sent Amarjit and Jarnail out of the room and they both ran upstairs as fast as they could. So there I am looking at Divinder and he's got eyes like a rabbit in headlights! I wanted to laugh but had to find out what happened."

Kamran was literally hanging on every word that came out his grandmother's mouth "So I said "Divinder do you know anything about what happened next door?" Divinder looked at me like I'm the idiot and says "I didn't throw the fire cracker!" That's when I said "Did I mention anything about a firecracker?""

Kamran jumped off his seat "I hope you shouted at Daddy!"

I glared at my mum and then at Kamran "Shouted at me? Kamran, my face isn't dark, it's still bruised from the beating I got that day, son!!"

Everyone laughed out loud, including Sonya.

My mum waited for the laughter to die down and then spoke again, only softly "The reason I'm reminding you about this story is because I want you to give your kids a break in the next few months. You were the worst kid ever but you have grown up so much since then."

She gently caressed my forehead and then hugged me before moving onto Kamran.

I saw her shed a single tear.

I hugged my dad who didn't try to hide his tears.

"Son look after yourself, Anisha, Kamran and Sonya. Be brave and remember that impossible is nothing."

I stepped back "Wow Dad! Impossible is nothing?! That's quite profound! Did you make that up?

My dad shook his head "No, I just saw it on that man's Adidas vest!"

I laughed and then kissed my dad on the cheek, hugged him tightly and then moved along the line that had formed.

We got to the last two people, Anisha's parents.

I looked to my left and saw Anisha crying with Jane.

I stepped forward and embraced my mother-in-law Rani.

She was blubbering and spoke between her tears, "Divinder please look after my Anisha, Kamran and Sonya. Promise me that you'll not be too proud and come back if Canada isn't all that you hoped it would be. Take my blessing and love with you."

She kissed my cheek and started to cry uncontrollably as a red-eyed Anisha approached her.

I finally reached the last person in the line-up, my father-in-law Mohan.

Before hugging him I reached into my jacket pocket and handed him my mobile phone.

"Here Dad the mobile phone is all paid up to midnight on Monday so feel free to use it for today. Thanks for, well, everything really."

Mohan hugged me tightly and then leaned in close and whispered "Son, you know, it's not too late to admit you've made a mistake! I promise you, no-one's going to judge you for changing your mind."

I wasn't able to speak, instead I simply stepped back and shook his hand.

I joined the queue of five passengers as I waited for Anisha and the kids to finish their goodbyes. Once they had hugged and kissed Mohan they joined me at passport control and the awaiting Zoom employee.

Anisha had puffy, blood shot eyes.

I pulled her in close as she started to cry again.

This in turn started Kamran and Sonya bawling their eyes out.

It took all my effort not to break down as Mohan's words "Son, you know, it's not too late to admit you've made a mistake! I promise you, no-one's going to judge you for changing your mind" were playing in my head like a record on repeat.

"It's OK Ani. Just don't look back."

Well as soon as I said that, Anisha turned and saw her mum crying.

She tried to run back but I held onto her shirt.

"Ani, trust me, you have to let go."

We got to the desk and the Zoom employee, Brian, asked for our boarding passes that I handed over.

Brian looked at Anisha and the kids crying "Is everything OK sir?" I gave a half-smile "We're emigrating to Canada so we're all a little upset at saying goodbye."

Brian nodded "Oh I see. Well good luck with your new life."

I said "Thank you" and then did one final look back and waved at our family and friends one last time and moved towards the X-ray machine.

I said a silent prayer "Here we go guys, a new life in Canada. Please don't let this be a mistake!"

About the Author

Divinder Purewal is a middle aged man who always wanted to write "his book".

In July 2005 he emigrated from the suburbs of London to Surrey, BC, Canada with his wife Usha, 8 1/2 year old son Kieran and 5 1/2 year old daughter Simran, in the hopes of having a better life with his family.

Once they were settled in Canada, Divinder asked his wife Usha for "6 months off to write my book", Usha agreed to give him 6 months off to write his book if he also settled their kids in school, unpacked all 104 of their moving boxes and repainted the entire inside of the house!

Divinder was upset as he actually wanted Usha to deny him permission as he wanted to be bitter for 40 years and be able to point a boney finger at her, on his death bed, and say "You killed my dream of being an author! Given 6 months off, I could have written the greatest book EVER!" and then pass away all angry!

Divinder has a wonderfully supportive and loving wife Usha and two equally wonderful kids, Kieran and Simran and this book is dedicated to them for putting up with me for all these years.

THANK YOU!